CARDINAL
AND GOLD

CARDINAL AND GOLD

THE ORAL HISTORY OF
USC TROJANS FOOTBALL

STEVE DELSOHN

CROWN
ARCHETYPE

New York

Published in the United States by Crown Archetype, an imprint of the
Crown Publishing Group, a division of Penguin Random House LLC,
New York.
crownpublishing.com

Crown Archetype and colophon is a registered trademark of Penguin
Random House LLC.

Library of Congress Cataloging-in-Publication Data is available upon
request.

ISBN 978-0-307-88840-2
eBook 978-0-307-88842-0

Printed in the United States of America

Jacket design by Gregg Kulick
Jacket photograph by Stephen Dunn/Getty Images

10 9 8 7 6 5 4 3 2 1

First Edition

CONTENTS

CARDINAL
AND GOLD

I grew up playing football in Chicago and I still recall watching the Rose Bowls with my father and brother during the late 1960s and early 1970s. Most of the memories involve USC, but not only because they appeared in Pasadena almost every January 1. Watching from the frozen Midwest on our Zenith color TV made the images so vivid: the pretty USC Song Girls, the striking white Trojan horse, the cardinal and gold uniforms lit by the sun.

The scores of those games have faded but not *how* those USC teams played. As a high school running back, I admired the purity of Student Body Right and Student Body Left. That didn't mean I wanted the Trojans to win, though. Kids in Chicago pulled for the Big Ten in the Rose Bowl, even while knowing deep down the Big Ten would lose.

I got a job in California after college, married an Angeleno, raised three children here, and never left. But I still wouldn't call myself a USC fan. Nor am I anti-USC. I was drawn to this book in the same way I was drawn to my previous three oral histories on American firefighters, Notre Dame football, and the Los Angeles Dodgers. I like writing about classic institutions.

Cardinal and Gold is based on the first-person accounts of those who *lived* the story of USC football over the last 40 years. I interviewed more than 125 players, coaches, athletic department members, and a handful of plugged-in writers and broadcasters. Most of the interviewees are the former USC players, who I found as a group to be funny, direct, and perceptive. Some were tough on their head coaches and athletic directors, just as firefighters tend to grumble about their commanders. But I never heard one bad word about the university itself. The opposite was true. They often used the words *love* and *great education* when discussing their alma mater.

Still, their particular school and the game of football are synonymous. USC has produced 11 national championships and 7 Heisman Trophy winners. It has sent 31 players to the College Football Hall of Fame and 12 players to the Pro Football Hall of Fame. The NFL has drafted more Trojans (488) and more of them in the first round (79) than it has drafted from any school in the country.

In 2009, the ESPN research department created a formula to determine the top football programs since 1936, the year the Associated Press started ranking teams and naming a national champion. USC finished No. 2 to Oklahoma. Then again, every true Trojans fan knows what happened when the two schools last met: USC demolished the Sooners, 55–19, in the 2005 Orange Bowl.

Before the birth of USC football, there was a fledgling university, and before that a region known as California. In 1850, two years into the Gold Rush, California became the 31st state in the union. In 1880, USC opened its doors in the lively frontier town of Los Angeles. The original 53 students and 10 teachers convened a few miles away from what is known today as downtown LA.

USC took up football in 1888. The first team went 2–0 and did not allow a point in both of its games against the Alliance Athletic Club. The program began its ascent in 1919 with the hiring of Elmer "Gloomy Gus" Henderson, who went 45–7 before being dismissed in 1924 mainly because he never beat rival California. USC attempted to hire Notre Dame's rising star Knute Rockne, but he chose to stay in South Bend. Rockne then recommended his friend Howard Jones, who made his reputation at Yale and Iowa.

That was when everything changed. After hiring Jones in 1925—two years after starting to play in the newly built Los Angeles Memorial Coliseum—USC emerged as a national power. As college football surged in popularity, Jones and Rockne became America's most famous coaches during the Great Depression. Jones's 16 USC teams won all five of their Rose Bowls, seven Pacific Coast Conference championships, and the school's first four national titles in 1928, 1931, 1932, and 1939. Jones retired after the 1940 season and died the next summer of a heart attack.

By the late 1950s, the program had lost its way. The Trojans hit bottom in 1957 when they went 1–9 while under heavy sanctions from the Pacific Coast Conference because the players had received cash from an outside foundation. By 1960 the school was off probation when it named the relatively unknown John McKay as its head coach. First he returned USC to national relevance. Then he established it as the country's leading program in the late 1960s and early 1970s.

In 1976, McKay left USC after 16 seasons for a much better-paying job in the NFL. That pivotal time, 40 years ago, is where *Cardinal and Gold* begins.

1

THE SHADOW OF JOHN MCKAY

1976–1977

In 1976 in the state of California, Jerry Brown dated the enormously popular singer Linda Ronstadt while serving his first term as governor. Two years after resigning over the Watergate scandal, Richard Nixon lived in exile in San Clemente and the Warner Bros. studio in Burbank released its Oscar-winning film *All the President's Men.* A San Francisco jury convicted Patty Hearst of participating in an armed bank robbery with the revolutionaries who had kidnapped her. The first year of a terrible two-year drought battered farmers and ranchers and ended up producing nearly $1 billion in economic losses. On a more pleasant note, Napa Valley rejoiced when one of its red wines *and* one of its whites were deemed superior to the finest French wines at a legendary blind tasting in Paris.

In 1976 in Los Angeles, the fabled John McKay left USC to become the first head coach of the newly formed Tampa Bay Buccaneers. McKay later said, "I wanted to make some money—it's that simple." In 1975, USC had paid him $48,000 a year to be its coach and athletic director. Tampa Bay, the new NFL expansion team, had reportedly offered him a ten-year deal at $250,000 per year.

Back in 1960, he was still an obscure USC assistant when he replaced the struggling head coach Don Clark. Los Angeles wasn't thrilled at the news of McKay's promotion or when his first two teams won a total of eight games. Then, in 1962, USC went 11–0 and won its first national title since 1939 under Howard Jones. McKay went on to win three more national championships in 1967, 1972, and 1974. His 16 USC teams also won nine Pac-8 titles and five Rose Bowls and three times went undefeated.

McKay did not invent the Power I formation, but he nearly perfected it. The five dynamic running backs he coached—Mike Garrett, O.J. Simpson, Clarence Davis, Anthony Davis, and Ricky Bell—earned the school the nickname Tailback U. Garrett and Simpson won USC's first two Heisman Trophies in 1965 and 1968. Davis should have won the third in 1974, but the player known as AD perhaps had too much swagger for the predominantly white Heisman voters. They awarded it instead to Ohio State's talented and more reserved Archie Griffin.

Off the football field, McKay had a famously dry sense of humor. When the Buccaneers turned out to be awful, losing their first 26 games, he was asked to comment on their execution. "I'm all for it," McKay said. When asked about the importance of emotion, he said, "Emotion is overrated. My wife is emotional, but she's a lousy football player." Another time he reminded the Los Angeles press: "There are still over 600 million Chinese who don't care if we win or lose."

That was the witty McKay who charmed the writers, boosters, and alumni. Gary Jeter, an All-American defensive tackle, says McKay was distant with players. In Jeter's case that began when McKay recruited him at his Cleveland high school.

GARY JETER: He was the only major college coach who didn't visit me. I took that as, *I'm not good enough.* Then my mother got on the phone and kind of threatened him. She said, "You're the only coach that hasn't been there. Joe Paterno and Ara Parseghian and Tom Osborne and Woody Hayes—they've all been here but you." And he still didn't come to visit. But it worked. I wanted to prove myself to John McKay.

On Saturday he would give you that pregame speech, that halftime speech, that postgame speech. During the week, man, you got nothing. He rarely told his players anything directly. He would drive around practice in his electric golf cart. It was so finely tuned, you literally couldn't hear it. Then suddenly he'd hit that horn, and it would stop practice. McKay would point at an assistant coach. He would *run* over to McKay, and McKay would chew out the assistant. Then the assistant would chew out the player or the two or three players. That was just how it worked there then.

If you really wanted to know how John McKay felt about you, you had to read it in the newspaper. He had a little quotation that he would put behind a player's name. Those words were "I've ever seen." As in "Gary Jeter is the toughest I've ever seen" or "Gary Jeter is the quickest I've ever seen." If he said those words, you were anointed, man. It went across the country like wildfire. And it was like he put money in your pocket with the pros.

McKay also was known for his willingness to recruit and *start* the best players regardless of their race. During the 1960s, when black players were not allowed to play at most southern schools, and many northern schools such as Notre Dame were still primarily white, McKay's progressive and pragmatic stance brought many top black athletes to USC. In 1970, it was the Trojans' famous "all-black" backfield—quarterback Jimmy Jones, fullback Sam Cunningham, and tailback Clarence Davis—that led them to their historic 41–21 victory at Alabama.

GARY JETER: You ever hear the line "Sam Cunningham did more for integration in the south than Martin Luther King Jr.?" That was a true story. Bear Bryant and John McKay were good buddies. And the one thing Bear's Alabama teams lacked was speed. They had all these white kids—gutty white kids that couldn't run. So McKay said to Bear Bryant, "Why don't I take my team down there and we'll play a game?" So they go down to Birmingham in 1970, and Sam Cunningham runs buck wild. Then all these predominantly white fans go, "Wow!" They are in awe. As a result of that game, that's when the black players started coming into Alabama and the rest of the SEC. Before that game, they weren't there. That's what actually got the SEC going.

By 1975, McKay's final year, Pat Haden had graduated and a junior named Vince Evans became USC's third black starting quarterback. Before Evans there was Jimmy Jones, the first black quarterback to appear on the cover of *Sports Illustrated,* in 1969, and before Jones there was Willie Wood, the first black quarterback in Pac-8 history. Evans had grown up in segregated Greensboro, North Carolina.

VINCE EVANS: Before USC I played one year at Los Angeles City College. During that era, there still weren't very many African American quarterbacks at the D-1 level. But I had seen Jimmy Jones. He was starting at USC, and he was excelling. I thought, *They have a white coach and an African American QB.* But when I actually got there, I was thinking USC might make me a running back. Coach McKay said, "No, you're a quarterback. That's what we recruited you for." Those were encouraging words from an icon like John McKay.

But in 1975, his first year as a starter, Evans threw for three touchdowns and nine interceptions while completing just 31 percent of his passes. There were bumper stickers on campus saying SAVE USC FOOTBALL. SHOOT VINCE EVANS.

VINCE EVANS: I'd been getting hate mail since I had been there. That year was the worst because USC was used to winning national championships and Rose Bowls and that year we went 8–4. I got another unsigned letter before the UCLA game. It basically said, "Nigger, you go out there today, we're going to blow your brains out." I took that letter to Coach McKay. He called the LAPD. I was later told there was extra surveillance around the stadium.

Coach McKay asked me if I wanted to play that game. I said, "I grew up in racist environments. I went to theaters where African Americans sat in the balcony and whites sat on the main floor. Separate bathrooms and all of that. I didn't come 3,000 miles to be intimidated by something like this."

USC lost, 25–22, and Evans played so poorly in the second half, *Sports Illustrated* wrote that "he couldn't have thrown a football into the Grand Canyon while standing at the rim." Evans would return for his senior year with that criticism still fresh in his psyche and without McKay, the coach who had given him a chance.

In 1975, McKay's farewell season, defensive back Danny Reece was a team captain. He is still second all-time at USC with 18 career interceptions.

DANNY REECE: We had no stars on those teams. Coach McKay was the only star. As a freshman, I had never flown on an airplane. I was scared to death. But once I got on the plane and Coach was on there, I said to myself, *This plane's not gonna crash. We got Coach McKay on this thing.*

He was coach and athletic director, so he had to keep some distance. Not all the players liked that. A lot of kids coming into college were needy. But he wasn't the type who would put his arms around you and hug you. He would sometimes say, "If you guys win, I'll treat you like men. If you don't, we'll practice on Sunday."

Quarterback Rob Hertel played two seasons for McKay and started as a senior after McKay departed.

ROB HERTEL: John McKay was Catholic, and he respected Notre Dame. But I remember one game we were standing on the sidelines. He's talking to us, but he's looking at their coach, Ara Parseghian. McKay says, "Right 28 pitch. Right 28 pitch." He was looking straight at Ara and challenging him! Like, *I'm coming after you, Ara. I said 28 pitch. Did you hear me?*

By then McKay and Parseghian were two of the epic figures in the Trojans-Irish rivalry. The most popular origin story for the glamorous series has the wives of USC athletic director Gwynn Wilson and Notre Dame coach Knute Rockne laying the ground-work for the first USC-Notre Dame matchup while riding a train together in 1925. In reality, the series probably began in 1926 because both schools envisioned large payoffs from an annual game against another national power. The big money started flowing in 1927, when USC-Notre Dame drew an estimated 115,000 fans at Soldier Field in Chicago.

In 1974, McKay's most famous win came at the expense of Parseghian and the Irish. In their regular-season finale, sixth-ranked USC and fifth-ranked Notre Dame played at the Coliseum before 83,552 fans and millions more who watched on ABC. Dave Farmer was a sophomore running back.

DAVE FARMER: Notre Dame went up on us 24–0, and you could hear a pin drop in the Coliseum. We were getting the shit kicked out of us, and we never got the shit kicked out of us, ever.

GARY JETER: 24–0 and it wasn't even halftime! So I'm getting emotional and I almost get thrown out in the first half. I run over to their sidelines, and I'm chasing their quarterback, Tom Clements.

He goes to step out of bounds, but he's not out of bounds yet and I blast him. Steve Sylvester, their offensive tackle, gets in my ear. Then here comes Ara Parseghian. Here's a guy [who] a year ago wanted me to come to Notre Dame. He was in my living room. Now he's screaming and hollering at me. So I gave him a few expletives: Go to hell and screw you.

I go in our locker room at halftime. Now we're down 24–6 and my tears are coming. We can't lose to Notre Dame like this. So I sit down, and it's quiet as a church mouse. McKay is in front of us with that doggone cigar. He made a couple comments, and then he got down to it. He said, "I just signed a new contract. I'm going to be here. You guys play like this in the second half, a lot of you guys won't be."

DAVE FARMER: We go back on the field, and they kick off to Anthony Davis. He runs it back for a touchdown, and the Coliseum lights up. What I remember about the rest of the game is that we had the perfect call against every defense. We clicked like nothing else you've ever seen.

Most of those calls were made by John Robinson, the offensive coordinator who would later succeed McKay as head coach. In a surreal second half, the Trojans outscored the Irish 49–0. After USC won, 55–24, *Sports Illustrated* called it "one of the most remarkable scoring blitzkriegs in college football's history."

I asked Jeter whether as USC poured it on against Notre Dame, he and his teammates went wild or remained professional on the sidelines.

GARY JETER: Are you kidding me? Professional what? That's Notre Dame over there. Stanford, Cal, UCLA—put them all together and it's not even close to the hatred that we had for Notre Dame. I'll spell it out for you. The Methodists versus the Catholics. The blacks versus the whites. Let's be honest. That's what it was. You'd look over there at their sideline and they'd have a few brothers and a whole bunch of white guys. You'd look at our sideline and we had a few white guys and a whole bunch of brothers.

Of course, at USC, there have always been plenty of white guys who can't stand Notre Dame either.

In October 1975, as the rivalry resumed one year after the 55–24 pounding, there were persistent rumors that the NFL might lure away McKay. By then he had turned down several legitimate offers, most of them coming from the Los Angeles Rams.

DAVE FARMER: We knew Coach McKay would leave one day, but when? And the more talk about him leaving for the NFL, the more distracted we got. Then he told us in a team meeting after the Notre Dame game.

VINCE EVANS: When the announcement came, it was almost like there was a death that happened.

DANNY REECE: Everything was going great that season—we were 7–0—until he announced he was leaving. Then the wheels came off. A lot of guys didn't know how to handle that. They were in a fog. They came to USC to play for John McKay.

GARY JETER: That Friday before we left to go play Cal, he calls a meeting. McKay walks in and says, "Hey, I'm going to Tampa Bay." He was matter of fact, like he always is. But shit, you'd have thought we were all on the *Titanic*. It was chaos, man. The assistants didn't know what was going on with their situation. A lot had been offered jobs in Tampa by McKay, but some didn't want to go and it was really a mess. There were all these questions being asked by the press. Then we lost our last four games. Went from 7–0 to 7–4.

DANNY REECE: We went to the Liberty Bowl in Memphis. The last ten practices, Coach McKay let us have a little more freedom. We were coming home from one practice two or three days before the Liberty Bowl. I was on the defensive bus, and it pulled over and our assistant Marv Goux went into a liquor store and bought a couple cases of beer. We were allowed to drink the beer. They were treating us like men because we *were* men by then. Well, at least the seniors.

GARY JETER: We played Texas A&M in the Liberty Bowl. We were only 7–4 and they had a good team, but we dogged them 20–0. That was McKay's last game. So he did go out a winner. But it wasn't emotional before that game. It wasn't a "win one for coach" thing. Maybe some guys will lie and say yes. But we weren't close to McKay. He wasn't close to us. He was a very distant coach who got his point across.

I think McKay left USC for the money and because he wanted a new challenge. He wanted to see if what worked at the college level could work in the NFL. And I thought he had a great chance. He didn't kill us in practice. He got the best players and the best assistant coaches. There was no yelling and screaming. It was very, very professional. That was one of the reasons why we sent so many guys to the NFL. It was like a semi-pro team, the way he ran everything.

DANNY REECE: Coach McKay didn't say much before the Liberty Bowl game. He said, "I'm leaving. Win this one." But I was very emotional during that game. Four years at USC had gone by in a blink. Then one of the A&M players said something about McKay—he *needs* to leave or something like that—and somebody started a fight and I jumped in. This one dude from A&M stuck his finger into my helmet, and I snapped my helmet down and it just *popped* his finger.

I was closer to Coach McKay than most guys. I was his last captain. It got to the point where he was my second father. I loved him. I would fight you today if you said something bad about him.

USC had announced that John Robinson would be its next coach back in November, before the Liberty Bowl. He had started his career as an assistant at Oregon for 12 years. In 1972, after two straight 6–4–1 seasons at USC, McKay wanted to spend more time with the defense and brought in Robinson to run the offense. During Robinson's three-year stint from 1972 to 1974, USC won two national titles while averaging 32 points a game. Robinson called the plays with confidence but rarely did anything slick. Like his predecessor, Robinson believed that a well-executed running game was the key to great offensive football.

JOHN ROBINSON: In 1975, I went up north to work for the Raiders. By then the question of who would replace McKay was already boiling. Everybody figured it would either be Dave Levy or Craig Fertig or Marv Goux, and they were all really good coaches and guys who were loved by the USC alumni. Plus, John Madden was coaching the Raiders. He and I were best friends all our lives. He would call every year and ask if I wanted to come up there. In '75, I said yeah.

Jack Hubbard contacted me when McKay left. He was the school president when I was there. He had come out to practice and watched me coach and saw that I had more of an in-charge position on offense. So later he basically hired me by himself. There was no committee. Nobody knew about it. We were getting ready for a playoff game in Oakland, and Hubbard called me from a phone booth in Washington, DC. He said, "Hey, I gotta catch a plane. Do you want to be the head coach at USC?" I thought about it for about two seconds and I said, "Yes."

The LA Times had some kind of headline the day I was hired: USC HIRES JOHN WHO? People were shocked. I was not a popular choice. I also had the problem that McKay took two or three assistants to Tampa. He took Dave Levy and Wayne Fontes, and Craig Fertig got the head-coaching job at Oregon State. The whole thing was a real shock to everybody, and there was a lot of mistrust about the whole thing.

On top of all that, Robinson was only 41, had no head-coaching experience, and was replacing a legend who had won four national championships.

GARY JETER: John Robinson was with the Raiders. When McKay left, I thought Dave Levy should have gotten the job. He was the assistant head coach under McKay. He was the heir apparent. It was just really weird when they picked Robinson. I had no idea why they picked him. I was like, *What? Who?*

DAVE FARMER: With McKay, you had to make an appointment to see him. With Robinson, you just walked in and said, "Hey, how's it going?" He was kind of happy-go-lucky. Coach McKay, if you did something wrong, he would embarrass you in front of everybody to pull you out of it. Coach Robinson was the opposite: He wanted to coach you up. He had more of a father-figure approach.

ROB HERTEL: McKay had an intimidating persona. Robinson was the exact opposite: a big, emotional, energetic guy.

As the 1976 season approached, senior quarterback Vince Evans appeared to be the biggest question mark, but Robinson named him the starter before the eighth-ranked Trojans opened at home against unranked Missouri. It was Robinson's first game as a head coach at any level and the first time in 16 years that anyone but McKay had led USC.

JOHN ROBINSON: Vince Evans had struggled the year I was with the Raiders. He had just been awful. I hired a quarterback coach, fella by the name of Paul Hackett, who did a great job of working with him on fundamentals. Still, Vince Evans was not a popular choice. I named him the starting quarterback, and that pissed everybody off. Then he plays terrible in the Missouri game and we coach terrible. With about one minute to go, Vince gets hurt and he's lying out there on the field. I go out on the field, and I'm bending over him. He gets up, and we walk together. And 90 percent of the people at the Coliseum are booing me and Vince Evans as loud as they could boo.

VINCE EVANS: They wanted to run him *and* me out of SC. The hate mail continued to come. And even just the regular naysayers weren't pleased that Robinson had picked me to lead the team.

DAVE FARMER: Missouri beat us 45–26! Our defense played so bad, we had to practice in pads the next day on Sunday. We had tackling practice! *Tackling* practice? This is not Pop Warner.

GARY JETER: We got plastered, at home. That was ridiculous. But Robinson did not screw up that game. The players did. And boy, did we get shellacked by the press. We had all these potential first-round draft choices, and Missouri just killed us.

JOHN ROBINSON: The team had only been 8–4 the year before I got there, but it looked like our team would be good in '76. Also, I had been aggressive in saying I *thought* we would have a really good year. So the *LA Times* said the next day, "How could one man ruin a great program so fast?"

After that game, they had a big alumni event: 7,300 people at Heritage Hall. I got up to speak, and people were just in a state of shock. I said, "This will never happen again. I will never have a team that is not prepared to play."

That was my first week as head coach. I still kind of knew the team would be good, but the trouble with something like that is that everyone sort of loses confidence in you and you lose confidence in yourself. But I just told myself that I knew the answers.

Keith Van Horne was a freshman offensive tackle. By his senior year, he was a consensus first-team All-American and a runner-up for the Outland Trophy, given to the best college lineman on either side of the ball.

KEITH VAN HORNE: It was our very first game ever under John Robinson. And we literally got booed off the field. Then we got into the locker room. John is a pretty laid-back guy, but he's not so laid-back at this point. He said, "Gentleman, I will never be booed off my home field again. Do you understand me?"

Under the tutelage of Hudson Houck, the great USC offensive line coach, Van Horne later would add to the school's fabled offensive line legacy. Before Van Horne came Ron Yary and Ron Mix, and after him Anthony Munoz, Roy Foster, Bruce Matthews, Tony Boselli, and others. In 1976, Van Horne's teammate Brad Budde started at guard as a freshman, a rarity at the time in college football.

BRAD BUDDE: I'm from Kansas City, so losing to Missouri was a double nightmare for me. After that game, Coach Robinson felt he was trying to do too much. From that point we really simplified things and went back to the basics, which meant being a physical team and wearing people out with the 28 pitch play. That became our trademark, and we proceeded to keep on winning the next four years.

Known to the public as Student Body Right or Student Body Left, 28 pitch was a quick pitch to the tailback, who tried to get to the edge with most of the offensive line leading the way. It was no coincidence that 28 pitch resembled the power sweeps run by the Green Bay Packers. McKay borrowed the play from Vince Lombardi and tweaked it until it suited McKay's I formation.

The Robinson era began righting itself immediately with a 53–0 win at lowly Oregon. As the Trojans played power football, Evans became more proficient, and the defense stiffened, USC won eight straight games after getting embarrassed at home against Missouri. Then the third-ranked Trojans defeated No. 2 UCLA, 24–14, in Pasadena.

JOHN ROBINSON: That was Terry Donahue's first year and it was my first year. The winner would go to the Rose Bowl. Mid-fourth quarter, we're ahead 14–0 and we call a quarterback draw, and Vince Evans runs through the whole UCLA team and scores a touchdown. He was going so fast that he ran almost up the tunnel. As he came back, I ran down there and we hugged each other, and it flashed through my mind: *Vince, you and I should turn around and give all these people the finger.* Because the USC fans were cheering us and I was thinking back to that first Missouri game.

The next Saturday at the Coliseum, third-ranked USC beat No. 13 Notre Dame, 17–13, a signature victory for Robinson in his first season. The 10–1 and second-ranked Trojans were now headed to the Rose Bowl to meet 10–1 and third-ranked Michigan. After USC won a brutal defensive battle, 14–6, *Sports Illustrated* wrote, "The Wolverines arrived in Pasadena leading the nation in total offense, rushing offense and scoring. But they left exposed as just another tough, solid upstanding Big Ten football team without a passing attack."

An efficient Evans completed 14 of 20 passes for 181 yards, ran for one touchdown, and was named the game's most valuable player. USC, at 11–1, argued that it should win the national championship, but the AP voters gave it to 12–0 Pittsburgh.

GARY JETER: After that loss to Missouri, we won 11 in a row. Pittsburgh had that schedule—that Notre Dame schedule—playing Temple and all those other goofy teams. Pittsburgh went 12–0. But we went 11–1 with a much harder schedule.

Still, Robinson won a Rose Bowl in his rookie season. Evans completed 54 percent of his passes, up from 31 percent the previous year, and threw for 1,440 yards, up from 695. I asked him what he recalled most fondly from his senior year at USC.

VINCE EVANS: Winning the Rose Bowl with my teammates, and John Robinson standing behind me.

In 1977, Evans played for the Chicago Bears, Rob Hertel replaced him as starting quarterback, and the Trojans entered the season ranked No. 4. By the time USC hosted Alabama in October, it was 4–0, ranked No. 1, and had won 15 straight games since the Missouri loss. Linebacker Steve Busick and tight end Hoby Brenner, who later would play 20 NFL seasons between them, recall the big game against the 4–0 and seventh-ranked Crimson Tide.

STEVE BUSICK: We were ranked No. 1, but we may not have been as good as our ranking said. We were very young. I was a freshman and I was playing, so that tells you something.

HOBY BRENNER: Our defense wanted to be ready for Alabama's wishbone. So we had a full-contact practice on the Sunday before we played them. That was the only time in college or in the NFL that we had a full-contact practice the day *after* a game.

ROB HERTEL: We were down 21–14 at the Coliseum. Then we scored in the final minute to make it 21–20. There was no overtime in those days. Coach Robinson and I discussed it on the sideline. He said, "What do you think?" I said, "We have to go for two. We're number one in the country. We can't settle for a tie." We went for two, and the play didn't work. I threw an interception.

Hertel actually played a strong second half, passing for 230 yards as USC charged back from a 21–6 deficit. Still, it was a crushing loss as the 5–1 Trojans headed into their rivalry game at Notre Dame. I asked Budde and Van Horne, the hard-nosed offensive linemen and close friends, if they were among the players who hated the Irish.

Budde tends toward diplomacy. Van Horne has no filter.

BRAD BUDDE: Did I hate Notre Dame? I don't know. I think hate and respect are synonymous in a way.

KEITH VAN HORNE: I've heard many people say, "My favorite team is whoever is playing Notre Dame." And it's not just USC people. That's people all over the country. It's their self-entitlement and their arrogance. They say they have a higher standard for who they take there. That's bullshit. They have guys who get in trouble too.

It's a great place to get an education. Don't get me wrong. But when I went to USC, of course that rivalry became ingrained in me. What really bugged me was their players' arrogance. Not all of them. Actually Joe Montana was a real nice guy. And they produced some solid citizens. They've produced judges and whatnot. But they really do believe God is on their side. To have the nerve to call their mosaic on the side of the building Touchdown Jesus? I mean, please. Brad Budde and I used to look at that thing, and I won't even tell you what we used to do. Touchdown Jesus, my ass. Every time we scored a touchdown, we'd look straight at him.

I actually received a letter from Notre Dame in high school. They said, "We'd like to review your film and see if you're somebody we'd be interested in." So we sent them my game film. Then I got a letter back signed by Dan Devine. It said, "We reviewed your game films and we've come to the conclusion that you're not the quality of player we desire here at Notre Dame."

Van Horne became a first-team All-American and a first-round draft choice of the Chicago Bears, where he protected Jim McMahon, opened holes for Walter Payton, and played on the 1985 team that won the city's only Super Bowl. Then again, Devine also had been flat-out wrong about Joe Montana, who began his junior year in 1977 as the No. 3 quarterback behind Rusty Lisch and Gary Forystek. Despite the public protest, Montana still wasn't starting by the third week against Purdue. Then he entered the game with 11 minutes left and the Boilermakers ahead, 24–14. Montana drove Notre Dame to 17 straight points and a thrilling 31–24 victory. By the USC game three weeks later, the "quarterback controversy" that never should have been finally was put to rest.

HOBY BRENNER: At Notre Dame, Joe Montana wasn't advertised much. I knew Rusty Lisch's name more than I knew Montana's. It was really the 49ers and the NFL that set his name on fire.

KEITH VAN HORNE: Starting Rusty Lisch instead of Montana? And Montana was like third string, right? Hey, I had to play with Rusty Lisch on the Bears. That guy was terrible.

In October 1977, the Trojans were 5–1 and ranked No. 5 when they faced the 4–1 and 11th-ranked Irish. The game was in South Bend and Montana was in place, but USC was favored anyway. Over the last ten years—nine of them under McKay—the Trojans had lost the rivalry game just once.

BRAD BUDDE: The '77 game was when Notre Dame wore their green jerseys. I remember looking at their uniforms during warm-ups and thinking, *Who's the color coordinator for this team?* At that point they still had their blue jerseys on, but they had yellow and gold socks. Then they went back inside before the kickoff, and that's when they changed into green.

ROB HERTEL: They brought out this Trojan horse in the middle of their field. Their four captains jumped out in these four Kelly green jerseys. It sounded like a bomb went off in the stands.

KEITH VAN HORNE: An actual Trojan horse. They built it, they wheeled it out. Then the rest of their guys run out in their green jerseys, which they hadn't worn in like 20 years. Then the place *really* goes crazy. I never heard a place get as loud as that. And it's kind of like, *Oh, shit, here we go.*

I got in at the end because the game was over. They were talking trash because they were kicking our ass. But that score was misleading. We played a physical game, but we had a ton of turnovers. And they had a quarterback—his name was Joe Montana. So they did hand it to us that day. But they had to resort to their little tricks to do it. That's what I say, anyway.

JOHN ROBINSON: It was a good old-fashioned ass kicking. They had been unsettled at quarterback, but they were really good. They won the national championship that year. I always thought Joe Montana was the best player I'd ever seen, and that was the beginning of it.

Some people said the green jerseys were the turning point. But I never thought that. I always liked playing on the road and the opposing fans' enthusiasm. I used to tell the team that those were the best games: when you win on the road and their fans are silent filing out of the stadium. I used to bullshit our team like that all the time. And they would believe me. So I don't think we were intimidated by the crowd. They were really good, and Joe Montana went on to have a great season.

Montana passed for two touchdowns and ran for two others. Notre Dame thrashed USC, 49–19, in the famous "green jerseys" game and then went on to win the national title as the DUMP DEVINE bumper stickers went back into storage. The Trojans ended up just 7–4 and went to the lower-tier Bluebonnet Bowl, where they beat Texas A&M, 47–28.

Still, 8–4 at USC was equivalent to 6–6 at most other programs, and the 30-point loss in South Bend was embarrassing. In Robinson's second year, he and his Trojans took a step backward.

2

"HEY, ALABAMA, WE WHIPPED YOUR ASS":
1978–1979

After going 8–4 the previous year, the 1978 Trojans entered the season ranked No. 9, a pretty nice accolade for the standard college football program. At powerful USC, it was the lowest preseason ranking since 1966, one of the aberrational McKay years.

The Trojans had bountiful talent—37 of them ended up on NFL rosters—but as Robinson said before the first game, "This will be a very interesting team. It has great potential, but in six years as an assistant and head coach, it's the youngest USC team I've ever been associated with."

Dennis Smith was part of the strong sophomore class, which included Ronnie Lott, Keith Van Horne, Hoby Brenner, and Jeff Fisher. Smith would establish himself as one of the most ferocious USC safeties ever, a reputation he later burnished as a six-time Pro Bowl selection with the Denver Broncos.

DENNIS SMITH: That season we were young, but we thought we'd win every game. The thing about USC, they brainwash you to believe you've got the best coaches, you've got the best players, and the only way you lose a game is if you run out of time. That's a great attitude to have as a college player and a great attitude to take into the pros.

The raw and gifted Trojans were 2–0 and ranked No. 7 when they ventured into the south to face 2–0 and No. 1 Alabama. The rankings were reversed from the previous season, when the Crimson Tide, ranked seventh, upset the top-ranked Trojans, 21–20, at the Coliseum. USC wanted payback, but even more than that a national title.

It was also the Trojans' first trip to Alabama since the historic 1970 game, which helped break the SEC's racial barrier. But according to linebacker Riki Ellison, who later won three Super Bowls with the 49ers, the Trojans were still perceived as foreigners.

RIKI ELLISON: It was the late '70s, and their fans saw us as these long-haired hippies coming in from LA. And there was this SEC, Alabama arrogance, like we were not at their level. But it was still pretty badass seeing Bear Bryant on the other side of the field.

STEVE BUSICK: We were in our hotel lobby, and all their fans were clones of Bear Bryant. They were all wearing the same hat he did.

KEITH VAN HORNE: It was hot and humid and loud, and there's Bear Bryant, a legend, with his hat and his checkered coat or whatever the hell he wore. Houndstooth, right? That was an electric atmosphere. It's the SEC and Alabama, and here come the Southern California guys.

JOHN ROBINSON: That was the biggest game of the season. It was a nationally televised game. And the thing about those big games back then, they were nationally televised for the whole country. There was no other college game on TV that day. So if you lived in Florida, you watched USC-Alabama.

Alabama was ranked number one and they were ten-point favorites, and we really dominated them. We won 24–14, but it was an ass kicking. I remember meeting Bear Bryant at the middle of the field after the game. He was about 6–4, a big man, and he was like a god. Bear Bryant just drawled, "Y'all just beat the living shit out of us." I said, "Thank you, sir! Thank you, thank you!"

After routing Michigan State in Los Angeles, the surging 4–0 and second-ranked Trojans made the short trip to Tempe to play unranked Arizona State.

KEITH VAN HORNE: That was the year the Pac-8 became the Pac-10. So that was the first game ever between ASU and USC. They were all fired up for that, and of course everyone gets fired up to play against USC. No excuses, they beat us, but by then we had lost all three of our centers. We had a defensive lineman playing center. And there were multiple quarterback-center exchange fumbles. Their place was going crazy, and they beat us. Mark Malone was their quarterback. I think that was the highlight of Mark Malone's life, frankly.

USC fumbled the snap six times, something you don't see in high school. ASU recovered four of the fumbles, leading to 13 points and a shocking 20–7 Pac-10 upset. But even with defensive lineman Ray Peters starting at center, the Trojans won their next six in a row, including a 27–25 thriller over Joe Montana and the Irish. Then, at 10–1 and ranked No. 3, they finished the regular season at unheralded and unranked Hawaii.

DENNIS SMITH: Our players were drinking that week like they were on vacation. Game time comes and they weren't ready. They were thinking, *This is just Hawaii.*

The hard-drinking Trojans beat the Rainbow Warriors, 21–5, but led only 7–5 early in the fourth quarter. Still, at 11–1, they managed to retain their No. 3 ranking. Then they defeated fifth-ranked Michigan, 17–10, in the Rose Bowl, thanks partly to the famously blown call that everybody in the stadium saw except for the officials on the field.

USC had the ball and a 7–3 lead in the second quarter. With second and goal at the Michigan three-yard line, Charles White ran into the end zone without the football he had just dropped, but line judge Gilbert Marchman signaled a USC touchdown. Oddly, Marchman was a Big Ten official.

The phantom touchdown put the Trojans ahead, 14–3. Dennis Smith intercepted a pass on the next Michigan drive, USC kicked a field goal, and at halftime it led by two touchdowns, one of them so bogus that even the Trojans admit it.

Most of them, anyway.

BRAD BUDDE: I was under the pile. So I didn't get a good look at it. That'll be my way out.

JOHN ROBINSON: He definitely fumbled. Thank God there was no replay then. Today they would have turned that over in a second. There *was* instant replay for the TV viewers, and everyone on TV saw it. It was clearly a fumble.

I reminded Van Horne that O.J. Simpson announced that Rose Bowl for NBC, Simpson called it a fumble, and the USC fans did not appreciate that.

KEITH VAN HORNE: Yeah, well, they don't appreciate him now anyway, right? We used to call that play the earthquake touchdown. There was an earthquake, and that's why the ball came loose. I remember the front page of the *Los Angeles Times.* There was a picture of it. Pretty obvious.

But you know what? They called a touchdown. And Michigan had a chance to beat us in the second half. They didn't. We won. That's it. *We* won the Rose Bowl.

College football is full of surprises and unforeseen heroes. One of the Rose Bowl stars was Hoby Brenner, who later played 13 years for the New Orleans Saints. But until he opened the scoring with a nine-yard touchdown reception in the first quarter, he was largely unknown outside his own family.

HOBY BRENNER: I got three balls thrown at me all year. The third one, I scored our first touchdown of the Rose Bowl. Then you're getting interviewed on TV and the whole nine yards and you're thinking, *This is so cool.*

I thought John Robinson did a great job that season. He was a very good motivator in a subtle way. He wasn't fire and brimstone, but he knew how to get a team ready. That year was a good example. We were talented but very young. And we went 12–1 and then won the Rose Bowl.

Robinson was 3–0 in the postseason, two of them Rose Bowl wins, and his three teams had gone a combined 31–6. Though clearly up to the task of following McKay, now he wanted something that McKay had accomplished four times: a national championship.

"I don't know if anyone knows who is number one," Robinson said in the victorious Rose Bowl locker room. "There are four or five good teams. I'm prejudiced and I'm going to vote for USC."

Freshman quarterback Scott Tinsley recalls what happened next.

SCOTT TINSLEY: There was an AP poll and a UPI poll. The UPI poll was the coaches, and they voted us number one. The AP poll was the writers, and they voted for Alabama, who we had beaten that season. So we had to split the national championship.

DENNIS SMITH: We knew we blew it when we lost that Arizona State game. We would have been 13–0 instead of 12–1. But for them to put Alabama ahead of us? When we beat them head to head?

RIKI ELLISON: We beat their ass. We're their daddies. They still know it today. Any of those guys, if we saw them today in person, they know who kicked whose ass in their home stadium. The facts are the facts.

HOBY BRENNER: That was total bull. Not only did we beat Alabama, we beat them up physically. But we were a West Coast team, and there was a lot more bias toward the eastern part of the country in the national polls.

STEVE BUSICK: How can you justify that? But it's Bear Bryant, and there were some politics. He pulled a lot of weight back in those days.

KEITH VAN HORNE: The Bear had some influence, yeah. But I still have a national championship ring that I'll show to any Alabama player and say, "You show me yours and I'll show you mine, and guess what? Hey, Alabama, we whipped your ass." And I still remember John Robinson telling us, "We know who the number one team in the country is."

JOHN ROBINSON: We kind of dismissed Alabama, as in hey, we *beat* them. But we didn't spend a lot of time being pissed about it. It was also not as big a deal back in those days. My wife and I were in Heritage Hall when they made the announcement that we were national champs in one of the polls. Somebody had a bottle of champagne, and 15 people stood around and had a sip of champagne and that was it.

It was a very big deal, of course. In only his third season— the same length of time it took McKay—Robinson won his first national championship. No one knew it would be his last. No one dreamed it would be USC's last until a coach named Pete Carroll did it 25 years later.

In 1979, almost every preseason poll placed the Trojans at No. 1. They had 16 starters returning from a 12–1 team that had won the Rose Bowl and the UPI national title. Paul McDonald returned at quarterback after a school-record 19 touchdown passes, which today sounds modest, but that was back in the day at run-oriented USC. Heisman Trophy candidate Charles White also returned as a senior, running behind an NFL-ready line featuring Anthony Munoz, Budde, and Van Horne.

The Trojans were 3–0 when they traveled to Baton Rouge for a characteristically crazed night game at Tiger Stadium. Or as Budde said afterward, "It makes Notre Dame look like *Romper Room.*"

JOHN ROBINSON: LSU is one of the most difficult places to play year in and year out. Their fans are fanatical. We were also ranked number one in the nation, and their coach, Charlie McClendon, announced that he was retiring after that season. So they were building this up as one of the biggest games in LSU history.

HOBY BRENNER: We pulled up to their stadium for a practice that Friday night, and there were thousands of LSU students yelling "Tiger Bait" at the bus.

JOHN ROBINSON: They wouldn't let us off the buses. They were rocking the buses. It looked like a '70s demonstration. But our guys were a pretty cocky group. Charlie White was running up and down the aisle laughing and saying, "They don't know who they're fucking with when they do this to us."

HOBY BRENNER: We had to wait until they got the police in there to escort us into the stadium. This was for a stupid Friday practice. It was crazy at LSU. The fans in Birmingham, at Alabama, were obviously active. But it was nothing like LSU and Baton Rouge. They were standing up and screaming the whole game, and you couldn't hear anything. My dad went to that game, and he told me afterward, "When you walk through a parking lot at a college football game, usually you see piles of beer cans. There were no beer cans. There were empty fifths all over the place."

KEITH VAN HORNE: Yeah, it's different down there. When we got off the bus, there were a few thousand LSU fans lined up. We could literally only walk single file through those fans. That's all the room they would give us. They were pointing at us and yelling—"Tiger bait, Tiger bait, Tiger bait!" And they had the damn fucking tiger in a cage. And they would stick him with the thing, so he would roar.

On the sticky and deafening evening at 20th-ranked LSU, the top-ranked Trojans trailed, 12–3, with 12:23 left in the fourth quarter. Then they scored two straight touchdowns, including the game winner with 32 seconds left. As Tiger Stadium went deathly silent, stout-hearted USC escaped with a 17–12 victory.

RIKI ELLISON: If you look at USC history back then, we took down the best the SEC had. We took down South Carolina and George Rogers. We took down Alabama at Alabama. We took down LSU at LSU. Man, we rocked back then against the SEC.

KEITH VAN HORNE: We won at Tennessee, too, and those people are a little wacko, too. And that song to this day makes me want to throw up. That "Rocky Top" shit?

After hammering Washington State, 50–21, the Trojans were 5–0 and still ranked No. 1 when they played at unranked Stanford in a game that haunts them still.

DENNIS SMITH: Going into that year, we thought we were better than the year before. We still basically had the same guys and we had more experience. Then that Stanford game blew our whole season for a second straight national championship.

RIKI ELLISON: They were coached by Bill Walsh, my coach later in the NFL. When I was at USC, we were the antithesis of Bill Walsh football. We were simple, big man on big man football. Bill Walsh loved to beat that kind of team because he hated that kind of football.

We had more talent that season than probably any USC team I played on. But John Robinson started pulling the starters out in the second quarter and third quarter of games. So prior to playing Stanford, I don't think our first units had ever played four quarters. Maybe the LSU game. So now we're up 21–0 against Stanford, and we put our second stringers in. They took advantage of that.

STEVE BUSICK: It was John Elway's freshman year. No one knew who he was at that time. Our coaches knew him, though. In film study that week, there was another quarterback we were watching, but one of our coaches said, "If this young kid gets in the game, their whole game plan changes because he can run all over the field and his arm is like a cannon. If he comes in, we may have some problems."

We're up 21–0 at halftime. Suddenly Elway comes in, as a freshman, and he's running all over the place and he just shreds us.

They ended up tying the game, 21–21. Then I played with Elway on the Broncos, and he never let me forget it. He used to rip me about that.

The Trojans took it out on their next five opponents, including a 49–14 crushing of UCLA in the regular-season finale. Then, in its second straight Rose Bowl, 10–0–1 and third-ranked USC faced 11–0 and top-ranked Ohio State. The day before the huge game, Robinson signed a five-year contract extension, but the deal was not yet made public.

One of Robinson's closest colleagues was Artie Gigantino, then in his second season as the USC linebackers coach. He later moved up to defensive coordinator, and *Sports Illustrated* once named him the second best recruiter in the nation.

ARTIE GIGANTINO: We were getting ready to play Ohio State in the Rose Bowl, and there was speculation that John Robinson would go to the NFL. John had been offered the Washington Redskins job before they gave it to Joe Gibbs. John is a renaissance man. He's more than just football. Likes music, likes politics. And I swear to God I thought he was going to take the job and move to Washington, DC. If he *had* taken it, USC would have done something unprecedented in the history of USC football. They would have hired John Jackson probably, who was an African American on our staff, as the head coach at USC. He coached at Illinois, coached in the Ivy League, very well respected, and he was John's initial running back coach. I believe Jack Hubbard, the president at USC, had the balls to do it. And I thought things were pointing that way if John took that Redskins job.

With Robinson fending off the NFL, Charles White rushed for a Rose Bowl record 247 yards and the one-yard game-winning touchdown with 1:32 left. That gritty final drive began with USC trailing, 16–10, from its own 17-yard line with 5:21 remaining. Then White carried six times for 71 of the 83 yards. The Buckeyes knew what was coming—Student Body Right and Left—but could do nothing to stop it. After USC won, 17–16, White was selected the Rose Bowl MVP for the second straight year.

He ended his senior season with 1,803 rushing yards and 18 touchdowns while averaging 6.2 yards per carry. That earned White the school's third Heisman Trophy, following his fellow tailbacks Mike Garrett and O.J. Simpson.

Many felt that the country's two best teams had just played in Pasadena. But even though third-ranked USC defeated No. 1 Ohio State, the 21–21 tie with Bill Walsh and Stanford kept the Trojans from winning back-to-back national titles. Alabama instead won it all by defeating Arkansas, 24–9, in the Sugar Bowl. This time the Crimson Tide, at 12–0, didn't have to share their grand prize with the team from Southern California.

3

THE TURBULENCE BEGINS:
1980–1982

Trouble came to the football program on August 12, 1980, when the Pac-10 placed USC on one year's probation. Four other schools (UCLA, Oregon, Arizona, and Arizona State) received the same punishment for various offenses. Thus, half the conference was barred from playing in that postseason, including the Pac-10's own Rose Bowl.

USC was punished for "unwarranted intrusions by the athletic department into academic processes," a reference to three speech courses in which 34 football players had done very little work or none at all. USC reportedly discovered the academic misconduct itself and then reported it to the Pac-10. Jim Zumberge, the school's new president, was on campus for only two days when he summoned Robinson to a meeting in August. "I had read what he said in the paper about dealing with the problem, and it all sounded good," said Zumberge. "But I wanted to look him in the eye and see if he had credibility. Because if what he said didn't have any teeth, than we're in big trouble."

Zumberge succeeded John Hubbard, the USC president for the

last ten years. Although Hubbard had improved the school's academic standing, *Sports Illustrated* once described him as an "unabashed athletic booster." Then Zumberge came in talking tough about academics, and Robinson also vowed to be more vigilant. "If I find out the week of the Notre Dame game that my tailback hasn't been going to class, he doesn't play against Notre Dame," Robinson said.

JOHN ROBINSON: We only had a slipshod academic advisory thing during that time. We had two part-time guys that worked there, and we had one guy who was a graduate student. And all of a sudden everyone found out that it was an easy speech class. And then they just carried it way too far. It started out as a legit class, but it crossed over pretty fast.

Ken Ruettgers later became an All-American offensive lineman, a first-round draft pick of the Green Bay Packers, and a member of the Packers Hall of Fame. In August 1980, he was a USC freshman wondering what he had stepped into.

KEN RUETTGERS: A few months after I signed with USC, they were put on probation. It was interesting. Before you even start college, your team is penalized for something that you had nothing to do with, no involvement with at all. I thought: *Should I have gone to one of those other schools that recruited me?* There was Notre Dame, Nebraska, Michigan State, all the other Pac-10 schools. But what I liked about USC was the players I got to meet on my recruiting trips. They were All-Americans, national champions, but they were regular hardworking guys.

When they announced the probation, I remember John Robinson saying, "We can still be number one in the nation. We can still have a national championship." So we set our goals on that. And at least for that year, we took on the underdog role because we were on probation.

ARTIE GIGANTINO: We got put on probation because of a speech class or two that some of the players took and never showed up. I wasn't 100 percent sure what was going on because I was just a young kid, just going to sleep every night thanking God I was coaching at USC. Now I know what happens in situations like that. Guys get too close to academic people, especially the young girls who are helping. And suddenly the guys stop showing up to class and all the work is getting done anyway. I also think USC at the time thought they were invincible, and sometimes you get a little more cavalier than you should.

That was also Jack Hubbard's last year as president. As Hubbard is going out the door, they bring in Jim Zumberge from SMU, and he has a different agenda. He's gonna clean up USC and try and crack the whip a little bit.

KEITH VAN HORNE: There was something with tutors and guys not going to class. I wasn't part of that. I was an actual student. But there was definitely a pall hanging over us, the fact that we went on probation and couldn't go to a bowl. I was one of the captains, and it was my senior year. All the seniors were like, *Shit, we can't go anywhere.*

STEVE BUSICK: Back then you could take advantage of some very easy classes that catered not just to football players but to other athletes. Those classes, if you walked in, it would be *nothing* but athletes. Speech was a big one. Drama was a big one. Another big one was Russian, believe it or not. A lot of guys would just show up the first day and then the last day, and they would still get by. I think this was happening at just about every high-powered program. And there was probably worse going on, and this stuff probably still goes on today. They just do a better job of hiding it.

Some universities still get caught, however. At North Carolina, the largest academic scandal in college sports history was revealed by a whistle-blowing tutor in the athletic department. That academic fraud at Chapel Hill lasted for 19 years.

In 1980 on the football field, USC's junior tailback Marcus Allen rushed for 1,563 yards and 14 touchdowns. Although more of a slasher than a power runner, he could deliver a blow when necessary. Allen had played fullback as a sophomore and had proved a capable blocker for Heisman Trophy winner Charles White.

Tight end Hoby Brenner led the 1980 team in receiving with only 26 catches for 315 yards and zero touchdowns. The starting quarterback was Gordon Adams, who perhaps you've never heard of but who, to his credit, graduated from USC magna cum laude.

RIKI ELLISON: Probation was a huge deal. That deflated us, knowing we had no chance to win a bowl game. But the quarterback position was the biggest issue on that team. Our defense was still bringing it, as I remember.

USC finished the season 8–2–1, including a 20–17 loss to UCLA, which the Los Angeles press dubbed the Probation Bowl. In the season finale, the 17th-ranked Trojans hosted 9–0–1 and second-ranked Notre Dame, which was in pursuit of Dan Devine's second national title. Back during the summer, Devine had announced this would be his final season, but rather than wait until the season ended, Notre Dame named his successor during USC week. The Irish chose Gerry Faust, who came straight from Moeller High School in Cincinnati. He had no college coaching experience.

Note Dame lost, 20–3, at the Coliseum, ending its quest for a national championship. USC might have won regardless—it was 8–2 in its last ten Notre Dame games—but the stunning announcement created a major distraction for the Irish.

JOHN ROBINSON: Gerry Faust seemed like a nice guy. But I was kind of like everyone else, scratching my head a little bit and asking, *Why would you do this?*

KEITH VAN HORNE: We couldn't go to a bowl my senior year. But Notre Dame was ranked No. 2, and we spanked them 20–3. So that kind of left a better taste in our mouth.

STEVE BUSICK: Of course, we wanted to win a bowl game again. But 1978 to 1980 was a great run at USC. We lost three games in three years.

The 1981 Trojans came off their one-year probation with a No. 5 preseason ranking and then pounded Tennessee and Indiana by a combined score of 64–7. USC was ranked No. 1 when it hosted second-ranked Oklahoma in the first enormous game of the season. The Trojans won a thriller, 28–24, scoring the go-ahead touchdown with two seconds left. Marcus Allen rushed for 208 yards and then made the cover of *Sports Illustrated* under the headline ROLLING THUNDER.

Still, USC would have lost if Oklahoma had not fumbled a ridiculous ten times. The Sooners rolled up 444 total yards, including 307 yards rushing, as their fabled wishbone made the Trojans look clueless.

ARTIE GIGANTINO: Here's a little background, and I don't give a shit who gets offended by it. We had hired R. C. Slocum as defensive coordinator. And I told John Robinson, "The next time that job opens, I'm out of here the next morning if I don't get it." But John thought I was too young to be DC. Maybe he was right; I was 27. So we brought in Slocum to be the DC. You don't know me, but I'm an Italian from New Jersey who wears Gucci loafers with no socks on and leather jackets. And this was at USC. That's like bringing me to the middle of Mississippi and saying I'm the new governor of Mississippi. It's not a fit. So instead we bring in Slocum, and one of the reasons John wanted him is that John wanted a guy from the South who had a pretty good understanding of option football. We got *slaughtered* by the option against Oklahoma.

The good news was, our offense was great. End of the game, we're driving. John Mazur, our quarterback, throws the ball to one receiver, and it goes by that receiver and right to Fred Cornwell, and we win the game. Later on, I saw the TV replay. Prior to that last play, their coach, Barry Switzer, is on one of the sidelines, kneeling down, smoking a cigarette! On the sidelines! John Robinson is talking to Mazur. And John Robinson was great when the camera was on him. And trust me, you know when the camera is on you. It's right in your face. So John is laughing with Mazur, trying to loosen him up. Obviously this is serious business, but John's trying to put him in a little bit of a relaxed mood. And ABC shows a double screen of Robinson and Switzer. It was classic. And it helped us in recruiting like you wouldn't believe.

JOHN ROBINSON: Of course I remember. On the last play of the game, we called a time-out with two seconds left. Mazur was a freshman quarterback, and he was scared to death. His eyes were rolling. Hell, I was scared to death, too. But I put my arm around him, and I figured I had to loosen him up. I said, "Look at all these people. They don't care who wins. This is just a fun afternoon." And we both just started laughing. Barry Switzer is on the other side of the field, and he didn't have anything to do with the defense, so he kind of half crouches down, smoking a cigarette. I sent the play in, and everybody thought it worked. But the play went to shit right away. But Mazur rolled out and scrambled and threw it, and we won. But Barry Switzer was a great coach. He's one of the few that won a national championship and a Super Bowl.

USC also beat Notre Dame again, this time 14–7, making Robinson 5–1 against the Irish. Marcus Allen gained "only" 147 yards that game before going on to end his senior year as college football's first 2,000-yard rusher. His 2,342 yards and eight 200-yard games earned him the fourth Heisman Trophy given to a USC tailback. Even more prestigious for the program, Allen and White won two Heismans in three years.

Still, the 1981 Trojans finished the regular season 9–2 overall and a middling 5–2 in the Pac-10. So after the one-year bowl ban, USC didn't go to its Mecca, the Rose Bowl. Instead the eighth-ranked Trojans faced 9–2 and seventh-ranked Penn State in the Fiesta Bowl. The Trojans still started John Mazur, not quite an A-list college quarterback, which was compounded by Nittany Lions coach Joe Paterno outsmarting Robinson.

KEN RUETTGERS: Penn State ran a defense that they had run earlier that season. We didn't spend as much time on that as we probably should have. Penn State had a good defense, but we were not as prepared as we should have been for that game.

JOHN ROBINSON: Yeah, we got killed. I don't think I did a very good job. My brother was dying at the time. He was in the hospital with cancer. I remember being distracted. I also remember an NFL team was offering me a job. I wasn't going to do it, but I was distracted. We also ran up against a great team, and the next year they came back and won the national championship. Penn State was good, and they killed us.

USC's 26–10 loss was Robinson's first defeat after three postseason wins. Linebacker Keith Browner Sr. was a sophomore that game. He was one of the six boys in a royal football family. Keith and his brother Joey played at USC. Three other brothers played for Notre Dame. Four of the Browners played in the NFL. Now, at the Fiesta Bowl on January 1, 1982, Keith says he was sure there would be more postseason games to come.

KEITH BROWNER: But that was the only bowl game I played in there, because we were about to go back on probation. By the time I left USC, we had been on probation three out of the four years I was there. It was disheartening. You work your butt off every year and you can't go anywhere. The regular season ends, and then that's it.

In April 1982, this time the NCAA sanctioned the Trojans, and the penalties were stiffer than those the Pac-10 had handed down in 1980. USC received three years' probation, with no bowl game appearances in 1982 and 1983 and no TV appearances in 1983 and 1984. The allegations included more academic fraud, but the main charge was the selling of USC football tickets, allegedly headed up by assistant coach Marv Goux. Some of the ticket money reportedly had gone to the players.

Back in 1980, USC president James Zumberge had just arrived on the job when the Pac-10 punished the football program. Now his own regime was under fire, and Zumberge's public response was far more combative. He called the NCAA penalties "unreasonable, inequitable, wholly unjustified and vindictive." Robinson mostly stayed silent as the pressure on him increased.

SCOTT TINSLEY: The ticket thing became a national story when one of our former players in the NFL said he made more money selling tickets when he was at USC than he made in the NFL. I thought that story was bush league, but it kind of blew up.

ARTIE GIGANTINO: There was a little girl by the name of Kim Kardashian whose father Robert Kardashian had been the student manager here one time at USC.

He and Marv Goux had a great friendship. They sold tickets. The one good thing—and everybody will tell you the exact same thing—

was that when the tickets were sold, Marv Goux did it all. So the rest of us as coaches never really knew what was going on. And that was a great thing because it protected everybody. Marv had been there forever and Marv kind of handled that. And he did it through Robert Kardashian.

JOHN ROBINSON: There were tickets being sold prior to when I was there. That was a fairly common thing with everybody in college football. It wasn't something that was being talked about, but it was universally done. I think a lot of people in the country said, "I'm glad they got USC and not us." But we were doing it, and we got nailed.

I asked Robinson if the ticket selling was really Marv Goux's thing or if he became a scapegoat.

JOHN ROBINSON: I think some of both. I think it was his deal. He did kind of do it by himself. But it wasn't as though anybody stood up—me or anybody else—and said, "Well, if you're gonna do something to him, then you gotta do something to us."

RIKI ELLISON: We were banned again from a bowl game that season, this time for tickets. Then we lost at Florida in our first game. It was hot and humid, a difficult first game. It was a difficult season. But we did beat Oklahoma at their place and we shut them out. Nobody used to do that against Oklahoma.

ARTIE GIGANTINO: We go down there and beat them 12–0. It's the first time Barry Switzer had ever gotten shut out at Oklahoma. They rushed for 43 yards. And it's the worst rushing total Barry Switzer ever had.

That was the 1982 season's third game. I asked Gigantino how it happened, given that Oklahoma had shredded the USC defense for 307 rushing yards the previous season.

ARTIE GIGANTINO: R. C. Slocum left, and I took over the defense. All due humility.

On November 20, USC fell to 7–3 when it lost, 20–19, to UCLA. The Trojans scored a touchdown as time ran out but failed on the two-point conversion while playing for the win instead of a tie. Three days later, Robinson shocked USC fans and all of college football by resigning from his coaching position to become the school's vice president in charge of university relations. He would coach against Notre Dame in the season finale, but then his seven-year run would suddenly end.

"The decision was a difficult one for me," Robinson said at a news conference. "The concept of changing careers in midstream is frightening. I've spent 25 years in coaching." Several times Robinson said, "The timing seemed right."

Nobody knew what Robinson really meant. Was he leaving coaching or just college coaching? Less than a year before, he had turned down a multiyear offer to become head coach of the New England Patriots. Now the rumors flew that the Seattle Seahawks and the Los Angeles Rams had interest in him. The Rams speculation came true three months later when Robinson made the move from downtown Los Angeles to Anaheim.

At the same news conference before the Notre Dame game, Robinson said he made the announcement that week because he wanted to beat the news being leaked.

KEN RUETTGERS: I thought maybe he announced it then as a way to motivate us for the Notre Dame game. He called a meeting and he told us about the "win one for the Gipper" story. Then he made fun of himself. He said, "Win one for the fat guy."

He probably did have some indications from the NFL, but it wasn't a done deal yet. And it seemed like he was getting a little tired of the probation years. That was draining on him. I think he wanted to take a step back. Maybe he thought he could get an NFL job, but if he couldn't, he still had the VP job.

KEITH BROWNER: I was a junior and I was sad. We were all sad. And I wanted to play for him my senior year. So I didn't want to play there my senior year. I didn't want to be coached by anyone else.

RIKI ELLISON: It was big news, but we were seniors, on our way out. I had been there for all but one year that he was at USC. From my perspective, the talent wasn't the same as when I first got there. The probation hurt our recruiting. So it looked like Robinson had peaked himself out. I think he was done. But I couldn't really see him as just the USC vice president. So yeah, I figured the NFL was looking at him.

KEN RUETTGERS: I don't think the school pushed him out. I don't know. It's hard to know. There was some heat on Marv Goux because Marv was most directly linked to the ticket thing. Then Robinson took Marv with him to the Rams.

ARTIE GIGANTINO: When John resigned as coach at USC, the job wasn't open at the Rams yet. But John is a very restless guy. He's a very smart guy, and that's a characteristic of extremely smart people: They get bored and they get restless. So John resigns, but he doesn't really know what to do. They offer him a job in the president's office, and he takes it, but Christ, he was still over at the football office almost every day for the next few months. Then the Rams job opens on Valentine's Day, 1983. The next day John became head coach of the Rams.

I think his restlessness was part of it. I also don't think he and Zumberge were in love with each other. John was more popular than Zumberge, and I think that made Zumberge uncomfortable. John's got a big ego, he's the man, he wanted to be John McKay, though he never quite reached that status. I think if Zumberge would have come in on his knees and said, "John, I'm gonna give you a contract tomorrow for the rest of your life, and your staff," John would have stayed. So yeah, he *could* have stayed. But things were pointing at him.

Linebacker Sam Anno adds his perspective. Anno's 23 tackles in one game against Illinois is still a USC record. He later played seven years in the NFL before going into coaching. He's now a defensive assistant with the Oakland Raiders, working under former USC linebacker Jack Del Rio.

SAM ANNO: If you're the CEO of something, and the shit is coming down a little bit, and you have a chance to get out for something good like the Rams, most people will make that part of their decision process. At the time the Rams had Eric Dickerson. They had an offensive line with Jackie Slater, Irv Pankey, Dennis Hannah. They had receivers, they had defense. As a coach, that would put a little more bounce in your step than staying where you're at and saying, "I'm fucked."

I asked Robinson about his decision, including whether he felt pressure from the school.

JOHN ROBINSON: No. I don't know what I was doing when I made that decision. When you look back on your career, you don't consider that one of your most intelligent ones. But I think like a lot of people in coaching, you get to the point where it's repetitive. On September 12 every season, you're doing the exact same thing. So I think there's a yearning sometimes to change things up. I think I was going through these feelings, and the people at the university came up with this idea about being a vice president at the school. It sounded good, but when I took the job, it wasn't long before I realized that I wasn't the right guy to do this. As soon as I wasn't a football coach, I said, "I gotta find a way to get back into this."

I asked if he knew the Rams would hire him when he stepped down at USC.

JOHN ROBINSON: No. I was committed to doing that vice president job. The Rams job came up later. They didn't start talking to me until after I stopped coaching at USC.

The same day Robinson announced his resignation, his offensive coordinator, Ted Tollner, was named to replace him. He was still relatively new to USC, having joined the coaching staff before that season.

ARTIE GIGANTINO: It was a chaotic time because everyone was trying to position themselves to get the job once we knew John was leaving. Marv Goux wanted the job. Paul Hackett had once been the offensive coordinator at USC, and he was at the Dallas Cowboys and he was trying to position himself to get the job. And quite frankly, a couple of people were talking to me about it.

You just couldn't hire Marv Goux. There was too much baggage. I was too young. And there were a lot of people who didn't like Paul Hackett. He's a good coach, but when he ended up coming to USC ten years later, he sucked. It was not a good fit. This first time, when Robinson left, Hackett rubbed some people the wrong way, including the USC chancellor, so they picked Ted Tollner, which was a surprise. Ted was a good guy, but he had only been at USC since that spring and he wasn't a USC guy. He didn't look like a USC guy, didn't talk like a USC guy. I'm not ripping the guy's character or any of that crap. He's a good man and he's a good football coach. It *wasn't* a fit.

The 42-year-old Tollner had made his reputation as an offensive coordinator at San Diego State and Brigham Young before joining Robinson's staff. At BYU he tutored Jim McMahon, who set a staggering 71 NCAA passing and total offense records. In his junior year alone, McMahon threw for 47 touchdown passes and 4,571 yards.

But this was Tailback U in Los Angeles, not pass-happy BYU in Provo, Utah. Furthermore, Tollner's only other head-coaching positions had been in junior college and in high school.

Amid the inevitable alumni grumbling, Tim Tessalone says Tollner seemed to maintain his perspective. That was Tessalone's first year as sports information director, a position he still holds today as the country's longest-tenured SID. He also has been an associate athletic director since 2012.

TIM TESSALONE: Ted Tollner had survived a terrible tragedy when he was a college player at Cal Poly, San Luis Obispo. Their team's plane crashed and killed 22 people. We talked about it. Ted had changed his seat before the flight left. Where he would have been sitting was an area where there were no survivors. Ted was very open about it: the trauma of losing your friends and knowing that it also could have been you.

I'm sure that weighed on him, obviously. I think it also affected him in terms of seeing the bigger picture in life. If you could live through that, fourth and goal in the fourth quarter of a football game is what it is. And to me, Ted Tollner always remained calm in everything he did.

"This is obviously a big day in my life," Tollner said upon signing his five-year contract. "I haven't been here that long, but I have always known about USC. Among all the other schools, this is the place. To be part of USC is all a man in my profession could ever ask for."

TED TOLLNER: At first, I didn't see John's resignation coming. I left BYU and became his coordinator, and we never discussed him getting out. Then, two-thirds through the season, he told me he was thinking of going into the fund-raising part of the program. It surprised me that he was going to recommend me to the president. Then I met with the president during the season, and they told me that when the season was over I would have the job. I was very surprised when it initially happened.

On November 27, 1982, Robinson coached his farewell game against Notre Dame at the Coliseum. Trailing 13–10 with 1:50 left, the Trojans produced a gritty 51-yard drive and scored the winning touchdown with 32 seconds remaining. As the gun sounded on the poignant 17–13 victory, Robinson thrust his fist up to the sky. Then Robinson cried as his players lifted him on their shoulders.

RIKI ELLISON: That was the "win one for the fat guy" game. And we beat Notre Dame for the fifth year in a row. For the seniors to beat them five times, or for some seniors four times, in John Robinson's last game was one of my greatest memories at USC.

But every game I played at USC was fun. John Robinson was a player's coach. Marv Goux was a player's coach. Bill Walsh, who I played for in the NFL, was not a player's coach. But Bill Walsh took the game to another level. I'll tell you what, though. If Robinson could take all the guys who played for him at USC to the NFL? John Robinson would have won a Super Bowl.

The 1982 Trojans finished 8–3 overall and 5–2 in the Pac-10 but could not go to a bowl game due to the NCAA sanctions. Robinson left USC with a seven-season record of 67–14–2, the third best winning percentage (.827) among active coaches behind Oklahoma's Barry Switzer and Penn State's Joe Paterno. Robinson went 4–1 in the postseason, including 3–0 in the Rose Bowl. In the rivalry games, he went 6–1 against Notre Dame and 5–2 against UCLA. His 1978 team split a national championship with Alabama, which his Trojans had defeated earlier that season at Alabama.

Still, his teams were sanctioned twice in his last three years. When he went to the Rams, the Trojans were still on probation for the ticket-selling violations, including one more season without a bowl game and two more seasons without any games on TV.

USC won consistently under John Robinson. And almost to a man, his players swear by him. But the program's reputation took a hit during the early 1980s on his watch.

4

USC IN TRANSITION, AGAIN:

1983–1984

In September 1983, *Sports Illustrated* placed USC at No. 9 in its annual preseason rankings. "This may be the year the Trojans come out throwing," wrote Jack McCallum. "Three reasons: They don't have a tailback of Heisman Trophy caliber; they do have two talented passing quarterbacks; and Ted Tollner is in charge."

Behind the scenes, however, the new coach faced skepticism from his predecessor's recruits.

KEITH BROWNER: I didn't know why they picked Tollner, and I didn't want anything to do with it. He came from BYU and just got to USC the previous season. I thought they should have hired someone else from Robinson's staff. Norv Turner or Artie Gigantino or somebody like that would have been good. So in truth I could have been a better player that season, but I was mad that Robinson left and I knew it was going to be a rough year.

SAM ANNO: It was his first head-coaching job in college. USC is a big job for someone in his first job. And great expectations can be killers. People thought USC would just roll on because it had rolled on for so long.

That first year was really hard on Ted. He didn't know what the fuck was going on. He was trying to figure it out. And when you're losing like that, and you're in that market, and you're the new guy, the assistants are also asking, *What the fuck is going on?* As players, we were like, *We're losing to these teams? We're SC. What the hell is happening?*

KEN RUETTGERS: I think Ted Tollner had a very good offensive mind. He kind of knew USC football. But he wasn't as dynamic a personality as a John Robinson or a Mike Holmgren or an Andy Reid or a Jon Gruden or a Steve Mariucci. He was more of an X's and O's guy. Ted's a good man. He just didn't have that charisma that some of the great coaches have.

Tim Green joined the Trojans that season after being rated as the top junior college quarterback in the country. In his two years at El Camino in Torrance, Green had set 12 national junior college records while passing for 49 touchdowns and 5,448 yards. His first season at USC, he mostly sat behind Sean Salisbury, but some players, including the confident Green, thought he should be starting.

TIM GREEN: USC was in transition when I got there. John Robinson and Marv Goux had gone down to Anaheim to coach the Rams. USC was still on probation and couldn't go to a bowl or play on TV. Everything was new. I would characterize the mood as uncertain.

That feeling intensified when the Tollner era began at the Coliseum on September 10, 1983. The ninth-ranked Trojans tied No. 18 Florida, 19–19, and the game would be remembered for its botched ending.

TIM GREEN: We tied the score on a last-second touchdown pass from Sean Salisbury to Timmy Ware. All we have to do is kick the extra point to beat them 20–19.

I was the holder. The snap was bounced to me, away from my hands, so I had to come out of my stance to get it and then get back in my stance so Steve Jordan could kick it. Steve Jordan never missed. He was automatic. But we never got the kick off. That was my first game wearing that uniform, and I was completely mortified.

To me, it felt like a loss. And that first game was pivotal. If we get that extra point, we win, and maybe our spirits are different and maybe we don't go 4–6–1. Nobody goes to USC to be 4–6–1.

The Trojans beat Oregon State the next week and then lost two in a row to unranked Kansas and unranked South Carolina. As USC fell from the top 25, a *Los Angeles Times* reader asked, "Does anybody think McKay or Robinson would be 1–2–1 with the 1983 Trojans?" Another disgruntled fan wrote, "When did USC de-emphasize football? The Trojans are playing like a bunch of walk-ons."

It was about to get worse. In a 34–14 defeat to Arizona State, the Coliseum crowd booed when USC went in at halftime trailing 27–0. At Washington the Trojans lost, 24–0, their first shutout in 187 games. They also lost to Notre Dame and UCLA, a double blasphemy that foreshadowed one of Tollner's crucial failings.

ARTIE GIGANTINO: We tied Florida in the opener, and then the thing goes downhill. Then we had a little bit of division—offense and defense—because none of the defensive kids related to him. He was an offensive guy. Never said a fucking word, to be honest with you, to anybody on defense. That season was bad. We were what, 3–8?

I told him they were 4–6–1.

ARTIE GIGANTINO: All right, whatever it was. That should not happen at the University of Southern California. Also, what was happening, there was some real division amongst the alumni. I don't think Jerry Buss was real happy that we hired Tollner. O.J. Simpson, who obviously had a voice at that time, was extremely unhappy about it. The *Los Angeles Herald* with Allan Malamud and Doug Krikorian: those guys were ripping Tollner all the time. So it just got off to a bad start.

SAM ANNO: We were banned from a bowl game, and that affected us. I think the feeling was, *What are we fighting for? Let's just get through this season and go for it next year.*

KEITH BROWNER: On defense we went into the games thinking, *Oh, my God, man, are we going to score a few points this week or what?* It was a brutal year, and the boosters weren't used to that. The players weren't used to that. That's how I remember leaving USC, unfortunately: wanting to get out of there, wanting to just stay healthy and get to the NFL. It's also never a good year when USC loses to Notre Dame and UCLA. And that year Notre Dame really hammered us.

The 27–6 rout on a wet, foggy day in South Bend came after five straight wins over the Irish during the Robinson era, which numerous fans and alumni already pined for. Scoring six lousy points against the Golden Domers was bad enough. On top of that their coach was Gerry Faust, then in his third season in South Bend after coming straight from Moeller High School.

SAM ANNO: That was weird for us. We're losing to a guy from Moeller High. Fuck. Keep going to the next topic.

ARTIE GIGANTINO: Dan Devine was there before Faust, and Devine did not treat people very nice. So they decided to get a warm-blooded guy who was a messiah in high school football. Faust had sent 10 or 12 guys from Moeller to Notre Dame. They thought it was a match made in, quote, heaven. And he campaigned for the job for five years. I thought it was an insult to college football. I heard him speak a couple times; the guy knew nothing about football. He had that raspy speech, and he was like a preacher at an Amway convention. But he didn't do good job of recruiting at Notre Dame because he was recruiting nationally against Oklahoma, Texas, USC instead of some high school in downtown Cincinnati.

But here's the thing: I don't blame Gerry Faust. I blame the people at Notre Dame. Why do you hire a guy who is completely out of his element? It's the best job in the country, or it can be. You see what happens when they get a decent coach. Obviously, Lou Holtz was very good. Tyrone Willingham was good at the beginning, and then he wore out his welcome a little bit. George O'Leary would have been great if he didn't screw up on his résumé. It's a great place, but how you can make a mistake like hiring Gerry Faust is beyond me.

Steve Jordan is perhaps the best kicker in USC history. He is second all-time with 51 field goals, including a school-record 23 makes from 40 yards or more. His 52- and 53-yarders are the third and fourth longest field goals by a Trojan. On extra points, he converted 109 out of 112.

STEVE JORDAN: Faust was a bigwig in high school. When Notre Dame hired him, we were like, well, okay. Then their students were wearing buttons that said "Oust Faust."

Notre Dame beat us that year, though, for the first time in a while. I was a three-year starter by then, so I was asked to speak at a lot of the booster club meetings in Southern California. People wanted to know what was going on. I told them not to worry. And personally, I did not doubt Coach Tollner. I did some research on him and found out he was a survivor from a plane crash. He also kind of reminded me of my own father. My father was in D-Day. I just felt like, *Goddamn, I can relate to this guy.*

But that first year must have been brutal for him. I know it was for me. I wanted to win every game, and I was tired of this shit. It became very frustrating for the whole university and for our whole team. Everybody, collectively, was like, *This really sucks. 4–6–1?*

It was the program's first losing record since 1961, when McKay went 4–5–1 in his second year. The next year McKay won his first national championship, but that was then at USC and this was now.

KEN RUETTGERS: The 1983 season was mediocre at best. The popular thinking was: *It's a talent issue. This is kind of the result of the last few years of some slack recruiting. Maybe John Robinson was thinking about leaving and he kind of lightened up on the recruiting.*

So Robinson got a little bit of heat for the downtick in recruiting. The media also started to write some stuff about Tollner, but it was his first year and you get a lot of grace in your first year. I also blew my knee out that season. Sean Salisbury blew his knee out. There were other injuries and people gave Tollner some grace. But there was also pressure going into that 1984 season. At USC, they won't tolerate too many years like 4–6–1.

TED TOLLNER: I think when you don't have a winning record, you're not coaching well enough to win. I think there is also a certain amount of, *Are you talented enough? Are you as talented as you want to be?* We didn't feel like we were. So we had to go out and get some help in that regard, and we had to do a better job ourselves.

But to answer your question, I didn't feel any I pressure that first year. I didn't feel any pressure until later when they made the AD change to Mike McGee. I didn't have a great relationship with the new AD.

In July 1984, Mike McGee replaced Dick Perry, who resigned under pressure after nine years as the athletic director. The Trojans won 20 national team championships during Perry's tenure, and he had been excellent for the USC women's programs. But the football team had just suffered its first losing season in 22 years. There were other men's teams in decline, and that was enough for Perry to lose his job.

The blunt and abrasive McGee wasn't a product of the so-called USC family. He arrived from the University of Cincinnati, where according to a *Los Angeles Times* profile written several years later, 89 people in his athletic department had resigned, were fired, or were reassigned during his four years.

TIM TESSALONE: The toughest thing for Mike was that he was viewed as an outsider. He had no USC connection. But I think he was hired for that reason. We were coming off some issues with the NCAA. Part of his directive from the president was to clean things up and run a clean ship. Mike was a no-nonsense guy but very clear in his directives. You knew where you stood with him.

Some people liked him, some people didn't. But say what you will about Mike, he modernized the USC athletic department. He really got it ready for this explosion of where college athletics was going. Mike formalized our business operations. Mike instituted things like a marketing department, which we never had and nobody else really ever had.

McGee was more than a forward-thinking AD, though. He was a former head football coach at East Carolina University and Duke, where his players called him Mad Mike. As an ex-coach he knew how coaches felt about athletic directors frequently telling them how to perform their jobs. Tollner says McGee did it anyway.

TED TOLLNER: The relationship wasn't good. We just did not have a good fit. Right away he wanted to tell me too many things about how to run the football program, which in my opinion was *my* job.

So I told him, "Listen, I'll run the football program, and if it isn't what you want, then you got to decide what you want to do. But I'm going to run it the way I think it should be run."

In 1984, USC still couldn't play on television because of the NCAA sanctions, but the two-year bowl ban ended. The rejuvenated Trojans started 7–1 and rose to No. 12 when they hosted 9–0 and No. 1 Washington. Their 16–7 upset clinched the Pac-10 title and a Rose Bowl berth, a significant achievement in Tollner's second season.

KEN RUETTGERS: The year before had been a shocking wake-up call: *We can't just show up at USC and have a winning season just because we put our cardinal and gold on.* So we worked very hard that next spring and summer. But it didn't seem like we had any standouts. When your best player is probably an outside linebacker—Jack Del Rio—it says a lot about your offense, not in a positive way. When you look at USC history, usually you got a running back, a quarterback, a Heisman Trophy candidate, some *Sports Illustrated* standouts on the cover. We looked around that year, and it was pretty lean. But it was one of those no-name USC teams that played well together.

In the Trojans' feel-good season, Tim Green was one of the no-names who stepped up. The senior quarterback from a nearby junior college became the starter when Sean Salisbury went down with an injury in the fourth week. Tollner once described Green as having "the style and temperament of a linebacker." The *Los Angeles Times* wrote after he graduated: "The press loved him, because he said whatever he wanted. The school hated some of the things he said, so they banned him from talking to the media."

TIM GREEN: When I got to USC the year before, I had just finished up a pretty good junior college career at El Camino. Started 20 games and won a lot. And like I said, nobody goes to USC to go 4–6–1. So I told one of the writers at the *Los Angeles Times*, "Hey, I should be playing." I was in Ted's office the next morning. I had hurt some feelings with Salisbury and our relationship. I didn't mean anything toward him personally. I hate losing, you know?

In 1984, sometimes Ted and I butted heads on play calls. I threw the ball an average of 45 times a game at El Camino. I get to USC and we're lucky to throw it maybe 15 or 20 times a game. So if we were third and long and I saw something with their cornerback, I would change it to Power Pass instead of Power. And 99 percent of the time I would complete that ball. Then I would tell Ted and Norv Turner that I missed their signal from the sideline. I never really got in trouble for it, especially when we went on a six-game winning streak, won the Pac-10, and beat the No. 1 team in the country, Washington.

KEN RUETTGERS: Washington was a big win. We needed that because it clinched the Rose Bowl. But then we lost to UCLA and Notre Dame. Everyone was like, *Wow, way to get back into the Rose Bowl.* Then Ohio State came in the Rose Bowl with Mike Tomczak and Keith Byars and some other first-round draft picks. So we were the underdogs.

By losing to the Bruins and the Irish (for the second straight year), USC surrendered its momentum and most of its national stature. As a result, the 8–3 Trojans were ranked just No. 18 versus the No. 6 and 9–2 Buckeyes. One perhaps inebriated Big Ten writer predicted that Ohio State would win by 38 points.

When the Trojans shocked the Buckeyes, 20–17, it proved yet again that the Pac-10 owned the Rose Bowl. In the last 11 meetings between the two conferences, the Big Ten had now lost ten.

Steve Jordan kicked a 51-yard field goal, which was a Rose Bowl record until the Ohio State kicker nailed one from 52 yards. Then Jordan kicked a second 51-yarder. Green threw for two touchdowns for the first time all year in the biggest game of the season. Green also threw a nice block when one of his receivers ran a reverse. He and Del Rio were named co-MVPs.

KEN RUETTGERS: Who would have ever thought that a junior college transfer, Tim Green, who was undersize and probably undertalented but had lots of guts and gumption, would lead us to a Rose Bowl win over Ohio State?

And who would have thought that Tollner, the passing guru who came from BYU, would win USC's first Rose Bowl since 1979 with a conservative offense and a rugged defense that allowed 14 points per game while being coached by Gigantino?

ARTIE GIGANTINO: After we won the Rose Bowl, there were a lot more people hugging me than hugging Ted. We killed Keith Byars in that Rose Bowl. He was the Heisman Trophy runner-up, he led the nation in rushing, blah blah blah. Except for one long run, we killed him.

TED TOLLNER: That first year we didn't get off to a good start. But we went out and got some immediate help with our recruiting. We got some real good young freshmen. The next year we won the Rose Bowl and the Pac-10, and they hadn't won that for a number of years. It was a fast recovery for us in my opinion.

KEN RUETTGERS: That was a good year for USC. It started us out of the hole that probation put us into. The fans were feeling good. The administration was feeling good. But at the same time, I think some people were thinking: *We can't tolerate continuously losing to UCLA and Notre Dame.* So there was still that pressure to beat those two schools.

Four months after the Rose Bowl victory, Tim Green did not get drafted by the NFL. At the other end of the spectrum, Ken Ruettgers went to the Green Bay Packers as the seventh player selected in the first round. Like so many USC players, the great offensive tackle says it was difficult to say good-bye.

KEN RUETTGERS: The fans in college football are so loyal. And you have those great rivalries. I played for Green Bay, and that probably comes the closest to that college feeling. You had the Bears and Packers. But it never felt as big as USC-Notre Dame or USC-UCLA. And going from USC to Green Bay at the time, it felt like a step down. The equipment room and the equipment manager weren't quite up to snuff. The locker room was a downgrade. The medical training staff wasn't quite as good.

We played on Saturdays at USC, so Friday before every home game we would practice, and then the USC marching band would come out. The Song Girls would do three or four songs. Then we'd take a shower and get on the bus and go to a different restaurant every home game. And it wasn't like we were going to this Denny's or that Applebee's. We were going to top-notch restaurants. We used to go to Lawry's, the Mexican one off La Cienega. The mariachi band would be playing the USC fight song. The red carpet would be rolled out, and we'd be treated like royalty. Then we'd get back on the bus and drive to Paramount Studios and watch a movie in a private screening room, sitting in leather chairs with Red Vines licorice. Then we'd go back to the Hyatt on Wilshire Boulevard and have a snack with all kinds of burgers and fried chicken and fresh fruit and pasta. It was amazing.

Then you go to Green Bay and you're staying in a two-story motel the night before a road game. For three of our home games back then, we would take a bus to play the game in Milwaukee and we would get McDonald's and eat it on the bus. That was our meal. And I'm thinking to myself: *This is the NFL and it's a step down from USC.*

5

TED TOLLNER UNDER FIRE:

1985–1986

The glow from the Rose Bowl triumph lasted exactly two games into the 1985 season. After beating Illinois in the opener, the third-ranked Trojans lost to unranked Baylor, 20–13, in front of a grumpy crowd at the Coliseum. The next Saturday morning, a reader named Frank Peters wrote to the *Los Angeles Times,* "If Ted Tollner doesn't get with it, he will soon be known as the Gerry Faust of the West."

That Saturday evening in Tempe, the Trojans had already slid all the way to No. 18 *before* getting thrashed, 24–0, by unranked Arizona State. Losses to unranked teams can get USC coaches fired, and Tollner already had two in the month of September.

By October 26, the Trojans were 3–2 and the Irish 2–3 when they met in South Bend. Amid the newspaper stories saying the rivalry had lost some luster, there were rumors that the beleaguered Gerry Faust would need to beat USC to keep his job. Shockingly, Notre Dame won, 37–3.

After USC flanker Randy Tanner fumbled the opening kickoff, the Irish recovered at the two-yard line and went in for the touchdown. Then the Trojans rolled over and trailed, 27–0, at halftime.

When Notre Dame came back out for the second half, Faust had his players wearing green jerseys, an emotional ploy that baffled even his players. As their defensive tackle Jay Underwood told me years later for a book I wrote on Notre Dame, "I remember thinking, *This is horseshit. This will make the news. Notre Dame came out in green when it was already up by 27 points.*"

Some USC players were irritated, but Tollner said, correctly, "We were responsible for our embarrassment. If we had taken care of our own program, we wouldn't have been behind 27–0 at halftime." Tollner also said, somewhat implausibly, "We were ready mentally and physically, but Notre Dame came out and just pounded us."

It was USC's worst loss to Notre Dame since a 51–0 debacle in 1966. It wasn't enough for Faust to salvage his job, though. He resigned under extreme pressure in late November with one game left on the schedule. Then his players didn't exactly win one for Gerry, losing 58–7 to Jimmy Johnson's powerful Miami Hurricanes.

USC's Aaron Emanuel was a talented freshman tailback from Palmdale, California. As the most coveted high school running back in the country, Emanuel had been pursued by at least 100 college programs. When USC beat out Nebraska—which flew him to Lincoln by Learjet for his campus visit—it was regarded as a Tollner recruiting coup.

Emanuel recalls the 37–3 Notre Dame beat-down.

AARON EMANUEL: They totally clowned us that day. They embarrassed us and had no respect for us. In 1985 we weren't that good. But after that year, we had some good teams and we still never beat those guys when I was at USC. That still stings today, as a grown man.

Tollner was 0–3 against the Irish. He was 0–2 against UCLA as the Trojans and Bruins prepared to play at the Coliseum on

November 23. By then Tollner had benched his erratic veteran quarterback Sean Salisbury for the raw but promising freshman Rodney Peete. Still, the Trojans were just 4–5, creating speculation that Tollner might be gone if he lost a third straight year to UCLA.

It certainly didn't help that he and his adversary, USC athletic director Mike McGee, were barely speaking to each other. When asked by the Los Angeles media to comment on Tollner's status, McGee said carefully, "The university is obviously tremendously interested in having a successful and winning football program within the context of the university. No one is more interested in seeing that happen than Ted Tollner. We have expectations that the program will turn around." It was later reported that McGee already was talking to other potential head coaches, including San Diego Chargers offensive coordinator Dave Levy, a former long-time assistant on John McKay's USC staff.

Terry Donahue's Bruins were 8–2 and ranked No. 8 when they hosted the 4–5 and unranked Trojans. Tollner's players perhaps saved his job when they delivered a 17–13 upset. A 20–6 win over Oregon in the regular-season finale lifted USC to 6–5 and earned an invitation to the Aloha Bowl against 15th-ranked Alabama on December 28. The Trojans still weren't ranked, though, and hadn't been since late September.

SAM ANNO: The Aloha Bowl is a lesser bowl game. Unfortunately, sometimes when USC is not in the Rose Bowl, it's kind of like, *Oh, God, what are we doing here?*

So there was partying before that game. But I can remember that even before the bigger bowls. It was a different time back then, too; the drug testing wasn't so much. And then coming over to Hawaii? Shit. The interesting thing about Hawaii, when you're getting off the bus, they're selling marijuana to you. They're like, "Hey, we got some weed; you guys want to come around the bus?" And you're kind of going, "Uh, my coach is right behind me; I can't talk right now."

If both teams had smoked weed during the national anthem, it still would not have produced a more boring first half than this one. The Trojans went in their locker room tied, 3–3. They reemerged and lost, 24–3, to the Crimson Tide. Freshman cornerback Ernie Spears recalls the somber five-hour flight back to Los Angeles.

ERNIE SPEARS: The mood was that the hammer was going to drop and bad things were going to happen. Rex Moore was this really crazy inside linebacker. He was singing a song and putting in his own words about Tollner getting canned. We also had alumni on that plane ride, and they were just not happy.

If upsetting UCLA in 1985 had salvaged Tollner's job, it still hung by a cardinal and gold thread as the 1986 season arrived. After going 6–6 and losing, 24–3, at the Aloha Bowl, the word in Los Angeles was that USC would need at least an 8–3 record and a respectable bowl game bid or Tollner's fourth year would be his last. By then there were also financial implications. The Coliseum held 93,000, and attendance had dropped to an average of 58,000 per game during the last three seasons. On top of all that, McGee already had fired men's basketball coach Stan Morrison and pushed baseball coach Rod Dedeaux into retirement. All Dedeaux did at USC was win 11 national championships and have the baseball field named after him. McGee, in contrast, had been at the school for two years.

TED TOLLNER: Mike and I were just not on the same page, and it led into my final year as the head coach there. I had different alums that were loyal to me, and they were telling me, "Hey, be careful. Mike is out there trying to muster up some support."

ARTIE GIGANTINO: With the other coaches, all Ted did was bitch about Mike McGee all the time, who I thought was a pretty good guy. He was more of a hard-ass than his predecessor, but I liked Mike. Ted couldn't stand him. So that thing had no legs. It had no chance of survival because of the animosity between Ted and Mike McGee. But Mike McGee didn't hate him. He came in and was asked to do a job, and I think the job was to fix the football department.

Led by sophomore quarterback Rodney Peete, USC started out 4–0 before getting blasted, 34–14, at lowly Washington State. The last time the Cougars had defeated the Trojans, it was 1957 and America liked Ike.

USC lost the next week against Rose Bowl–bound Arizona State but fought back with three straight wins over Stanford, Arizona, and California. The 7–2 Trojans were ranked No. 10 and riding some momentum with two regular-season games left against UCLA and Notre Dame. Then McGee undermined him, Tollner says.

TED TOLLNER: We were 7–2 and the Orange Bowl wanted us, but they would not commit unless we beat UCLA or Notre Dame. We also had a commitment from the Citrus Bowl, regardless of what happened, that we could go there and play Auburn. So I talked to our players and said, "Here's the situation, guys. We can guarantee the Citrus Bowl right now or we can win our way into the Orange Bowl."

Our players were unanimous. They said, "We want to take our chances against UCLA and Notre Dame and whatever happens, happens." Well, we took that vote, and later that same week Mike decides to take the Citrus Bowl. I felt like I was misled about whether we would have an opinion or not, and it seemed like I hadn't been truthful to our players.

The Trojans did not merely lose, 45–25, to UCLA at the Rose Bowl. They trailed 31–0 at halftime and 38–7 at the end of the third quarter. USC fans were stunned, and so were the officials from the Citrus Bowl, who flew out to watch the game. Tollner told one of them in the dazed USC locker room, "We'll put on a better show; we'll guarantee that. We didn't show it today, but we'll make you feel good about your invitation."

TIM TESSALONE: That night was the most awkward plane flight I ever had to take in my life. The Citrus Bowl officials were going to have a big press conference on that Sunday in Orlando. So me and Ted Tollner and Mike McGee had to jump on a red-eye after the UCLA game. I was sitting between those guys, and I don't think anybody talked for the entire flight. First of all, it was a red-eye, so we were trying to sleep. But the real awkwardness came because I think everyone knew that a coaching change was about to be made. So there was the three of us—me, the head coach, and the athletic director who's about to make the change—sitting next to each other for five hours.

After the bad defeat to UCLA, the 7–3 Trojans fell seven spots in the polls to No. 17. Next up were the 5–6 and unranked Fighting Irish, coached by Lou Holtz in his first season and steadily improving but nowhere near as strong as Holtz would soon have them. USC played tougher and better than it had against UCLA and went into the fourth quarter leading by 17 at the Coliseum. The subsequent collapse and its aftermath would be remembered as the epitaph for the Tollner years.

Linebacker Bill Stokes and center Brad Leggett recall those dramatic moments.

BILL STOKES: Tim Brown led this furious comeback. He was the best college football player in the nation during those years. We went into the final minutes still leading, 37–35. Then Tim Brown ran back a punt. I was on that punt return team. We had a guy, I won't tell you his name, but he didn't contain properly. Tim Brown cut back in, and that guy missed the tackle. So we had one guy screw up, and Tim Brown ran it back 56 yards. Put them in great field position. John Carney kicked a short field goal as time expired, and we lost 37–35.

BRAD LEGGETT: Steve Mariucci was our special teams coach. Before the Notre Dame game, Mariucci was saying during the special teams meetings, "We're not afraid of Tim Brown. We're gonna kick it to him." And sure enough, we were winning, we punt to Tim Brown, and he returns it all the way down there and we lose. The writing was on the wall that they would get rid of Tollner. And I remember Pat Morris, my offensive line coach, in the locker room. He said to Mariucci, "Hey, great fucking work. You just cost us our jobs."

A few minutes earlier, Tollner had stood outside on the Coliseum field with his senior players. He had a microphone and was ready to follow the USC football tradition by introducing each senior after the final home game of his career. As Tollner began to speak, the intense booing drowned him out. No one knew for sure if the fans were booing just him or also the seniors. Regardless, it was ugly.

SAM ANNO: By then I was out for the season. I tore my ACL. But I'll never forget the Notre Dame game. I'm a senior and I'm on my crutches after my operation.

I knew how they introduced the seniors in the past. But as soon as Ted started talking, the whole crowd booed. Ted said to the seniors, "Let's go; we're out of here."

Sometimes I look back and think it would have been neat if Ted said to the crowd, "Fuck it. Go fuck yourselves. I'm gonna say some stuff about our seniors. You can boo the whole time, but I'm still gonna talk about these guys." But that was a brutal spot for him to be in. And I thought it was very chickenshit of our whole student body and all the fans.

Dan Owens and Don Gibson were young and talented defensive linemen who later would be named first-team All-Pac-10.

DAN OWENS: At the end of that Notre Dame game, plays needed to be made, and we didn't make them. I think the fans were booing the coaching staff and how that game ended more than the players. But you can't fire the players anyway. After that game, we thought something was going to happen coaching-wise.

DON GIBSON: It was *very* disrespectful not only to the coach but to all those seniors. When I came in as a freshman, those were the guys you looked up to. Tim McDonald, man, he was one of the classiest guys I'd ever met. Guys like that, you see what's happening to them after the Notre Dame game, you are in disbelief.

McDonald was a consensus All-American safety and later a six-time selection in the Pro Bowl. He is now a defensive backs coach for the Buffalo Bills.

TIM MCDONALD: I honestly don't remember the USC fans booing that day. Maybe I blocked it out. I did think Tollner had a chance to keep his job, but not after those last two games. You come to USC to beat UCLA and Notre Dame. Not to play them, to *beat* them. And at that time in my life, I hated them both. Today, it's still rough on me, to be quite honest. I didn't get a win against Notre Dame. Are you kidding me?

ARTIE GIGANTINO: It was a bad scene on the field, but I was so distraught after that game, I just walked into our locker room. I knew what was coming. I knew we were gonna be fired. You could tell.

Jerry Buss was always on our sideline. He was a USC graduate and a huge booster. He was saying, "We gotta get this thing cleaned up." He's got Magic Johnson standing next to him, and Henry Winkler, and Steven Spielberg, and Jerry Buss is just ripping Tollner.

TED TOLLNER: We lose to Notre Dame. The tradition is to introduce your seniors after the final home game. So we went over to do that, and the players felt the bitterness. But the bitterness was really directed toward me, and I could deal with that. I could not deal with the players being embarrassed because they had just busted their ass against a good Notre Dame team. So we left the podium. I said, "Let's go in the locker room. I'm not going to expose you to this."

It was not a pleasant time for anyone, especially the players who had just lost a difficult game. We would have been 8–3 instead of a 7–4 year, and they wanted that in the worst way. It was also hard for the players' families who were at that game and hard for the coaches' families. But you've got to have thick skin if you're going to go into the athletic arena, especially at a big-time level.

BILL STOKES: Everyone called him Coach Ted. Everyone on the team liked him. I really think his issues were with the USC alumni powers that be and that we didn't win against UCLA and Notre Dame. But guys like Ted Tollner, Lou Holtz, these are all good coaches. They all got these premium jobs for a reason, because of who they were and also where they came from. Tollner was Jim McMahon's coach at Brigham Young and had an incredible relationship with Jim and also a lot of success. He brought him by USC a couple of times when Jim was with the Bears, and they still had a great relationship.

AARON EMANUEL: You can't survive very long at USC without the alumni behind you. They don't like six-win seasons, seven-win seasons.

Maybe coaches can get by winning six or seven games at other schools, but not at that school. The alumni association is just too strong.

SAM ANNO: That was a big job for someone in their first head-coaching job. And USC was different from anywhere else in the country. Back then you had the Rams, the Raiders, the Dodgers, the Lakers. You had some professional teams that were *legendary*. So the bar was high.

On December 8, 1985, nine days after the Notre Dame loss, USC President James Zumberge announced Tollner's dismissal. Zumberge said he made his decision with a recommendation from Mike McGee.

TED TOLLNER: If your administration or management and the coaching staff aren't close to being on the same page, it's not best for the program. So something's going to change. When it was all done, Mike McGee went to the president, Jim Zumberge. Jim and I had a good relationship. He gave me a chance to say why I thought we needed to get more time, because we had a lot of good young talent and 7–4 is not great, but it's not the end of the world either. I lost out on that deal, and the rest you know.

Zumberge and McGee said a search for a new coach would start immediately. In reality, the search already had started, but that's typically not what presidents and ADs say on the same day they fire someone. As for the Citrus Bowl on January 1, Zumberge and McGee said Tollner would coach it, an awkward scenario that pretty much never happens.

Clarence Shelmon had been an assistant on Larry Smith's coaching staff at the University of Arizona. Although it wasn't announced yet, Smith soon would be named the next USC head coach.

CLARENCE SHELMON: When we came over from Arizona, that was part of the deal: that Tollner was going to finish out the season and coach in that bowl game. I don't know why it happened that way, but that's what happened. In my own experience, 21 years in the NFL and 15 years in the NCAA, normally they move out the coach who has been fired and let one of his assistants serve as an interim coach. Because typically when a head coach is fired, he doesn't leave on the best terms, so most of the time they want him out of there.

ARTIE GIGANTINO: Mike McGee wanted to fire him. And he did fire him. But Ted talked Zumberge into keeping him through the bowl game. And that was hell. That was 30 days of hell. Ted kicked Mike McGee off the practice field one day. Can you imagine that? The fired football coach is kicking the athletic director who fired him off the fucking field during practice for the Citrus Bowl. It was insane.

TED TOLLNER: The president gave me the choice. I said, "It's our team, and our staff is going to coach it." We had a good enough record to get to a bowl game. Normally when you get to a relatively major bowl game, it's supposed to be a good feeling. So we were going to coach it if we had that option. They could have said, "You don't have it; you're gone."

To me, it was the way that it should be. Why run away from the negative? Our staff had earned the right to go there. So let's coach, and then when it's over, you guys will have your new staff and our staff will move on.

AARON EMANUEL: I don't know why USC did that. Maybe they thought guys would play harder for him. But looking back on it, it was just a weird deal. I remember him talking to the team, and a lot of our guys were sort of like, *Whatever. You're gone. You're a nice guy and all, but you're not gonna be here next year.*

DAN OWENS: That was not a good deal in Orlando. The players that weren't playing at the time and the older players—for them it became a party time atmosphere.

DON GIBSON: When you're an 18-year-old kid, you don't know what's normal. That *was* my normal. And I really liked Coach Tollner. I really liked Artie Gigantino. I was happy they were there with us.

BILL STOKES: The way that Gigantino and Tollner were talking was like they had just found out their wives had cheated on them. There was surprise. There was anger. They were spouting off to us on who they were angry at, but we didn't really know what they were talking about because we didn't know what happened behind the scenes. Gigantino especially seemed really fired up. I think he was really pissed.

I know Ted Tollner was pissed because of his attitude in the pregame speech. It was laced with some jazz toward the alumni, the ones who had sway and say in that decision. And maybe he was talking a little bit toward Mike McGee. But whoever he was speaking about, in his mind they were the reason he got fired. And he was not in agreement with it. Then, during the game, we were losing at halftime to Auburn. Artie Gigantino was like, "What the hell is the matter with you guys? This is our last game. We're on national TV. You should be killing these guys."

Gigantino was being his fiery self. In truth, Auburn had been the superior team all season. The 9–2 Tigers came in ranked No. 10, whereas 7–4 USC entered unranked. Tollner's team played hard in his last game, particularly on defense, but Rodney Peete threw four interceptions and passed for just 113 yards. The Tollner era ended with a 16–7 defeat.

TED TOLLNER: After the game was over, that's when it hit me the hardest. I mean just personally, emotionally. When you walked off the field after the Notre Dame game, you didn't know what was going to happen. Then all this stuff happens and you're going to be replaced. But you're still coaching, getting ready for the bowl game. But when the Auburn game was over, you talk to the players and you say all the things that need to be said. We had a lot of young players. I told them, "You guys are going to have a great career, and all the reasons you came here are still going to happen. You'll get your degree from a tremendous school and have success on the field."

Then I got back to our hotel with my family and friends, and then it really hit me. It was a blow. It was a very difficult emotional blow.

I'm telling you how I felt about it because you asked, and I wouldn't trade the experience for anything. I was there five years, four years as a head coach. It was a great experience, and two of my three kids got their degrees there. And they both married USC students who got *their* degrees there. There's a lot of good that came out of coaching there. It ended with them making a change. Coaching changes are part of life.

TIM TESSALONE: I always felt like he never quite got the chance to see things through. You're coming off an era in the '70s when the program had great, great success. The fan base was used to that. And the standards at USC, no matter the year, are extremely high. So sometimes the patience wasn't there.

But remember, when Ted got here, we still had a postseason ban. I thought he was building a really good thing here. It was very evident that he recruited well. The three years after he left, Larry Smith took over, and those were three Rose Bowl teams

In his four seasons at USC, Tollner went 1–7 against UCLA and Notre Dame. His overall record was 26–20–1, including 1–2 in bowl games. His teams lost 12 games to unranked opponents and lost ten games by 20 or more points. In retrospect, Tollner was perhaps a better offensive coordinator than head coach. That seemed apparent again when he became head coach at San Diego State in 1994. Tollner went 43–48 there before his firing in 2001.

On the positive side, his second USC team went 9–3 and won the Rose Bowl. His record against top ten teams was 6–1. His essential decency appealed to high school recruits and their families, an important factor in a program tainted by academic misconduct and a ticket-selling scandal before Tollner arrived there. Not only would his recruiting benefit the Trojans over the next few seasons, Tollner managed to do it while hampered by the NCAA sanctions he had inherited.

6

LARRY SMITH VERSUS HIS PLAYERS:

1987–1988

USC introduced Larry Smith as its new head coach on January 2, 1987, one day after the Trojans lost in the Citrus Bowl. The *Los Angeles Times* headline the next morning read: "Larry Smith, the 'Outside Choice,' Named USC Football Coach." As the Trojans beat writer Mal Florence explained, "Smith is the first non-connected USC person to get the job since Howard Jones was hired in 1925."

Smith had learned his trade as an assistant for six years under Bo Schembechler, first at Miami of Ohio and later at Michigan. A prodigious winner known for his explosive temper, Schembechler was idolized in the Midwest and sometimes described outside it as a "tyrant." Smith said after arriving at USC, "Bo influenced me in what it takes to be a successful head coach. Number one is discipline."

Known as a defensive specialist, Smith had his first head-coaching job at Tulane, where he turned the struggling Green Wave into a 9–3 Liberty Bowl team in his fourth season. Arizona was also a middling program when Smith took over there in 1980. He produced six straight winning seasons in Tucson and five consecutive wins over rival Arizona State. In 1986, Arizona went 9–3 and finished No. 11 while the 7–5 Trojans fumbled around in Tollner's final year.

"This is clearly an important time and a crossroads for the football program," McGee told reporters at Smith's introductory media conference. Said the 48-year-old coach, "I consider this opportunity one of the highlights of my life. This is by far one of the finest football jobs in the United States."

It was also a job, according to Gigantino, that he was in the mix for before USC settled on Smith.

ARTIE GIGANTINO: We were practicing at the time for the Citrus Bowl. Mike McGee calls me and says he wants to interview me for the fucking job. I said, "Great, Mike," knowing full well it's going to cause a little bit more of a rift with Ted Tollner. But McGee also says to me, "You'll be one of four finalists."

So it ends up being Dave Levy, Paul Hackett, Larry Smith, and me. And I got some pretty good people backing me. O.J. Simpson wants me—blah blah blah. But McGee just felt he couldn't turn it over to a young guy who was part of the staff that just got fired. So he hires Larry Smith. Now, Larry Smith, if you portray this properly in your mind, when he got to USC, was an Arizona coach. Meaning, that small-time rah-rah-rah tough guy who should have been coaching at Bowling Green or something.

TIM TESSALONE: He had great success at Arizona, a Pac-10 school, so he knew the conference. He had a Big Ten background and a Bo Schembechler background. They had a lot of success at Michigan. So Larry Smith made sense in a lot of ways to the people doing the hiring.

Larry also brought in a new coaching staff with hardly any connection to USC. That was probably the biggest thing at the beginning: You've got an athletic director with no USC background, and now you've got a head coach and staff with little or no USC background.

Smith brought eight of his assistants with him from Tucson, including tight ends and offensive line coach Gary Bernardi.

GARY BERNARDI: Mike McGee was interested in someone tough and demanding and someone who had had success against his rival school. When we first got to Arizona, our record against ASU had been like 3–15 the last 18 years. The last five years we were there, we beat ASU. USC at the time wasn't beating Notre Dame and UCLA.

Pat Harlow was a 6-foot-7, 270-pound defensive lineman who later became a highly aggressive offensive tackle. His senior year he won the Morris Trophy as the Pac-10's top offensive lineman and then was selected 11th overall in the NFL draft. Harlow was a freshman when Smith and his staff arrived from another Pac-10 program.

PAT HARLOW: Chris Allen was Arizona's defensive coordinator. He had been recruiting me out of high school. He showed up at my school on a Monday wearing all Arizona stuff. Then they hired him at USC, and he showed up on Friday in all USC stuff. Same message, different colors.

DON GIBSON: My older brother was going to be a senior at Arizona, and they had also recruited me heavily there. It came down to USC and Arizona. First they were selling me on why I should go to Arizona. Then these guys were saying they love USC. I was like: *You were just saying you love Arizona.*

USC was still USC, but the vibe definitely changed. Artie Gigantino used to bring me into his office every few weeks and ask me, "How is it going? How is school going? Everything going okay with your family?" Smith's staff was more regimented. You had one coaching staff, Tollner's, that seemed more pro-player, and another staff, Smith's, that seemed more pro-administration.

Scott Lockwood was a freshman who ended up starting at tailback that season. While starring at his Colorado high school, he had narrowed his choices to Notre Dame and USC, where his father had played for McKay. He says he chose USC partly because of Smith but quickly realized that his tenure would be contentious.

SCOTT LOCKWOOD: He was an old-school coach who worked for Bo Schembechler. All of our watches were always set on Smith Time, which meant five minutes faster than the other clocks on campus. Smith told us at the beginning, "You're on my time now. My time is five minutes ahead of everyone else's."

If there was a meeting set for nine o' clock and you weren't there by 8:55, the doors were locked and you missed the meeting. One day our cornerback Dwayne Garner wasn't there early enough. He was banging on the door, wanting to get in. The other coaches were looking at Larry Smith, and he was like, "Who the fuck is late to a meeting? It must be a freshman." So Larry Smith gave the so-called freshman a break and told one of the coaches to let him in. Dwayne Garner, this sophomore, walks in, and everyone's looking at him. Larry Smith says, "Dwayne Gardner, you used to be a starter at USC. You're no longer a starter. You're fourth string. You can work your way up." Dwayne didn't start again until the third or fourth game. Everyone got the message: If you're late, you're screwed.

BRAD LEGGETT: We went from a loose ship to hiring a guy like Tom Roggeman. He was this old-school assistant who Smith brought from Arizona. USC had signed a junior college defensive lineman, a big steroid guy. Roggeman and the coaches started undressing this guy verbally, and it was like, *Holy shit, what the hell is going on?*

They were getting our attention. There was a lot of talent there from the Tollner years. It needed to be cultivated and coached. So they came in with a hard hand and changed the culture. My dad was a defensive line coach in the NFL. He played in the NFL. He was *always* hard on me. When he saw how my new O-line coach John Matsko was, my dad said, "Look, I was preparing you for this. Now you have a coach who's gonna get on your ass." And boy, you did not want to lose with our new coaches. Those practices the next week would be brutal.

In April 1987, the *Los Angeles Times* ran the flattering headline USC'S LARRY SMITH: IN A WAY HE'S LIKE MCKAY; PRACTICES UNDER NEW COACH REFLECT SAME KIND OF ORGANIZATION AND INTENSITY. Mal Florence wrote, "This doesn't necessarily mean that Smith will be as successful as McKay, who won 4 national championships and made 8 Rose Bowl appearances in 16 years at USC. But there is a similarity in coaching style and organization."

Comparing Smith to McKay five months before Smith's debut was a serious reach. Still, Smith had scored locally by saying he intended to revive the once-powerful USC running attack. Although Tollner had not ignored the running game, implementing it was not his strength. USC averaged 137 yards rushing in his final season, the lowest at the school since 1949.

In 1987, Pat O'Hara was a redshirt freshman quarterback. In 1988, he ended up not playing much behind Rodney Peete. The next year O'Hara engaged in a three-way quarterback battle with Shane Foley and the wild child, Todd Marinovich.

PAT O'HARA: When Larry Smith brought in his staff, they were cracking the whip, and some of the older guys had a tough time adjusting. Then we opened the season at Michigan State. We lost, 27–13, and we didn't look good at all. We all looked at each other like, *Man, we're not a very good team.*

CLARENCE SHELMON: At USC, losing isn't really tolerated. So there was some grumbling from the alumni. But that's part of it. You sort of accept it when you come to coach at USC.

The Trojans had entered the opener ranked No. 19 against the 17th-ranked Spartans. It was their first loss to a Big Ten team since the 1974 Rose Bowl, but the bigger oddity was their school-record 47 passes. Yes, USC had to pass after falling behind, 24–6. But 47 passes no matter the circumstances was hardly a return to the program's storied rushing attack.

The Trojans also looked nervous in the national TV game played on Labor Day night. Peete fumbled three times and threw two interceptions before Smith benched him. Smith tore into his players after his debut. Then he told reporters that if USC kept making that many mistakes, "We'll be 0–11."

The good news: There was a bye week before playing unranked Boston College.

The bad news: The players endured two weeks of hellish practice.

On September 19, when the now-unranked Trojans played the lowly Eagles, only 46,205 fans showed up at the Coliseum. When USC won, 23–17, that didn't placate Smith.

BRAD LEGGETT: The hardest practice we had at USC was the Sunday after we played Boston College. It was only helmets and sweats, but it was the hardest practice we ever had in our lives. We beat Boston College, but not by enough.

The Trojans were 4–2 and still unranked when they traveled to South Bend to face the 4–1 and tenth-ranked Irish. The disparity in the rankings despite the similar records probably had to do with Michigan State. After easily beating USC, 27–13, the Spartans had been drilled, 31–8, by Notre Dame.

As the pollsters scorned the Trojans, Irish coach Lou Holtz lavished them with praise. He said USC had shown "dramatic improvement" and had "a great chance to go to the Rose Bowl." Then Notre Dame beat USC for the fifth straight year. The 26–15 final score was misleading since the Trojans scored a touchdown with 50 seconds left. Smith, the defensive specialist, looked furious on the sideline as the Irish rolled up 351 yards rushing.

Full of blarney or not, Holtz was right about the Rose Bowl. The Trojans won their next three games to improve to 6–1 in the Pac-10, setting up a showdown for the Rose Bowl against 7–0 UCLA. The eighth-ranked Bruins came into the Coliseum as nine-point favorites and led, 13–0, after three quarters. Then unranked USC rallied for a rousing 17–13 victory.

After a shaky start, Smith had steered his team to the Rose Bowl in his first season. In an unusual rematch from the opening week, 8–3 and 16th-ranked USC faced 8–2–1 and eighth-ranked Michigan State. The Spartans won again, 20–17, in the Pac-10's first defeat after winning six straight Rose Bowls and 16 of the last 18. The legendary Jim Murray wrote in the *Los Angeles Times*: "The Big Ten won in the Rose Bowl! Cross my heart! Would I lie about a thing like that?"

The following season (1998) marked the 100th year of USC football, but *Sport* magazine wasn't feeling sentimental. According to its college preview, "Rodney Peete's biggest problem is that he's the second-best quarterback on the second-best team in town. The City of Angels will belong to UCLA and Troy Aikman in 1988."

Maybe. But maybe not. The eighth-ranked Trojans came out smoking. While winning their first nine games, they demolished Arizona, Oregon, Cal, and Arizona State by a composite score of 165–32. As the lopsided wins piled up, writers in other cities lauded Smith while Tollner's reputation took a beating.

"Leave it to a coach with Midwest virtues to instill passion and desire into the laid-back lads from Southern Cal," Ed Sherman wrote in November in the *Chicago Tribune.* "Before Larry Smith's arrival, USC was the California stereotype personified. Ted Tollner was a great guy, but his teams preferred to be at the beach. So what if the Trojans lost on Saturday afternoon? There still was going to be an oh, wow, really-happening party on Saturday night."

On November 19, the 9–0 and second-ranked Trojans faced the 9–1 and sixth-ranked Bruins in a second straight showdown for the Rose Bowl bid. Back in the 1970s, USC had dominated the rivalry with a 7–2–1 record. UCLA was 5–2 in the 1980s, and there was talk in Westwood of a paradigm shift.

I asked Leggett and Harlow how they used to view their crosstown rivals.

BRAD LEGGETT: UCLA wore polo shirts. We wore T-shirts. They drank beer with straws, in a glass, and we drank beer out of a bottle. That was our mentality: We felt we were tougher than them.

Jeff Peace was this big-time recruit out of Mission Viejo High School. He told me the story about his recruiting trips. He went to UCLA first, and they took him to the strip club and everyone was wearing polo shirts. He goes to USC, and they're sitting around drinking beer and someone says, "Hey, Jeff, where do you want to go?" He says, "Well, at UCLA, we went to the strip club last week." So they go to the strip club, and they get in a fight. He said, "*That's* where I want to go."

PAT HARLOW: My son plays at Oregon State, but he had been recruited by UCLA. He talked to Coach Mora, and Coach Mora said, "Why don't you want to come to UCLA?" My son said, "Because you guys are soft." Mora is changing that now, but we always thought we were a little tougher than them, living and working in South Central LA versus living in Westwood. UCLA always had the mystique of being soft.

PAT O'HARA: We played at ASU the week before we played UCLA, and we beat them 50–0. I actually got to play, and I was the backup. We get home from ASU, and my roommate Rodney Peete falls super ill. It turned out he had the measles.

I had never started a game in my career—I was a redshirt sophomore—but Rodney was sick as a dog. There was a lot of talk that week about who would start, and Larry Smith shielded me from the media. Then Rodney gets off his deathbed after losing 15 pounds and he goes out and beats UCLA and Troy Aikman.

USC won the famous measles game, 31–22. Peete completed 16 of 28 passes for 189 yards and one touchdown and also ran for a touchdown. Aikman was even better: 32 of 48 for 317 yards and two touchdowns. The difference was Aaron Emanuel, with 27 carries for 113 yards and two touchdowns.

The win gave USC its second straight conference title and Rose Bowl berth. Even better, it came at UCLA's expense. But one week later, the regular-season finale was flat-out monumental when 10–0 and second-ranked USC hosted 10–0 and top-ranked Notre Dame. In a series that had begun in 1926, this was the first time both schools had perfect records.

That week Smith and Holtz avoided talking about national championships. They also danced around questions about the previous year's game, when the Fighting Irish controlled the line of scrimmage in a decisive 26–15 victory.

Then Holtz tried making the case that this season's Trojans were bigger and stronger than his little Notre Dame squad.

"They are little?" Smith said. "His defensive tackles are 283, 277 . . . I will not discuss it."

The game didn't match the hype when Notre Dame won, 27–10. Still, the Trojans didn't perform as badly as the scoreboard indicated, gaining 356 total yards to Notre Dame's 253. But they also committed four turnovers, all at bad times: two interceptions by Peete, a fumble by Emanuel, and a fumble by Ricky Ervins, the small but powerful sophomore tailback.

Not only would there be no national title, it was USC's sixth straight loss in the rivalry. The last time the Trojans won, in 1982, Robinson was coaching his final season. Now Robinson was with the Rams, and the matchup was Smith-Holtz. Did that give the team from South Bend a major advantage?

RICKY ERVINS: They definitely did something different against us that game. Most teams didn't blitz Rodney Peete. Then they blitzed Rodney Peete every play it seemed like. That disrupted our flow because he wasn't used to that. We weren't used to that. Lou Holtz made a great call: Nobody's blitzing these guys, so why don't we blitz them and see what happens?

SCOTT LOCKWOOD: They outschemed us defensively. They blitzed every single play, and our blitz pickup wasn't good enough to win the game. Ned Bolcar was one of their linebackers. He was 6–5, 250. I'm a 5–11, 200-pound running back, and I have pass pickup protection every single blitz. I'm not gonna win that battle too many times.

On defense the Trojans were hurt by Notre Dame's option quarterback, Tony Rice, who threw for just 91 yards but rushed for 86 while making several clutch plays.

BRAD LEGGETT: Dan Owens was my roommate for three years at USC. He was a defensive guy, so he knew more about it than I did. But he and I would talk. For example, that year we played Oklahoma and we shut down their option. Against Notre Dame, we didn't play the same defense even though they ran the option. You see things that like, you start to look at the play calling. Not against UCLA: I never thought the coaches got tight against UCLA. But against Notre Dame, our coaches got tight.

DAN OWENS: We coached differently and we played differently against Notre Dame than we did against Oklahoma or Auburn or any other good team we played. We would play two safeties deep, and Notre Dame ran the ball on almost every play. As a former player and now as a coach, I don't understand why we would not play an extra linebacker or a D lineman when we were having trouble stopping the run.

SCOTT LOCKWOOD: Tim Brown. Rocket Ismail. Jerome Bettis. Ricky Watters. Tony Rice. If you look at their offense during that stretch when they were beating us, they had several players who are collegiate Hall of Famers or NFL Hall of Fame–caliber players.

Holtz was also an incredible motivator and leader. With Larry Smith it was more fear by intimidation. So everyone played tight, with so much anxiety. USC was also fragmented during those years. The offense hated the defense. The DBs hung out with DBs; the receivers hung out with receivers. We had all these cliques in the locker room. I think Holtz had his teams playing together. For years I used to turn on college football to listen to Holtz as an announcer. And he was still full of a bunch of shit. But it's like going to church and listening to a sermon. If there's a couple different things that work for you, then you got something out of it.

AARON EMANUEL: Notre Dame was really good that season. But so were we. We were outcoached, probably, once again. Lou Holtz was a master at getting his teams prepared. And that game still stings today. We were No. 2 and they were No. 1. If we win that game, we go into the national championship game. And they came into our house and handed it to us.

Matt Gee was a freshman linebacker who lettered all four years and became a team captain as a senior.

MATT GEE: We were going to the Rose Bowl no matter what because we won the Pac-10. Then Notre Dame comes out here and kicks our asses in the Coliseum. And that had been such a great season. It seemed like it was time for us to be No. 1. The last time USC had finished No. 1 was 1978, so this was ten years later. Then we just dropped the ball and Tony Rice ran all over us.

GARY BERNARDI: Lou Holtz did a phenomenal job. But going into those games, he had a tendency to make you sound like you were a world-beater, and Larry Smith wouldn't ever buy into that. It would piss him off because that wasn't him. He was a meat and potatoes guy. So that stimulated the rivalry during those years.

Leroy Holt was a freshman who later became a team captain and the first USC fullback to start all four of his seasons. He broke two of Sam Cunningham's school records for fullbacks—most rushing yards and most carries without a fumble—and was also a bruising blocker.

LEROY HOLT: I hated Notre Dame. They always found a way to spoil our national championship aspirations. After the '88 game, Larry Smith was pissed because we lost. So he didn't shake Lou Holtz's hand out on the field. Then Lou Holtz got so pissed, he came out to our bus. We were ready to depart, and Larry Smith got on the bus and Lou Holtz jumped up on the bus right behind him. Holtz said if Smith stepped off the bus, he would kick his ass. That's my memory of Lou Holtz. He told Larry Smith, "You son of a bitch, that's disrespectful. Come off this bus and I'll kick your ass."

Holtz weighed about 150, so perhaps it was better for him that Smith kept his cool. Still, in his third season in South Bend, the pugnacious "little general" led the 12–0 Irish to their first national title since 1977 when they beat West Virginia in the Fiesta Bowl.

USC faced Michigan in the 75th Rose Bowl game, where the three main story lines were Bo Schembechler's 1–7 record in Pasadena, his 0–3 record there against USC, and his friendship with his former protégé, Smith.

"I joke about it, but underneath I'm ticked off just like everyone else," Schembechler said. "When you're 1–7, that's a lot of losses. Maybe I'll have better luck against Larry."

Smith said, "I'm just a young guy on the block. And I'm going against the veteran."

The 10–1 Trojans came in ranked No. 5, and the 8–2–1 Wolverines were No. 11. The oddsmakers had USC as six-point favorites, which seemed about right when it led, 14–3, at halftime. Then Michigan made better adjustments and outscored the Trojans, 19–0, in the last two quarters.

The second-half collapse and 22–14 defeat meant *Smith* was now scrutinized for his Rose Bowl record. Not only was he 0–2, the program had never lost two straight Rose Bowls before.

AARON EMANUEL: I think our hearts were still broken from losing to Notre Dame. We didn't quite recover the way we should have. A lot of guys didn't prepare themselves the way they should have. We were still reeling from the chance to be the No. 1 team in the country. Then Notre Dame went on to win it all that season. That only made it hurt worse.

MATT GEE: We lost to Michigan because we didn't care. We really did not give a shit about that game. All you had to do was win the last game of the season against Notre Dame. We're both 10–0 and we lose at the Coliseum? We were done. That season was done.

7

AND A FRESHMAN SHALL LEAD THEM:

1989

By August 1989, with Rodney Peete having graduated and no clear-cut replacement, a three-way quarterback battle finally had been won by Pat O'Hara. Todd Marinovich and Shane Foley appeared to be competing for the No. 2 spot. But ten days before the season opener, O'Hara tore up his right knee on a controversial play during a practice.

O'Hara and Foley were juniors who rarely saw the field while serving as understudies to the durable Peete. Before USC, both had been local prep stars. In his last two years at Santa Monica High School, O'Hara threw for 44 touchdowns and almost 4,000 yards. Foley was the 1986 California Interscholastic Federation (CIF) player of the year at Newport Harbor High School, passing for more yards (5,300) than anyone before in quarterback-rich Orange County.

Marinovich was a freshman who had redshirted the previous season. He'd been groomed since early childhood by his father, Marv Marinovich, a former USC captain and Oakland Raider whose special diets for Todd and strict training regimen had first been examined closely in a *California* magazine piece with the headline ROBO QB: THE MAKING OF A PERFECT ATHLETE. It was an excellent profile, but in lesser ones to follow, the son would be reduced to a caricature: his father's science project.

Their collaboration resulted in a prolific high school career. At Mater Dei and Capistrano Valley, Marinovich didn't just shatter Foley's Orange County record; he passed for more yards (9,914) than any high school quarterback ever. He enrolled at USC in 1988 as one of the most scrutinized and anticipated recruits in the program's history, and yet Marinovich says he almost went elsewhere.

TODD MARINOVICH: Right away I let people know I was staying on the West Coast, so that had eliminated a lot of schools. But then I was really close to going to Stanford. They put in the full assault since I was a freshman in high school. Jack Elway asked me at the end where things stood on a scale of one to five, five being signing with him, and I told him four. But I had promised SC I would take a trip even though I had been there on campus many times over the years. My family didn't put any real pressure on me, but after my SC trip, my grandfather took me aside. He said, "Where do you want to live when you're done with school?" I said, "Southern California." He said, "There's your answer." But I also didn't want to get my ass beat by SC every year either.

SHANE FOLEY: There was already a lot of media attention given to him, at a time in the late '80s when there wasn't nearly as much coverage as there is today. It wasn't just the sports media, either. *People* magazine did a story on him in high school. That was very unique, to have that kind of hype when you're entering a college program. But Todd was actually more of an introverted guy. Todd was pretty shy.

PAT O'HARA: In '89 I won the job over Todd during the spring. We got to preseason camp and had a scrimmage in late August. I was rolling out to my left, and a freshman linebacker was scraping to his right. He decides to commit to go after me. He goes low; my offensive lineman sees him and dives to block him. I got hit by my lineman's helmet on the outside part of my knee, and then both of their bodies kind of rolled over me. So my offensive lineman was trying to protect me, and this freshman linebacker was probably too overzealous in that situation.

I ripped up my knee, and that was that. I tore my ligaments in my knee and I broke my tibia. I had two surgeries. And I got really sick, too. I was in the hospital for two weeks, which is unusual for a knee. I was out for the entire season.

I asked O'Hara: After waiting three years to win the starting job, was he angry at the freshman linebacker?

PAT O'HARA: I was angry, period. When you're 20 years old, it's devastating. I had to learn who my real friends were, because you do get treated differently. Out of sight, out of mind. You were the starting QB at USC, and now that's dramatically changed. I became a bit of an outcast, and that was really an eye-opener for me. But hey, that's life. And that's the nature of the business in major college football.

TODD MARINOVICH: Until then, Pat was the guy. The question was, really, who would back him up? I remember when Pat got hit like it was yesterday. The sound really stuck with me. I think everyone knew it was something really bad with a sound like that. It was just a really freak accident. You don't see hits like that in a game, let alone in practice.

John Jackson was a senior flanker who graduated as USC's all-time leader in receptions and yards. He also starred in baseball and was a two-time Academic All-American. Jackson is now a Los Angeles sportscaster with ESPN radio and FSN TV.

JOHN JACKSON: I was livid. The rule is, never hit the quarterback under any circumstances. To this day I don't know what that defensive player was doing. And I've never felt so bad for anyone in my life. Pat had waited his turn, playing behind Rodney Peete. Then it's finally his turn, and I'm telling you Pat was ready. I love Todd Marinovich to death, but I think we win the national championship that season if Pat O'Hara is the starting quarterback. Todd was *going* to be a great quarterback, but he got thrown into the starting role so late in the process.

BRAD LEGGETT: Going into that season, we were loaded. Quarterback was going to be the question mark. Then Pat O'Hara was named to be our starter. We were good to go. Then a guy rolls over Pat's knee, and suddenly here we are, about to play Illinois. Next man up, right? They decided Marinovich was the guy.

RICKY ERVINS: The talk was that he never ate a Big Mac before, he never had any fast food, and yadda yadda yadda because of his dad. You hear all these things and you just want to know: Can he perform? Is he competitive? Is he *good?*

JOHN JACKSON: I was his leading receiver, and he was extremely, extremely accurate. Maybe only a receiver would appreciate something like this, but he never laid me out into a kill shot. He never put the ball where a linebacker or a safety would knock my head off. You could put a can 40 yards away on top of a garbage can and he could knock the can off.

BRAD LEGGETT: We open at the Coliseum against Illinois with an overly conservative game plan. We don't put anything on Todd. And it ends up biting us in the rear end.

Even with its freshman quarterback on a short leash, fifth-ranked USC led 19th-ranked Illinois, 13–0, after three quarters.

Then future NFL star Jeff George threw two touchdown passes, and the Illini won, 14–13.

Marinovich passed for only 120 yards, absorbed four sacks, and threw a key late interception. The *Los Angeles Times*'s Steve Springer wrote on Sunday: "The launch of a new era had fizzled." Not for long, however. Larry Smith put more faith in his young quarterback, and in the next two games USC crushed Utah State (a doormat) and Ohio State (still finding its way) 66–10 and 42–3, respectively. Marinovich threw a total of six touchdown passes, including a school-record 87-yarder to John Jackson.

At Washington State the next week, in what would be remembered as The Drive, USC had the ball on its own nine-yard line, losing 17–10 with 3:31 left in the fourth quarter. Marinovich converted twice on fourth down, including a huge 15-yarder on fourth and ten to Gary Wellman. Then Marinovich connected on two difficult third-down situations. Finally, with four seconds left, he threw a two-yard touchdown strike to Ricky Ervins. USC still trailed, 17–16. After Smith called time out and chose to go for the win, Marinovich hit Wellman in the end zone for a delirious 18–17 comeback win on the road.

RICKY ERVINS: You could tell in the huddle, Todd thought we would win. I said after that game, "This a baller right here. He's a straight baller."

PAT HARLOW: Todd hated practice. He probably didn't prepare as much as he could have. But when the lights came on, his eyes were big, and he was ready to rock and roll.

TODD MARINOVICH: That was the real momentum changer for us: that late drive in Pullman. It was the best moment I ever had playing football. I knew they had confidence in me, but they were looking at me to see how I would respond. And everyone did his part. You can't make that kind of drive without guys making plays. It was one of those things that you really play football for: to experience something like that.

Three weeks later, on October 21, in the biggest game of the regular season, USC and Notre Dame met in South Bend. The Irish were 6–0, ranked No. 1, and trying to win their second straight national title. USC had won five straight after losing to Illinois and was ranked No. 9.

The Trojans still recalled the severe disappointment of their 27–10 loss in 1988, when both teams had come in at 10–0. Notre Dame still recalled what Smith later told reporters: "People say we were outcoached and not physical enough against Notre Dame. That's not true. We outcoached them, outblocked them, and out-tackled them. We made about seven crucial mistakes, and Notre Dame, being a good sound football team, took advantage and turned them into points."

In South Bend during that same 1988 season, Notre Dame and Miami had been in a pregame brawl, and many had concluded that both teams were equally guilty. Now, one year later, the Irish and the Trojans had their own pregame scuffle. According to *Sports Illustrated*'s Doug Looney, the fault this time belonged solely to Notre Dame. "These are nasty, ornery pit bull Irish," wrote Looney, "who may be beyond the control of their own coach. Approach at your own peril."

Years ago I asked Chris Zorich, Notre Dame's intense All-American nose guard, if *SI* was correct and the Irish started the fight with USC.

"I hated the USC guys," Zorich said. "They lived in California. They had beautiful swimming pools on campus. They never shoveled snow."

I said, "But who started the fight?"

Zorich said, "They were a bunch of cocky California guys. Of course they started it."

For this book, I asked Gibson if he knew who started it.

DON GIBSON: I wasn't there. I blew out my knee my junior year, and I didn't go back for that trip, unfortunately. I was watching it on TV. But I'm sure it was Notre Dame's fault.

GARY BERNARDI: Our kids were confident hotheads, and they were confident hotheads. But obviously I'm on the USC side . . . so I would say they started it. And you could just feel it was coming. It felt like there was going to be a riot or something.

AARON EMANUEL: I remember exactly how it started. We were warming up before the game, and most of our guys had already gone into the locker room. We were doing a few last drills, and then we went to go inside. Most of Notre Dame's team was lined up across the back line of the end zone that led to our locker room. They were all locking arms, like, *Hey, you need to go around us.*

I was right behind our running back coach, Clarence Shelmon. He turned around and looked at us. He was fired up. He said, "Come on! We're going straight through! We're not going around!" Notre Dame was playing mind games, and Coach Shelmon didn't want to go around.

LEROY HOLT: I guess that was their idea of intimidation. I think it was Coach Shelmon who ran right through them. Then our players ran right through, and that's what started the fight.

SCOTT LOCKWOOD: I had broken my thumb in the first game against Illinois. So I was home, watching it on TV. The camera work wasn't as good as it is today. All you could see was players getting punched and kicked underneath the bench. I remember seeing Dwayne Garner under the bench getting kicked. It was chaos. Helmets were getting ripped off. I was sitting there wondering what the hell happened.

Clarence Shelmon was my running back coach. I loved him to death. He was more of a father figure and not just a coach. Half of our running back meetings would be about doing the right thing and getting good grades and becoming a doctor or lawyer, something meaningful with your life. But he would also cuss out the band at Berkeley, he would flip them off, he would throw cups of water at them. When he was pissed, he was pissed. At Notre Dame, I'm assuming he probably threw the first punch. I'm in firm belief that Clarence Shelmon, one of the coaches, started the fight.

CLARENCE SHELMON: Nah, I wasn't involved. I mean, I got knocked down. I was just trying to get through.

AARON EMANUEL: Before you knew it, all hell broke loose. I remember just trying to keep my helmet on because it was right near their people in the stands. And most of our team was already inside the locker room. We were outnumbered by *a lot*.

MATT GEE: It was 100 against 11 for a while. I was literally thrown into the stands by their O linemen. That fight was legendary. They started it. But I got some punches in. I got a coach really good, because we all kept our helmets on and their coaches were grabbing our face masks.

TODD MARINOVICH: I was in our locker room when it started. And then before you know it, people are running in and saying, "We're getting ambushed!"

Matt Willig was a 6-foot-8 sophomore offensive tackle who went on to play 14 NFL seasons and win a Super Bowl with the St. Louis Rams. He is now a successful actor and appeared last year in *Concussion,* the NFL-based movie starring Will Smith.

MATT WILLIG: Some of our guys came running inside and said, "They're fighting out there!" So we went running out, too. It was a bunch of Notre Dame guys on top of a few USC guys. I didn't throw any punches. I just started throwing some of their guys off of our guys.

GARY BERNARDI: More of our guys joined in, and it was a free-for-all. There were a lot of big kids at those two schools, and it was a full-ass brawl. It got pretty violent, and a couple of the security guards who traveled with our team had to go to the hospital.

CLARENCE SHELMON: We all went back inside our locker room when it got broken up, and the urgency of the situation got amped up even more. But that's not a game you need motivation for. If you're not motivated for Notre Dame, you're in the wrong game.

TODD MARINOVICH: There was a lot of emotion for sure. People were beside themselves, really. When things settled, that played a part in how we came out and got up on them quickly.

USC led, 17–7, as the teams left the field for halftime. Marinovich, the first USC redshirt freshman to start at quarterback against Notre Dame, already had passed for 156 yards and two touchdowns. Then the Trojans got too cocky for their own good. As the opposing teams entered the same narrow tunnel that leads to both locker rooms, several USC players sarcastically sang the Notre Dame fight song.

Precisely how it unfolded has always been unclear. Was it carefully planned or semi-spontaneous? Was USC assistant Tom Roggeman the true instigator, or was this one on the players?

MATT WILLIG: Before we went into that game, Tom Roggeman handed out the Notre Dame fight song to everyone and made us learn it. He gave everyone a copy. I remember thinking, *This is crazy; there's something morally wrong about this.* Because this was their song and it was so hallowed.

TODD MARINOVICH: Coach Roggeman thought it would be a good idea to learn the Notre Dame fight song. Little did I know that we would actually put it in their face at *halftime.* I don't know if *he* thought it would actually happen. But it did, and didn't go over well with Notre Dame.

MATT GEE: I don't remember why they made us learn it. But we were still so pissed off at Notre Dame, we went ahead and sang it.

AARON EMANUEL: Roggeman was a real fiery guy. Looked a little bit like Popeye. Old guy, short guy, chunky little guy with a Popeye face, always had this snarl on his face. He said the week before, "I'm handing out their fight song. Take it home and learn it. Get to know their words. By Friday, you better know this song. 'Cause we're gonna sing it while we're kicking their asses!"

So we're winning 17–7 at halftime. We're looking around at each other like, *Do we sing it now? When are we gonna do this? Do we wait until we win this game?* Literally, people are looking around and whispering, "Do we do it now, guys? When do we sing the song?"

Somebody said, "Yeah, do it now, do it now!" It started out pretty funny because a lot of us didn't remember the full song. A couple guys started singing the first couple words and then a few more guys joined in, and then before you know it, we're singing the Notre Dame fight song in the tunnel, right next to them. I remember a couple of their defensive players, Chris Zorich and Mike Stonebreaker, going crazy: "You hear those motherfuckers? Those fuckers are singing our fucking fight song!" They went berserk. They couldn't believe *we* were singing their fight song, rubbing it in their face, like, *here's* your fucking fight song.

LEROY HOLT: We didn't like them, and they didn't like us. Every opportunity to get in their face—especially if we were winning—we would stick it in their face. And that was one of those times.

GARY WELLMAN: I remember thinking, *What the hell are we doing? Why would we give them any more motivation than they already need during halftime?*

Did that affect the game? I don't know. But it was one of the more stupid things that we've ever done.

DON GIBSON: It was one of those ideas that sound good until they happen. Then you look back and see the momentum shifted. Notre Dame was asleep at the wheel. We were controlling the game and were cruising.

TODD MARINOVICH: Uh, it wasn't the best idea I've ever encountered.

Safety Stephon Pace grew up in South Bend and turned down Notre Dame to play for USC, where he anchored the defensive backfield as a three-year starter.

STEPHON PACE: We were all in the tunnel, and I saw Lou Holtz looking at us. You could read his mind: *You're going to sing our fight song? Okay.*

They come out in the second half, and they wipe us up and down the field. *We* started that. We were *winning.* And we may have had the better team. But suddenly you do this thing, and you give a coach like Lou Holtz the motivation he uses to his advantage?

SCOTT LOCKWOOD: I'm back home watching them on TV, and I'm thinking, *Please don't start singing their fight song now. All you're going to do is piss their guys off. And little tiny Lou Holtz is going to go in there and get their guys all jacked up.*

PAT HARLOW: It was a sign of respect. It was taken the wrong way. In hindsight, it was probably not the right thing to do because they came back out pretty fired up.

AARON EMANUEL: It wasn't out of respect. Why would we want to respect Notre Dame anyway? Whoever told you that is giving you a line of bullshit. I'm sure you knew that already.

I still don't understand why we did that. It was a bold move, put it that way. If we win the game, it's a great story. It's a *classic* story if we win that game. But you look back at it now like, *Did that really happen?* And they came roaring back out and kicked our ass.

The Irish outscored the Trojans, 21–7, in the second half. The 28–24 loss was USC's seventh straight to (clearly) its most hated rival. Still, it was a fantastic college football game. There were controversial calls (against the Trojans), dynamic plays by future NFL stars, and a mostly electric performance by Marinovich, who threw for three touchdowns and 333 yards. He also threw three interceptions, reminding everyone that he was still a freshman playing for his first time at Notre Dame. In the final two minutes, Marinovich drove USC to a second-down play at the Irish seven. Then he threw three incompletions under a furious Notre Dame rush.

TODD MARINOVICH: We should have won. As a quarterback, if you get that kind of opportunity to win a big game like that, it's all you can ask for. If there's one game I still lose sleep over, it's that game.

DAN OWENS: Lou Holtz was really good. He made the right adjustments in the second half of that game. On the other hand, we stayed in a base defense for almost the entire game. We were playing conservative, playing tight, playing not to make mistakes.

After losing to Notre Dame the year before in the regular-season finale, the disheartened Trojans lost, 22–14, to Michigan in the Rose Bowl. The 1989 Trojans showed their resilience by winning the next three games by a composite score of 91–9. They stumbled at the end of the regular season—tying unranked UCLA, 10–10—but by then had already clinched their third straight Pac-10 title and Rose Bowl appearance.

MATT WILLIG: We still had a lot to prove. We *lost* the last two Rose Bowls. So there was a feeling of, *Shit, if we don't do this now, this is going to be our lore. We can't beat Notre Dame and we can't win the Rose Bowl. We can get to the Rose Bowl, but we can't take it to the next level and win that game.*

On January 1, 1990, USC faced Michigan for the second consecutive year. The 8–2–1 Trojans came in ranked No. 12, and the 10–1 Wolverines were No. 3. Schembechler had announced this would be his final game after 21 years at Michigan, where he won 13 Big Ten titles but never a national championship.

USC had lost four straight bowl games—Rose, Rose, Citrus, Aloha—but the Trojans finally broke through with a 17–10 victory. Marinovich coolly led a game-winning drive that began on the USC 25 with 5:15 to play. Ricky Ervins rushed for 126 yards and scored the winning touchdown from 14 yards out. Ervins, who would clash with Smith the next season, was named Rose Bowl MVP. It was Smith's first postseason triumph, and it came against his fiery ex-boss, who did not go out gently.

MATT GEE: Late in the fourth quarter, I don't know what Schembechler thought happened, but he came walking out on the field. He was clear out to the numbers. He threw his headset down and he told the ref to fuck off, and he was flagged.

GARY WELLMAN: That was a huge win for us, and I've never seen Larry Smith happier in his entire life. Bo Schembechler was his mentor. Smith was the understudy.

I think Smith saw that game as making his tenure at USC. Winning the Rose Bowl was a big feather in his cap.

DAN OWENS: That was my senior year when we finally got it done and won the Rose Bowl. Since I'd been at USC, the bowl games had become a party-type atmosphere. Go out and have a good time and the football becomes secondary. That was kind of hard for me to deal with because I'm a football-first guy and a party-second guy.

It was a little different before that Rose Bowl as far as the parties go. It was our third Rose Bowl and we had lost the last two, and it was at the point of, *What the shit?*

BRAD LEGGETT: At the end of the game, we were on offense. We were in the victory formation. I snap the ball to Todd. Game is over. Todd puts his hands up in the air with the ball in his hand. I turn around and I grab the ball, and I say, "You'll get your own ball next year." I still have that ball.

That was it, my last game at USC. My family is from the South. My dad was an All-American at LSU. When I came out of high school, it was between LSU and USC. I remember sitting at our kitchen table. I didn't know anything about college football. My brother said, "You can't turn down a USC scholarship. Not only because of the linemen they put in the NFL but because of all the connections you're gonna make."

Sure enough, that's been true. And there's nothing like being a Trojan and having the USC band and Traveler and the Song Girls. There's no experience like that. No one can top what SC has to offer. It's just magical.

8

TEAM TURMOIL:

1990

On September 3, 1990, *Sports Illustrated* published its college football preview with Todd Marinovich gracing the cover and the headline GROWING PAINS AT USC. In recounting his freshman year, Douglas Looney wrote that Marinovch "had some awful lows and some awesome highs as he struggled to assume the mantle of leadership in one of the most glamorous positions in sport." Looney pointed out that both UPI and *The Sporting News* named Marinovich the college freshman of the year for 1989, he was the only freshman named to the All-Pac-10 team, and he completed 61 percent of his passes while throwing for 2,587 yards and 16 touchdowns. Yet when Looney asked Smith what he saw as "his team's primary need this fall," Smith said, "Improved efficiency at quarterback." It was a telling reply given that the 1990 Trojans returned only seven starters and probably would have bigger issues than their dynamic young quarterback's efficiency.

The *SI* cover story also reexamined Marinovich's relationship with his father. Never mind that Marv had starred for John McKay at USC and then been an offensive lineman and conditioning coach for the Oakland Raiders. Once Todd came along, according to Looney, Marv was "the prototypical stage father. In most ways, Marv didn't have a life. He had Todd's life."

TODD MARINOVICH: When I was at USC, he would give me coaching points and he would critique. But he was never really hands-on. He downshifted big time when I left for college. He still tried to make every practice he could, which had been a constant since day one with me. But his whole attitude was different by then.

TIM TESSALONE: Marv Marinovich would sit in games in the upper corner of the Coliseum, almost by himself. If he went to practice, he would stand in the corner by himself and watch. I never sensed he was looking over everybody's shoulder. Obviously he had a football background. He knew his stuff about training and conditioning people. Troy Polamalu swears by him. But people painted him as the mad scientist, and Todd was the experiment.

MATT GEE: Todd was my roommate. I think he loved working out with his father. I think he liked eating healthy food. But he wasn't the robo QB that the media made him to be. That was all bullshit. The first day I met Todd, we were at McDonald's eating. All that stuff in the media was just an attempt to pump him up. I also know his father very well. When Todd went to college, Marv let him go. He was around, but he wasn't the guy I heard he was supposed to be.

DON GIBSON: I used to train with Todd and his dad. When they were working out, they were laughing all the time. There was a lot of hard work but a lot of laughter, too. I think Marv has gotten a horrible rap. Did you know both of them were artists? And Todd was an amazing artist at USC. He's an amazing artist today.

I've known Todd a long time. I remember him as a freshman at Mater Dei. Even later when I was married and had kids, Todd would come over, and our kids loved him. He was as genuine as you could get. Obviously he got caught up in some things later. I'm sure if he could rewind the clock, he would. Addiction is a terrible thing. But I have never known Todd through any of it to be anything but Todd, which is a very fun-loving person. The only person Todd ever hurt was himself and some of the people who loved and cared about him.

MATT GEE: Todd did some drugs in college, which is kind of normal. People called him Marijuanavich. But honestly, who didn't smoke pot in college, at least a little bit? Everybody probably tried it. He wasn't addicted it to when I was around him, *ever.*

The Marijuanavich tag had clung since his basketball-playing days at Mater Dei High School. Other teams' students would chant it as he stepped to the free throw line. Marinovich did, in fact, frequently smoke pot in high school and college, and later in life he moved on to drugs as serious as heroin. Today he says he is sober.

TODD MARINOVICH: The partying at USC started on my recruiting trip, and it continued until my last game there. It never really stopped. Drinking a lot. Smoking a lot of pot. A little bit of cocaine, kind of just beginning with that. Sprinkled in with a little hallucinogenics.

The Marijuanavich thing started back in high school. It kind of died out in college, but yeah, I do recall it. It bothered me, yeah. It was the heaviest my junior year of high school. It wasn't cool in my mind at the time. My mom, my parents, my grandparents were at the basketball games, and it would just be echoing in the gymnasiums. Jesus.

I asked Todd if Marv's strict regimen when Todd was younger— all those years of being groomed and micromanaged—contributed to his drug use and various rebellions later on.

TODD MARINOVICH: My dad said to me many times that *not* allowing me to make more of my own decisions was one of his many mistakes but one which he also thought was of some value. And I can't disagree.

Was it the time? Genetic? Where I was, Orange County? All that stuff plays a role. That's what makes it so hard to answer that. There are also a lot of temptations when you play quarterback at USC. If I was an offensive tackle, we wouldn't be talking about this. That's just a hard fact. But I chose to play the quarterback position, and that comes with certain stuff that you might not like but you have to endure if you want to play the position. And you know? I really did. I really grew into loving playing quarterback.

The rumors about his drug use at USC were accompanied by whispers that he cheated on his drug tests. After he left the school, the *Los Angeles Times* reported that Marinovich wasn't alone. The 1991 investigation by several staff writers said, "The *Times* has learned of a pattern in which USC football players regularly cheated on their drug tests."

In 1990, Mike Salmon was a freshman safety who became a three-year starter and a big enough hitter to also play linebacker. He recalls the day in 1990 when he helped Marinovich pass a drug test.

MIKE SALMON: Let me preface my statements by saying Todd wasn't masking something that would enhance his performance. He was masking a recreational drug that a good chunk of the country uses. I was one of those guys who didn't take steroids, and I knew the guys who *were* taking steroids. Todd wasn't one of those guys.

My first drug test at USC, I had never been formally introduced to Todd. He was the golden boy, the poster child, and the face of the franchise. I saw him from across the cafeteria or at practice, but I never saw him up close. Then I went in for my first drug test, and he handed me a cup, and the first thing he ever said to me was something like, "Hey, you mind?" He said it with a smile on his face, and (a) I was totally caught off guard, and (b) I don't know if you've ever been face to face with a celebrity, but at the ripe old age of eighteen, I was blown away that it was Todd who was asking.

I had my pants down and I was going in my cup, and he handed me his cup. I just smiled back and filled up about a shot glass full of urine and gave it back it to him. We both kind of laughed and walked away, and that was the end of it. Then I realized the magnitude of it as I was riding around campus on my bike. I thought, *Did I just do that?*

Every other drug test I took after that, I made it a point to go inside a stall or to the side of the room where nobody was at, because I didn't want to be in the same position again and end up getting in trouble. But with Todd, it was spur of the moment. The last thing I wanted to do was upset the face of the franchise or to go and tell on him or something.

SCOTT LOCKWOOD: I've heard that some guys would pee for him. I've heard they would piss in a hot water bottle. Todd would tape it to his back and would run a clear tube from that to the front of his pants. When they said go in there and piss, he put their stuff in the cup and his own stuff into the toilet. Then they started changing the rules after a couple guys got busted. Then you had to drop your pants completely, all the way to the ground, in front of the guy who was monitoring.

TODD MARINOVICH: We knew when they were going to drug test. That was the whole key ingredient, really. Knowing when it would happen. There was a leak. Somewhere in the athletic department, from someone in the athletic department, the "memo" would go out. And just knowing a few days in advance was key. There were a lot of methods and ways to beat the tests, and I really tried them all, I think, while at SC.

DAN OWENS: I was in the NFL in 1990. In 1989, we had a strong senior class. When we left, we said, "Who's gonna control Todd now?"

In 1990 Todd became the focal point instead of another guy. Once he became the focal point of everything that goes right and everything that goes wrong, he had a lot on his plate and he had a lot to deal with.

SCOTT LOCKWOOD: Todd seemed so laid back on campus, walking around with his skateboard. So I don't really know if he felt the pressure. But he had Larry Smith on him. He had his father.

LEROY HOLT: Marinovich had some issues that were well documented. But on the field his freshman year, he and Larry Smith had seemed to be okay. Hell, he had started as a freshman and had won the Rose Bowl for us. Obviously, he had to be clicking with the head coach and the offensive coordinator in order for that to happen. Even at the start of our next season, I didn't see anything bad between him and Smith.

TODD MARINOVICH: The old saying is, "When you're winning, everybody is okay and there's no issues. But as soon as there's a little adversity, things change." And that was exactly the case in 1990.

But from day one of my first year when I was a redshirt, we didn't see eye to eye in regard to how he handled my fellow teammates. I didn't say too much. I just looked around and saw what was going on. So the writing was really on the wall when I was still a redshirt. The university is what got me to USC, not Larry Smith. I went there in spite of Larry Smith.

MATT GEE: At that time, the spread offense was starting to happen in college football. And Smith wouldn't do it. UCLA was doing it. They had Tommy Maddox at QB, and they were spreading the field. And we still have a fullback and tailback and two tight ends. That was the problem. He wasn't changing with the times. He was a Midwest guy. He wanted to play that boring Midwestern football. In California, the football was different. The kids were different. He treated us like we were 13-year-olds. After a while we were like, *Hey, we're 20-year-olds.* He couldn't get over that part: You're in California now and these kids are a little different. They're not as rushed. They're a little bit chilled.

TODD MARINOVICH: I think he struggled with that, no doubt. The era it was and where we were, in Los Angeles. This wasn't the Midwest or Arizona. It's tough being a head coach. I understand. And you have to deal with a lot of personalities. It helps if you have one.

JOHN JACKSON: Larry Smith had coached at Arizona. His teams there were full of blue-collar workers. Chuck Cecil is the perfect example. Nobody wanted him coming out of high school. He comes into Arizona with a chip on his shoulder, he lives in the weight room, he does everything the right way, and now he's knocking guys' heads off. That's the kind of guy who came through the Arizona program. Todd Marinovich is *not* the blue-collar worker. He's the elite superstar. But Smith wanted to treat everybody like a blue-collar worker.

TIM TESSALONE: Todd was a left-brain guy. You see that now in his art. He was very much a left-brain guy playing a right-brain sport, coached by right-brain people.

During spring football camp in 1990, USC students still wore their IN TODD WE TRUST buttons from the previous season. There was media talk of Marinovich perhaps winning the program's fifth Heisman. But when a reporter asked Smith if Marinovich could be replaced by his backup, Shane Foley, Smith said, "Sure, it's possible. Foley would be starting anywhere else." As for Foley, the dependable workaholic with an accurate arm, he says he thinks Smith gave Marinovich too much slack.

SHANE FOLEY: I don't think it was limited just to Todd. There were some exceptions made for certain players. And that did hurt the program. If there's a certain behavior that deserves a certain punishment, there's some gray area there. But if something takes place and a coach just looks the other way—and he may not look away for someone else—that becomes a problem.

STEPHON PACE: There was *always* turmoil that season. You're looking at two of your leaders, Larry Smith and Todd Marinovich, and they're at odds. Everyone could see it, and everyone could feel the tension. Honestly, to me, it was a power struggle. You have a head coach who is ultimately in charge of the program. You have a quarterback at one of the biggest universities in the country, getting his name mentioned as a Heisman candidate, who was feeling like he was bigger than the program.

SCOTT LOCKWOOD: There was a lot of division on that team. That came out in practice and in the locker room. There were a lot of cliques. You had Matt Gee and Todd and Scott Ross and Gene Fruge, and they were a tight little group. They would go out and party and drink and have fun. There was a big Christian contingent. The black guys did their thing. There were the guys who weren't playing much and wanted to be Academic All-Americans. There was a lot of tension. Also, we went to the Rose Bowl the first three years, and I think the pressure was on Larry Smith now because several of his assistant coaches had left. People were looking at him.

Even with only those seven starters returning, the 1990 Trojans were the defending Pac-10 champs and came into the season ranked No. 9. When they began with victories over Syracuse and Penn State, they moved up to No. 5. Then they traveled to Seattle for the Pac-10 opener against the 21st-ranked Huskies.

SHANE FOLEY: We're 2–0 going into the Washington game. Mark Brunell is their quarterback. And we get our heads handed to us. It's unbelievably loud, they're ringing that siren, and Todd is getting his butt knocked in. He's getting hit, he's getting hurried, we have barely crossed the 50-yard line. First half we go in and we're down 24–0. We go into the locker room, and you can hear a pin drop. We've just won three straight Pac-10 championships. We beat Bo Schembechler in his last game, at the Rose Bowl. We know Washington is on the rise, but nobody is expecting to be down 24–0.

Then they pulled out Todd in the fourth quarter. As I'm on the sidelines, getting ready to run out there, Todd says to me, "Have fun out there, bro." I said, "Yeah, dude, just have a seat."

MATT GEE: It was always real loud at Washington. But we were going the wrong way as a football team, and everybody was getting tired of Larry Smith.

CLARENCE SHELMON: That might have been my worst game in my four years as a coach at USC. They just kicked our ass. And USC should *never* lose 31–0.

TODD MARINOVICH: The Washington debacle. Bad dream. There's a quote up there in Washington that they loved, that I said after the game: "All I saw was purple. It was like being on the 5 freeway, going the wrong way." And that's actually a bad analogy, because the 5 up there is really slow. But it was a long day, to say the least.

It had been 30 years since any conference opponent had whipped the Trojans this badly. They recovered to win their next three, but then felt embarrassed again after losing at home to Arizona, not only Smith's former team but also unranked. The next week Smith announced that Marinovich was suspended one week for cutting classes. Foley says there was a story behind the official version the public received.

SHANE FOLEY: We had lost to Arizona, and now we were 5–2, with both losses in the Pac-10. We were getting ready to play at ASU, and Todd said he had an inner ear infection and couldn't practice that day. Smith got into it with him. They were clearly butting heads by then. Smith said, "You *are* going to practice." Todd said, "I already talked to the trainer. He hasn't cleared me to practice, and I'm dizzy." Smith says, "You don't practice today, you don't play." Todd said, "I can't. I can't practice."

So then Todd walks off. Smith calls the whole team around and says, "Todd's not playing this week. He's not traveling. Shane Foley's the guy. Get behind him. Let's go."

Todd and Larry both said that Todd was on academic probation and that's why he didn't play at Arizona State. Which wasn't true. He might have been on academic probation, but he didn't play that week because they butted heads and got into it at practice. It all ties in together with what I said before: being consistent with how you deal with your players. A guy gets an ear infection and says he can't practice after throwing two or three picks against Arizona, and then you cover it up and say he was cutting classes. Well, that might have been it, but it wasn't the *truth* of what happened. Players know what's true and what's not.

I was finally handed the reins the fifth game of my senior year. I started against ASU. It was televised on ABC. Dick Vermeil and Brent Musburger called it. Larry Smith called a conservative game. I didn't pass much. I ran some. We won, 13–6, at a time when we hadn't been beating ASU on the road. I was the ABC player of the game.

The next week I tore my quadriceps at practice. But this was my shot. Todd and I battled back and forth that week before the Cal game. At the moment, it didn't feel like Todd was necessarily the guy. Then the game is coming up, and they still haven't named the starter. But I can tell by the walk-through on Friday they're gonna start Todd. But Smith still doesn't announce it in the papers.

The day of the game, we're at the Hyatt, getting ready to go to the Coliseum. Todd comes late to our quarterback meeting. Ray Dorr, the quarterback coach, who is my guy, locks Marinovich out of the meeting room. Reggie Perry is in the meeting and Pat O'Hara and myself, and Ray Dorr won't open the door for Todd. We walk outside, and Dorr isn't pleased. He said to me, "You ready to start today?" I said, "Absolutely."

We go to the game. We get the ball and I start, and we go down 82 yards and score on our first drive. Then I get benched. They put Todd in. We were up 7–0. We just beat Arizona State with me starting after a loss the week before when Todd played the whole game. So now a lot of the Coliseum is booing. How does a guy go down and score and get yanked from the ball game and benched? How does that happen?

TODD MARINOVICH: I won't say it was scarring, but it was something I'll never forget. Smith had started the shuffling of the quarterbacks, with me and Shane. He decided to sit me down, and Shane took them right down the field for a touchdown. The next time we got the ball, Smith put me back in. It was a TV time-out. When I stepped out on the field, the rest of the huddle was already out there. And it just rained and showered boos. It was shocking and surreal. But I remember hearing from my inner voice: *If you play long enough, you* will *be booed.*

It was a tough pill to swallow, playing at home and still being a kid in college. But it really got down to the bone of why I played the game. My right tackle, Pat Harlow, was in a frenzy, just frothing at the mouth when I came into the huddle. First play, I can't recall who I hit over the middle, but he took it 70 yards. I didn't celebrate. I just walked to the sidelines, and I saw Harlow throwing his helmet toward the student section, with the double bird in the air. That's what I get warm and fuzzy about—shit like that. Because it's about you and your teammates, really. That's what it comes down to. Not who's coaching or even who you're playing. It's who you're playing with.

SHANE FOLEY: We ended up tying that Cal game, 31–31. They missed a field goal that would have beaten us. Smith by then in a lot of ways had backed himself into a corner. The media was asking why I had gotten benched. He just said something about Marinovich being more equipped to handle the game plan. I asked him about it myself after the game. He hemmed and hawed. At that point there wasn't much more to say. I just tried to stay positive and be a team guy. But it turned into a controversy that Smith wasn't looking for, and created by Smith himself.

Then the hot seat in Smith's kitchen started getting hotter pretty quickly. They had those Monday Morning Quarterback meetings. It was basically for the boosters. I heard there were some boosters asking how you bench a guy after he scores a touchdown and was player of the week in the game the week before. Instead of Smith taking the heat and answering the question, I heard he threw down the mic and walked out, and the athletic department guys basically got him to stay. Then he started making boosters write down their questions beforehand rather than just fielding questions, because I guess he didn't want to answer the tough ones.

PAT HARLOW: That was my senior year, and that was a hugely disappointing season. The turmoil between Todd and Coach Smith really kind of tore us up. I don't know if anyone is to blame; it's just what happened. Could Todd have done something different? Yeah. Could Coach Smith have done it differently? Yeah. But everything in hindsight is a whole lot easier.

GARY WELLMAN: Todd was in the spotlight of college football. Coach Smith knew he was partying and didn't like it. He talked to some other guys on the team and knew what was going on, but he couldn't catch him, because back then there wasn't any type of consistent testing method for drugs. Smith did everything in his power to try to catch him. He learned from the sheriff's department how to do an eye test—to see if your pupils are dilated or twitching. He did everything that he could, not only to Todd but to the whole team, about the drug issue and the partying issue. It didn't work. And they had the worst relationship I've ever seen.

AARON EMANUEL: The thing about Larry Smith, man, once you got on his bad side, you weren't even sure how you got there. If he had his eye out for you, he would go full speed, balls-out to make sure you knew it. Todd wasn't the type of guy who was disrespectful. There's only so much you could take, though. Smith played games with Todd a lot. He did it with a few players. Once you got on his bad side, that was pretty much it.

SCOTT LOCKWOOD: I think Todd's dad also had a lot to do with it. I don't think Larry liked the fact that Marv would show up at every practice and watch from Dedeaux Field, the baseball stadium. Marv would watch and kind of critique Todd afterward. Then he and Todd would grab some balls, and they would work on *Marv's* version of what it meant to be a quarterback. While Larry and all the coaches are walking off the field, Todd is being coached up by his dad.

Todd was also just too laid back for Larry. Todd had that long red hair, and Larry said no long hair. So Todd got a buzz cut. Before that he had it in a ponytail for a while. Matt Gee had long hair, too, and Scott Ross. They all kind of had long surfer hair. Then Larry said no long hair, and they all came back with short haircuts.

I think Todd just grew sick and tired of it all. The father kept telling him, "Todd, you're not doing that right." And there was constant harassment from Larry Smith. He was so critical of everything Todd did. I think Todd was finally like, "Fuck you. I'm growing my hair long again. I'm doing my own thing. I'm missing class."

After the disappointing 31–31 tie against unranked Cal at the Coliseum, the 6–2–1 Trojans, who had once been ranked No. 5, slid in the rankings again, to No. 23. Next up, fortunately, was abysmal Oregon State.

SHANE FOLEY: Marinovich and Smith started arguing on the sidelines. Smith told him to have a seat. I came in, and I had my best game statistically. Completed all nine of my passes and threw for two touchdowns and ran for one. We won 56–7.

The next week we play UCLA, and it becomes a quarterback controversy. Smith doesn't name a starter. On Saturday he comes up to me at the Hyatt before we bus over to Pasadena. He says, "Shane, this is the toughest decision I've made as a coach. I'm gonna start Todd today."

That was a big game for Todd and for our team. It was the 45–42 shoot-out against UCLA and Tommy Maddox, with Johnnie Morton making the catch to win it at the end. Things happen for a reason, and Todd did have a big game. He *was* a competitor. And that was USC's last win against UCLA before they beat us eight straight times.

In a wild and thrilling game before 98,088 in Pasadena, USC appeared to have lost when UCLA pulled ahead, 42–38, with 1:19 left. Then Marinovich drove the Trojans 77 yards, including the game-winning 16-yard strike to Morton with 16 seconds left.

TODD MARINOVICH: We played them at the Rose Bowl, and by then we knew we weren't going to *the* Rose Bowl. So that game was kind of our Rose Bowl. Exciting game. Yeah, I'm glad that one happened.

Smith had just unleashed his sophomore quarterback against UCLA, and USC had responded with 45 points. The following Saturday at the Coliseum, Smith returned to his cautious mind-set when playing Notre Dame. The Irish continued their mastery over the Trojans, winning, 10–6, for their eighth consecutive win in the rivalry. USC's nemesis, Lou Holtz, had won the last five.

It would have been much healthier for the program if the season had ended right there. But the 8–3–1 and 21st-ranked Trojans now faced 7–2 and No. 22 Michigan State in the lower-tier John Hancock Bowl, where this tumultuous season finally imploded. The postseason problems began with senior tailback Ricky Ervins, the previous year's Rose Bowl MVP in the win over Michigan, not even making the trip to El Paso, Texas.

RICKY ERVINS: We had played Ohio State in the fourth game. I had almost 200 yards. But I hurt my ankle the very first play of the second half. I kept going for about ten or 15 more plays. Then I couldn't play anymore.

I was out for about two weeks. Now I'm getting rehab, and I can run straight pretty good but I can't cut on it. Larry Smith calls me over one day, and I tell him I can't cut. He tells me to practice. So we run a screen to me, I plant, and I pop my ankle again. Now I'm out for three more weeks.

We're about to play Oregon State. I'm running with the physical therapy guy, but I'm not practicing yet. In the Oregon State game, he decides to put me in for four plays, says he wants to see what I can do. You *know* what I can do. Why would you put me in? We got UCLA and Notre Dame in the last two games, and those are on grass. Oregon State is on turf.

They put me out there anyway. First play, they call 24, which is to the right. I get it, and I'm thinking about my ankle, and I get hit real quick. Next play was 39, which is like an option. Todd pitches it, I cut up the field, and 15 yards down the field suddenly here's this DB. He comes up and hits me dead on my ankle. It looked like my leg was broke. They gotta help me off the field. I look at Coach Smith with this mean look, and that was it. That's when everything started between us.

I missed the UCLA and Notre Dame games. I'm trying to get ready for the John Hancock Bowl, working every day with the physical therapy guy. One day I'm talking to the other players right before practice starts. Coach Smith thought I was a nuisance. He called me over and said, "I don't want you going to the bowl game. I think you'll be a disturbance to the team." I said, "What are you talking about?" He said, "You're always hurt." I said, "I hurt myself for *you*."

So I went and told the players, right there on the field! I said, "He doesn't want me to go to the bowl game." I could have played in that game. I was *trying* to play. But I didn't even go. I watched the game on TV at my apartment.

MATT WILLIG: When we got to El Paso, it felt like things were brewing between Todd and Larry Smith. Todd was a guy who had fun off the field. Smith was like, *You're not taking this shit seriously enough; you're letting your teammates down.* And quite frankly the team was like, *Hey, Todd's fine. Todd's great. Todd gets it done on Saturdays.*

But I do wish that Todd had the sense to lay back a little instead of saying all the things he felt and thumbing his nose a little bit at Larry. There was also maybe a feeling throughout the whole team: *Not only are we not playing in the Rose Bowl, we're down here in El Paso at the John Hancock Bowl. Shit, this doesn't matter. It's not gonna be anything that anyone remembers.*

PAT HARLOW: The seniors had a meeting before we went about accepting the invitation or not. I didn't want to go. I told them I didn't come to USC to play in the Hancock Bowl. I came to play in the Rose Bowl. I had played in three of them, and this was not the way that I wanted to go out.

Back in 1990, not all minor bowl games were televised, but CBS broadcast this one on December 31. So a national audience witnessed what USC insiders knew for months: Marinovich and Smith were completely fed up with each other.

GARY BERNARDI: Punctuality, studying, preparation—that wasn't Todd's forte. On Saturdays, in those games, he was a competitive son of a gun. He was emotional, and he was into it. Coach Smith was the same kind of guy. He was a stubborn-ass German. They were both pretty stubborn. They were both pretty prideful. And it all escalated toward the end of that game.

Michigan State led, 17–13, with 9:01 remaining when Smith pulled Marinovich for Foley. Before then Marinovich had played poorly, with two interceptions, one fumble, and several missed open receivers. Still, the Trojans were down only four, and Marinovich was often best with the game on the line in the fourth quarter.

SCOTT LOCKWOOD: Something was different about Todd during that game. The way he performed, his reads, his accuracy. I don't know if he smoked dope before the game, or maybe some guys snuck out and they smoked the night before. I wouldn't put it past him. He could have been doing that for two years and nobody would have known. But that game in particular, Todd comes out and throws some terrible balls and misses some easy reads. He seemed mentally somewhere else. Maybe in his mind, he was like, *I'm out of here. Screw this. I'm going to play next year in the NFL.*

TODD MARINOVICH: I was kind of really upset when he took me out, almost beside myself. Smith didn't tell me himself he was sitting me down. John Matsko, the offensive line coach, came over and said, "We're going with Shane here to try and get something going." We were down by four, but you know, a touchdown wins it.

SHANE FOLEY: I got put in with us down 17–13. We go down and the drive stalls and we kick a field goal. We got about four minutes left, and we just cut the gap to 17–16. I come off the field, and Smith says to Todd, "Hey, if we get the ball back, I'm putting you back in." Todd points to some of our players and he says, "I'll go back in for them but not for you." That's when the F bombs start. And it's all captured on TV on CBS.

TODD MARINOVICH: Smith wasn't who said I was going back in. Smith wasn't talking to me. Matsko was taking messages back and forth. Matsko comes over and says, "If we get the ball back, he wants to go with you." And I said, *"What?"* Matsko walked away and came back and said, "He needs to know now." Finally, Smith comes over, steaming, because I won't really give him an answer immediately, like, *Yes sir, I'm going in.*

And that's when the tape was rolling, when he was in my face. Right before he actually blew up, he said, "Are you ready to go back in?" I said, "I will for these guys"—and I pointed at our offense. That's when Smith absolutely blew up.

SCOTT LOCKWOOD: They were going at it. Todd said, "Fuck you, I'm out of here." I just remember that part: "Fuck you, I'm out of here." When he said that, I knew he was not coming back. This would be his last game.

SHANE FOLEY: We never got the ball back anyway. We lost 17–16.

While Ricky Ervins had battled injuries and Larry Smith, Mazio Royster had emerged as the Trojans' leading rusher with 1,168 yards and eight touchdowns. He recalls what happened next in the locker room.

MAZIO ROYSTER: There was a confrontation. My running backs coach, Clarence Shelmon, went up to Shane Foley and told him,

"We should have kept you in there the whole game." He said that in earshot of Todd and our linebacker Scott Ross. Todd responded, and then Scott Ross *really* responded. He said "F you" to Coach Shelmon, and they had to be separated. It was chaos in there.

SHANE FOLEY: That was Todd's last game. But to me that game— and how that season ended—was also the beginning of the end for Larry Smith.

STEPHON PACE: Our thought process was: *Marinovich is gone, and Smith is gonna get fired.* Smith didn't get fired, but that was the thought: *We are finally done with the Marinovich era, and it might be the end of the Larry Smith era, too.*

Not quite three weeks later, on January 19, 1991, the Newport Beach police arrested Marinovich as he walked home from a bar. The officer later said he thought Marinovoch reached for a weapon, which Marinovich didn't have, but a search revealed that he did have cocaine and pot. He was charged with misdemeanors and allowed to enter a counseling program for first-time offenders. That winter he trained with his father for the NFL draft in April. Rumors had Marinovich dropping from the first round, and he almost did. Then Raiders owner Al Davis chose him as the No. 24 pick.

I asked Marinovich how much his relationship with Smith— and Smith's coaching style—had to do with him leaving for the NFL after his sophomore season.

TODD MARINOVICH: One hundred percent. Without a doubt. I had gotten to the point where I knew I couldn't play for that coach. I couldn't play another down. I also knew I didn't want to play for any other university. I knew that. So my hands were tied, really. The last thing I wanted to do was leave school at that point. By then I had found the art department. I was liking that part of school. Loving it.

It is what it is. But I have pondered the thought of whether I made the right choice. Who knows? It was one of the most difficult decisions I ever made, to leave. Would I do it again? Yeah. I would. Because it wasn't like anything was going to change with the atmosphere and with the head coach. He wasn't going anywhere.

I asked Marinovich what he considered the best part of playing at USC.

TODD MARINOVICH: Putting on the uniform. It was an experience like none other. People like to talk. He said, she said. All that does not matter. Because there's a history, and I'm a part of it. I'm really stoked just to be a part of that rich history. You can't talk about the USC–UCLA game without bringing up my team that year. And no matter what a shitty, up-and-down year that was, that's what people really remember—that we beat UCLA 45–42 in an amazing game. They don't remember the Cal game when I got booed. *I* sure do. Nobody really remembers the loss at Washington. Maybe the Husky fans do. It's special to be a part of something like USC football. I didn't realize it quite as much at that time. I understood it more the farther I got away from it. But it's super cool.

9

IMPLOSION:

1991–1992

In the early 1990s, Todd Marinovich wasn't the only elite talent to leave USC early for the NFL. One season before him, defensive stars Junior Seau and Mark Carrier had both left USC after their junior year. They didn't skip *two* full seasons as Marinovch did, but the three premature departures raised questions about Larry Smith's ability to keep his top players on campus.

And yet in August 1991, USC athletic director Mike McGee gave Smith a multiyear contract extension with one year still remaining on his original five-year deal. Many found this surprising after an 8–4–1 season capped by the ugly defeat in the John Hancock Bowl. Even Smith himself said, "I feel very good about it, my family feels good about it, and I think my coaches feel good about it. I hope the players feel good about it."

MATT WILLIG: That was amazing. I couldn't believe it. I also heard, at the time, that they had nobody else to hire. They had nobody waiting in line, so they didn't know who they could go to if they dismissed him. But they give him an extension?

TODD MARINOVICH: I didn't know the timing until you told me that. I didn't know that's when he got a contract extension. But it sure does sound like a move Mike McGee would have made.

Smith wasn't the only Trojan who received a vote of confidence as the 1991 season approached. Senior linebacker Matt Gee was named USC's only team captain.

The bad news for Gee: The Trojans went 3–8, their worst record in 34 years.

Back in 1957, when USC went 1–9, there were legitimate reasons. The Trojans had just come off three years of heavy sanctions from the soon to be disbanded Pacific Coast Conference. Thus, among other issues, the 1957 Trojans had *zero* scholarship quarterbacks or receivers.

The 1991 Trojans also had severe quarterback problems. With Marinovich playing for the Los Angeles Raiders, USC started sophomore Reggie Perry, who had taken all of three snaps in his college career. In 1991 he threw three touchdown passes and 12 interceptions before losing his job in midseason to freshman Rob Johnson. Meanwhile, the once-revered USC running game also faltered as opposing defenses packed the line of scrimmage and dared the Trojans to pass.

MATT GEE: We were going to have a really good season that year. Todd was going to be a junior. We had Curtis Conway and Johnnie Morton at receiver. These were NFL receivers who played for years. That team was ready. But Larry Smith and Todd could not see eye to eye, and Smith couldn't ease up with the California guys.

So Todd didn't play his junior *and* senior year. That was insane. And that's why we were so shitty my senior year. Smith couldn't swallow his fucking pride, and he left us with no quarterback. We ended up with Rob Johnson, who was just coming from high school. We got destroyed because we lost Todd. Period. Our quarterback most of the year was Reggie Perry? He was a fucking *safety* they turned into a quarterback. That's how bad we were.

SCOTT LOCKWOOD: That season was awful. I played in the Penn State game, second game of the season, got injured, and didn't play again after that. I was like, *Thank God I'm not playing.* We had Reggie Perry at QB and even Curtis Conway for a while. Like maybe we'll just run the wishbone now? To me, it felt like the coaches forgot to recruit a QB. USC was always able to throw the ball when we needed to. But now we can't throw the ball because we don't have a quarterback?

Assistant coach Gary Bernardi has a different perspective.

GARY BERNARDI: For two years before that, we couldn't recruit a top quarterback because we had brought in Todd, who was the national player of the year in high school. There was no top quarterback who wanted to come to SC knowing that Todd was there. Then we recruited Rob Johnson and he did a good job, but he was a freshman. And you weren't going to win ten games with him. Same thing happened at UCLA. In 1990, we had a shoot-out with them, 45–42, Todd Marinovich and Tommy Maddox. Then both of them left early, and it set both teams back.

The 1991 season began with USC ranked No. 16 and a seemingly easy home game against unranked Memphis State, which had gone 6–15–1 the last two years. But after leading, 10–3, at halftime, the Trojans did not score again in a 24–10 loss that the *New York Times* called "the first big upset of the college football season."

MATT GEE: Their head coach was Chuck Stobart. He'd been the USC offensive coordinator. He took the head job at Memphis State,

Larry Smith didn't change anything, and Memphis State kicked our ass. We thought we would just roll them because we were USC.

STEPHON PACE: You're expected to win against Memphis State. Regardless of whether you've worked as hard as them or not, you have the superior athletes. That's just the nature of the beast.

Once we lost to Memphis State we never recovered. We came back and won a few games, but that team was never together. The *players* were. We were close that season. But you could tell the coaches weren't getting along.

MAZIO ROYSTER: The situation is always grim if you're not winning games. Add to that, you have a history of winning at SC. So now it's the not the same feeling inside the facility. And people outside the program are asking, "What's going on? Are the players buying into what's being taught? Why aren't they winning?"

That season started going downhill fast. Coaches were concerned about their jobs. They were thinking about their livelihoods. When things were going well, Larry Smith used to say, "We have a tough opponent coming up, but nobody's butt hole is puckering. Everybody's relaxed." I would venture to say, toward the end of that year, even his butt hole was probably puckering. It was tight around there.

MATT WILLIG: That was my senior year, and it was really tough. Junior Seau had come in with me, but he left early. Todd left early. It was probably one of the weakest USC teams ever. I hate saying that, but it really was. We used to sit around and go, *What the fuck is going on here, man?*

At the same time, USC is a school where the alumni are so prevalent. You see these old-timers, and they can be brutal. Midway through the year, they're already talking about the next season: *Maybe we can turn it around.* That's really tough to hear when you're a senior and you're trying to be a leader on that team.

There was almost a feeling that USC might be done. Several other Pac-10 schools were building themselves up. A lot of recruits starting leaving California and going to these other Pac-10 schools. We just didn't have the players anymore. Ted Tollner's recruits were gone, and Smith couldn't keep it going. I really think there was a feeling that the dominance of USC was over.

The *New York Times* agreed with Willig's recruiting assessment. "Smith had the Trojans in the Rose Bowl his first three seasons on the job," wrote Tom Friend, "but that was mostly with Ted Tollner's recruits."

In many programs, however, recruiting partly depends on how much that school is willing to compromise on academics in order to win more games and please the wealthy boosters who write the largest checks. At Notre Dame in the mid-1980s, after Gerry Faust ran the program into the ground, Lou Holtz essentially told the priests who run the school that he couldn't turn things around with choirboys. The Irish promptly altered their admission standards and won a national title just three years after Holtz succeeded Faust.

By 1991 at USC, assistant coach Gary Bernardi and safety Stephon Pace say the cycle had turned in the opposite direction.

GARY BERNARDI: From the time we got there to the time we left, they were really trying to change the admission process. They made it harder to get guys in. I recruited Russell White. He was from Los Angeles and one of the best high school running backs in the country. If he didn't pass the SAT, USC wasn't going to let him in the school. Russell's mom was a prideful woman. If they would not let him in like they did Junior Seau—because I recruited Junior Seau, too—that was not gonna fly with Russell's mom. Meanwhile, Cal was going to let him in if he didn't pass the test. I don't know if he ended up passing the test or not. But Russell White went to Cal.

Russell White was Charles White's nephew. And I used to hear it

all the time: *Once a Trojan, always a Trojan. USC is for life. It's family.*
But you're not gonna let Charles White's nephew into the school?
Come on!

That was also part of the strain between the administration and
Coach Smith. They changed the recruiting guidelines. We made
recruiting mistakes like everyone else. I'm not saying we didn't.
But the playing field also changed. Somebody else might try and
sugarcoat it. That's the fricking truth.

STEPHON PACE: At that point in time, USC wanted to become
Stanford number two. So there were a lot of us 3.5 and 3.8 kids
coming into the football program out of high school. We were all
very intelligent kids. Later on, when Pete Carroll came in there, how
many kids did he take who had 3.8? Not many. He was able to go
into Long Beach, he was able to go into the inner city and then say
to USC, "I want this kid. I'll make sure he goes to class. I'll make sure
he does what he's supposed to do. But I need these kids to turn the
program around." Larry Smith didn't have that flexibility. The school
said, "We want to be Stanford."

Take a look at the Washington team that won the national
championship in 1991. Probably five to eight players were from
Dorsey High School and high schools in Los Angeles like that.
They wanted to stay home and go to USC, but suddenly they're in
Washington, and they win. Napoleon Kaufman and those other guys
who Washington got? Put them in the uniform at USC and Larry
Smith is probably still coaching there.

JOHN JACKSON: Once Ted Tollner's players graduated, there
weren't as many NFL-type players even being recruited by USC. You
have to get the elite players, who might have a Todd Marinovich
attitude. Mazio Royster is another one who Larry Smith didn't get
along with. But those guys are great players. You have to bring
them in, and you have to relate to them somehow, some way.

Pete Carroll is a master at that. He knows how to treat different personalities.

Larry Smith stopped recruiting that elite player. But there's a lot of guys that have come into USC and the odds were against them staying around for four years. Then at the end of the day, they graduate, get their degree, and become quality citizens. They grow while they're at USC. And that's where I think Larry Smith lost it. He stopped taking that blue-chip player who might have some rough edges around him. Instead of taking that guy and trying to smooth those edges.

MIKE SALMON: I'm a big fan of Larry Smith. You know where you stood with him. Yeah, he was coaching football, but I think he cared equally as much about what kind of guy he was putting out on the streets as he did about winning games. He might have cared more about that. I've played for coaches who don't give a squat about what happens off the field.

But his downfall was his recruiting. In 1991, from a defensive standpoint, I was making a whole lot of tackles. When your free safety is making that many tackles, it doesn't take a rocket scientist to figure out that you're having trouble stopping the run game. We didn't have those big defensive linemen we had when we got there. The cupboard was kind of bare, and we had depth problems all across the board.

They were bringing in recruits for their campus visits, and some of them were picking between USC and schools like New Mexico. A few guys told me they had *no* other offers. So the recruiting really killed us. We still got some blue chips, but we also took a bunch of guys that USC typically wouldn't. There was one defensive back who they brought in who literally couldn't backpedal. This is at USC.

SCOTT LOCKWOOD: There was a lot of resentment toward Larry Smith that season. The players felt like, *Larry, this is your fault. You* *forced Todd out of here. Now you're forcing Mazio Royster out of here.*

As the 1991 season unraveled, the Trojans lost their last six games, including five straight defeats in the Pac-10. Smith clashed with his players over generational issues, such as whether they could wear earrings. Smith clashed in print with Royster over his carries and his willingness to accept authority. Finally, after rushing for 1,168 yards the previous season, Royster found himself benched midway through his junior year.

He, too, would leave USC early. His story illuminates how a collegiate player's relationship with his head coach can affect that player's stock in the NFL draft.

MAZIO ROYSTER: I was on the cover of our media guide. I was being discussed as a preseason Heisman Trophy candidate. All-American candidate as well. That's how I went into that season.

Against Memphis State, I had about 20 carries in the first half for about 97 yards. But I was injured during that game. Didn't play in the second half. When I came back, I tried to shoulder the load and asked for more carries. It turned into a back-and-forth in the media. By me saying I want more carries, the great running backs here have gotten 40 carries and they didn't share the position, it looked like I was questioning Coach Smith. Then he said something like, "maybe he should be in the press box calling plays."

I was 21 years old, and I made some mistakes. In hindsight, I should have discussed it with him in private. It was immaturity on my part instead of going to him like a man and figuring this thing out. At one point, even my mom called Coach Smith and said, "Why isn't my son playing?" That was probably another reason why he was like, *Oh, man, let's just put Mazio on the shelf for a while.*

I was completely healthy for the last three or four games, but by then the relationship between us had soured. I didn't play at all in our last two games against Arizona and UCLA. Back then it wasn't common for college guys to leave early. It was *more* uncommon for Todd, who was only a sophomore. But I decided to leave after my junior year. I knew my stock wasn't that high. I had been injured. I had character issues, if you will, because here I am going at it with the coach. When I decided to forgo my senior year and enter the NFL draft, it was with the understanding that I could be a mid- to late-round draft choice. I didn't know it would be in the 11th round.

But for me the NFL was still the best option. The atmosphere at USC was bad then. And I was morphing into a bitter person.

At 3–8 overall and 2–6 in the Pac-10, the Trojans didn't participate in a bowl game for the first time since 1983, when the NCAA had banned them from the postseason.

I asked Matt Gee, the 1991 senior team captain, what he considered the low point of that dreadful season.

MATT GEE: We lost our last six in a row! There were some good teams. Notre Dame was good that year. Cal was good, and Washington was really good. But six losses in a row? I don't even know what the low point was. The low point was losing every fucking week. That's what the low point was.

Let me tell you how my career ended there. We lost to UCLA at the Coliseum. There are very few linebackers who make triple digits in tackles, and I had 90 tackles going into that game. I really wanted triple digits. I'm at 97 tackles in the third quarter. I'm getting ready to make a tackle, and here comes our D back Jason Oliver, and he takes *me* out. I tried to put a brace on and go back out there and make a few more tackles, and I couldn't even run out there. They carried me off on a golf cart. I'm on a golf cart, heading for the tunnel, and I'm looking around at the crowd and I'm thinking, *This is the last time I'm ever gonna see this.* That's how my career at USC ended.

Less than two months later, in January 1992, Larry Smith's reputation took another hit when former USC running back Jon Arnett, a retired Chicago Bear and an influential alumnus, cowrote a nine-page letter criticizing Smith's recruiting, his play selection, his ability to teach, and his overall management of the program. Arnett said Smith's career had revealed "a pattern of mediocrity," and if USC didn't act soon, "the team and university would suffer greatly." Arnett sent the letter to Smith as well as the board of trustees and a number of prominent boosters. Arnett also took a swipe at Mike McGee, saying that the AD and his department had "noticeably underperformed."

When the blistering Arnett letter became public, Jeremy Hogue had just finished his freshman year as a USC offensive lineman. He would become a three-year starter and an Academic All-American.

JEREMY HOGUE: I heard about that letter after the fact, many years later. I have really no issue with guys like Jon Arnett trying to be influential in a program that they were such a big part of. The guys who wore that uniform take pride in what goes on in that athletic department both on and off the field. Certainly there are means that may be more productive than others, and you may not always agree with the means. But when former players are chastised for making comments, I find that hard to swallow. I think guys like Arnett have earned every right to have a pretty strong opinion.

In August 1992, *Sports Illustrated* wrote a feature story with the deflating headline WHERE ARE THE GOOD OLD DAYS? The subhead read: "Southern Cal, a team of glorious tradition, is struggling to recover from a 3–8 season." At the time John Michels was a defensive lineman about to begin his freshman year. He would later be converted to an All-Pac-10 offensive tackle.

JOHN MICHELS: That 3–8 team was one of the worst football teams in USC history. So we were really aware of what was being said when the '92 season started. People said those three Rose Bowl teams should have been national championship teams; there was enough talent on those teams to win it all. People said we couldn't win the big games against Notre Dame and UCLA. We started to hear that murmuring a lot, and I think we felt that pressure even on the field. It just wasn't fun out there. It was tense all the time.

It became especially tense on the defensive side, where Larry Smith specialized. Says one star USC player anonymously: "Larry was very loyal to some assistants that he should have cut before that season. We had one defensive coach who benched Jason Sehorn. He benched Willie McGinest. Our defensive meetings were nuts. He was challenging guys to fights. He was throwing tantrums. Sehorn's NFL stock went way down. McGinest's stock went way down. Then Bill Belichick said, "Screw it, this guy's too big, too fast, too good," and he drafted McGinest at New England. But before that his stock went way down because of what went on that season at USC."

The 1992 Trojans entered the season unranked for the first time since Ted Tollner's final year in 1986. They opened on the road at unranked San Diego State, where future NFL superstar Marshall Faulk ran for three touchdowns and 220 yards in a 31–31 tie. Still, it felt like a loss, particularly since the Trojans *would* have lost if the Aztecs had not missed *two* last-minute field goals. Plus, Faulk was the type of exciting tailback who would have looked superb in cardinal and gold. Perhaps most troubling, as *Sports Illustrated* noted, "It appeared that San Diego State wanted to win more."

STEPHON PACE: It was the same feeling as losing to Memphis State to start the season before. We're the big boys in town, and we're not supposed to tie San Diego State. We can look at it *now* and say they had one of the best running backs to ever play football. But again, we're supposed to be USC.

By the end of October, the Trojans had bounced back to 5–1–1, but then they lost three of four games during November to finish the regular season at 6–4–1. In the November 21 defeat to the Bruins, UCLA quarterback John Barnes was a walk-on with three career starts, yet he passed for three touchdowns and 385 yards as UCLA overcame a 14-point deficit to win, 38–37. Twenty-four years later, the 1992 Trojans still say "walk-on" a lot.

STEPHON PACE: They started a walk-on who threw for 300-plus yards. We had a 5-foot-7 cornerback named Gerald Henry covering J. J. Stokes, a 6–4 receiver who could play football. We're asking our cornerback to be an island. We're not giving him a chance to win his one-on-one battle.

I coach football now, so looking back on that, I would never do something like that. And I think that was the end. That was probably the first time in my five years that the players had turned on the coaches. Because you had players telling other players, "That's a bad matchup. We shouldn't have done that." We had lost faith.

GARY BERNARDI: The Friday night before the UCLA game, we went to the Rose Bowl for a little practice, and Coach Smith told the team, "There's a good chance if we win the game against UCLA, we'll go to the Fiesta Bowl and play Syracuse." Fourth quarter against UCLA, we're ahead by 14 points, and we end up losing. Man, that was hurtful. They beat us with a walk-on quarterback.

The regular season ended the following Saturday at the Coliseum with USC's tenth straight loss (31–23) to Notre Dame. Although the Trojans had improved on their shocking 3–8 record the season before, no one was popping champagne over 6–4–1, a No. 23 ranking, and an invitation to play in nearby Anaheim against 8–4 and unranked Fresno State in the Freedom Bowl.

Daryl Gross was in his second year as an assistant athletic director. Before that he had been a scout for the New York Jets, where he worked for one season with a defensive coordinator named Pete Carroll. Years later Gross played a pivotal part in Carroll's hiring at USC.

DARYL GROSS: Back then the Freedom Bowl, from USC's standards, wasn't looked upon very highly. Fresno State, on the other hand, wanted that opportunity like it was a Super Bowl. So there were two different attitudes going into that game. They wanted it badly. We had some guys going pro who didn't want to get hurt and all that stuff.

JOHN MICHELS: We already finished the long drudgery of a regular season that was subpar for USC. Then they came to us with an invite to play in the Freedom Bowl against Fresno State. We sat down and had a players' meeting. As a team, we said, "We don't want to play. We've got nothing to gain here. We've got everything to lose."

Because if we win that game, well, of course you're supposed to beat Fresno State. But if we lose that game, then we're the laughingstock of USC. So we voted it down as a team. Coach Smith came in and said, "Unfortunately, you guys don't have that choice. You've got to play in it." So we practiced another two weeks in Anaheim. It was miserable. We were having two-a-days, kicking the snot out of each other at practice.

STEPHON PACE: As seniors, we knew we were done, and the younger players all knew there would probably be a new coaching staff coming in there. So there was no support for that game. There was no fan support, either. USC couldn't sell tickets. The other team, Fresno State, sold out all their tickets because their coach Pat Hill was saying, "We're gonna beat them."

Hill was a fiery leader and also a sharp tactician who had been an assistant with Nick Saban under Bill Belichick when he was head coach of the Cleveland Browns. In the Freedom Bowl, Hill's Bulldogs upset the listless Trojans, 24–7.

MIKE SALMON: Nobody wanted to play at the Freedom Bowl. It didn't affect my preparation, but I think it did affect some guys. But we also didn't have the players anymore. The school had tied Larry Smith's hands. Russell White went to Cal. He wanted to go to USC. Fresno State had more NFL players come out of their backfield than we did. They had Trent Dilfer and Lorenzo Neal. There was a lot of gloom and doom after that loss.

JOHN MICHELS: Fresno State lit us up. That was the nail in the coffin for Larry. I think he was done before that anyway, but that really sealed the deal.

TIM TESSALONE: After the Freedom Bowl game, I was walking off the field near Larry Smith. The venom that was coming out of the stands . . . I felt really bad for him. People were booing him and kind of spitting. I was like, *Really? It's a football game.*

He had set the standard so high in his first three years by going to the Rose Bowl, though he only won one of those. Then we went to the Hancock Bowl, and then we had that terrible 3–8 year, and then we lost to Fresno State in the Freedom Bowl. And right after that game, Larry made some comment about logos, which some of the media people took badly. They took it to mean that Larry said there was nothing behind the USC logo. So then the public took it that way, too.

Smith's exact quote after the 24–7 Freedom Bowl upset was "I'm not really surprised. Big names and logos don't mean anything in college football anymore."

Self-destructive choice of words for a USC coach, but by then he probably knew he was done there anyway. Three days later Smith resigned under pressure from Mike McGee and Steven Sample, the USC president in his second year on campus.

A couple of seasons later, in 1994, Smith showed some animus toward his former program when Missouri hired him as its head coach. "I'm going to call them Southern Cal from now on, because they hate that," Smith said. His seven Mizzou teams went 143–126–7 before his dismissal in 2000.

For now, at USC, Bernardi also was fired along with most of Smith's other assistants.

GARY BERNARDI: At USC, you don't go 3–8. When we came back in '92, we were 6–4–1, but we screwed up the UCLA game because we were up by two touchdowns in the fourth quarter. After our six years, we were 3–2–1 against UCLA. But we were 0–6 against Notre Dame.

Larry Smith and Mike McGee were also both hardheaded guys. McGee was very actively involved—or tried to be involved—in the football program. I'm speculating, but after we went 3–8, I think they were asking Smith to make changes in our staff. He was a loyal guy, and he wasn't gonna do that.

That press conference when he left, Larry was in the tank. Then I would go to see him afterward, bring my kids to go see him, and he was so depressed. He was mad but depressed, too. It was very hurtful to him the way that ended. He was a prideful guy and a damn good coach, and he had done a good job. But the recruiting guidelines had changed.

In his six years in Los Angeles, Smith compiled a 44–25–3 record, with Rose Bowl appearances his first three seasons. But his 9–13–1 record the last two years, his 1–4 mark in bowl games, his 0–6 futility against the Irish, and his failure to connect with a majority of his players were too much for USC to overlook.

10

JOHN ROBINSON REDUX:

1993–1995

On January 3, 1993, two days after Larry Smith's forced resignation, he was replaced by one of the program's own legends.

John Robinson was 57 when USC hired him a second time. Although he was no longer a young man, neither were many of the powerful boosters who had lobbied for his return behind the scenes. From 1976 to 1982, his seven USC teams had a flashy winning percentage of .819, won three Rose Bowls, and shared a national championship with Alabama in 1978. Against their two biggest rivals, Robinson's Trojans went 6–1 against Notre Dame and 5–2 against UCLA. On the negative side of his legacy, the program was sanctioned twice in his last three seasons, first for a few bogus speech classes his players rarely attended and then for ticket-selling violations reportedly committed by assistant coach Marv Goux.

In December 1982, Robinson resigned to become a USC vice president but kept that job only three months before the Rams hired him as their head coach. In his nine NFL seasons, he was good but not great, reaching the playoffs six times with an overall record of 79–74. Twice the Rams advanced to the NFC champion-ship game, but they never took that next step to the Super Bowl. In 1991 Robinson quit after going 7–19 the previous two years, calling his decision a "mutual" one with the team's front office. He then spent one restless season as a TV commentator.

JOHN ROBINSON: Larry Smith had had some success, but I think everyone felt the mystique was gone. So it became something like, *Well, if we hire him, we'll go back to the glory days.*

The athletic director was still Mike McGee. He came and said, "We'd like you to come back." So it wasn't an interview or anything like that. It was, "Hey, do you want this job?" And I was eager to do that. Then Mike McGee left USC In fact, he already knew that he was leaving, and I think hiring me was going to be his swan song. I was there two or three weeks, and Mike Garrett was hired as the athletic director.

As I started there again, people were disillusioned a little bit. But I think there was a sense of, *Everything will be okay now that we got Robinson back.* In retrospect, I regret not being more demanding with the school. Larry Smith suffered through an era in which the school wasn't going to reinvest in the program, so improving the football facilities wasn't really on anybody's mind. But your first day on the job is your most powerful day. You go downhill after that. So I probably missed an opportunity to create an atmosphere of reinvesting and rebuilding.

TIM TESSALONE: It was like Robinson Redux. He had always been beloved here. It just kind of made sense to bring him back and try and recapture the glory.

DARYL GROSS: It seemed like a natural fit. And by then Bill Walsh had also come back to coach Stanford. As a young administrator, I remember thinking, *What a great move.*

Gross's new boss in the athletic department was Mike Garrett. In December 1992, Mike McGee had announced he'd soon be leaving to become the athletic director at South Carolina. McGee said he wanted a "new challenge," but there was speculation that USC forced him out for supporting Larry Smith long after the alumni had turned on him. It was McGee who gave Smith the contract extension after Smith and Marinovich cursed each other out on national TV during the John Hancock Bowl. Marinovich then left USC two years early, and Smith's next two teams went 9–13–1.

McGee was an outsider when he came to USC from the University of Cincinnati. In January 1993, when Garrett was promoted from his job as associate athletic director, he was a famous member of the so-called Trojans family. In 1965 while playing for John McKay, he won the school's first Heisman Trophy and led the nation in rushing with 1,440 yards. Garrett played in two Super Bowls with the Kansas City Chiefs, earned a law degree, and later spent three years as director of business development at the Los Angeles Forum. He worked there for Lakers owner Jerry Buss, perhaps the most influential of the high-profile USC alumni. It was Buss's strong recommendation to university president Steven Sample that clinched Garrett's hiring despite opposition within Heritage Hall. As one athletic department employee told the *Los Angeles Times* anonymously before Garrett was selected, "There's already been a poll taken among the coaches, and none of them want him. He has no support internally from anybody who counts."

But none of them owned the Lakers.

As athletic director, Garrett would prove to be even more polarizing than McGee, but at first he and Robinson seemed downright chummy. Garrett said he admired Robinson and would have hired him if McGee had not done so already. Robinson said, "Nobody represents the past and hopes for the future more than Mike Garrett. I look forward to working with him, and it's a great day."

Behind the scenes, however, Artie Gigantino says Robinson's return was more complicated than it appeared.

ARTIE GIGANTINO: John's ex-wife was always great friends with all the alums at USC. Now he's divorced from his wife and he's got this young girlfriend who's about 20 years younger than everybody. She doesn't fit into the landscape at USC. The whole thing has changed. John has changed. He's not as energetic. He brings his son in to coach. He brings in Charles White and Doug Smith, two guys who played for him with the Rams, as full-time coaches at USC. They're non-coaches! So the thing doesn't work this time the way it did.

For the moment, though, the fans, alumni, and writers seemed to fully embrace the Robinson era part two. The *Orange County Register* ran the headline ROBINSON'S BACK IN NEIGHBORHOOD; FAMILIAR FACE RETURNS TO DIRECT USC FOOTBALL. The *Los Angeles Times* proclaimed, CHEERS ALL AROUND; ENTHUSIASM RETURNS TO USC WITH SECOND COMING OF JOHN ROBINSON.

JEREMY HOGUE: I remember our first team meeting when he asked for different comments and suggestions. We had a tight end named Brad Banta from Louisiana, and Robinson said, "Any of you guys have anything to kick off the meeting, any comments or things you've learned over the years?" Brad raises his hand and says in his thick Cajun accent, "Let sleeping dogs lie." Robinson said "Can you say that again?" Brad said, "Let sleeping dogs lie." Robinson looked at him and said, "I don't understand that Cajun shit."

Everyone busted up laughing, and it took the tension right out of the room. Robinson immediately was one of the guys. He would still give players shit when they needed to be given shit. But we knew he was on our side. All the sudden, the program felt fresh and clean. It was almost like you got to take a shower and get rid of the junk we'd been through the past couple years.

JOHN MICHELS: There was one huge difference between John Robinson and Larry Smith. The game of football got fun again.

Billy Miller was a freshman who would graduate from USC as No. 4 all-time in receiving yards. He played 11 seasons in the NFL, winning a Super Bowl with the New Orleans Saints.

BILLY MILLER: When I was still in high school, there were some college coaches who were like gods. Lou Holtz. Bobby Bowden. John Robinson. From a *guy* standpoint, what kind of guy he was, I remember falling in love with John Robinson. When you're 18 years old and you go to college, you're playing for someone who's going to take on a father role. Some coaches don't get that. They run it like a business, and they lose players to other schools. John Robinson made you feel like you were part of his family. Not the USC family, *his* family. I'm not sure Coach Robinson put together a great staff around him. But he was like Lou Holtz. He could get you to play for *him*.

MIKE SALMON: His hiring was kind of unusual because he had coached there several years earlier. But he had so much success at USC, and he could make anyone feel like a million bucks. He was also no dummy. The recruiting had really dropped off, and Robinson ran a bunch of those guys off.

JOHN ROBINSON: I don't think there's any question that recruiting had dropped off. It seemed like they had been recruiting a different kind of guy. For some reason, they had evolved away from recruiting the Southern California players. There's no question we were a pretty average team in my first year. I think we got the maximum out of that group.

The 1992 Trojans had ended their 6–4–1 season with the crushing 24–7 defeat at the Freedom Bowl to Fresno State. With Robinson returning, the 1993 team entered the season ranked a probably inflated No. 19. Then USC laid an egg in Robinson's second debut, losing, 31–9, to No. 20 North Carolina while allowing 291 rushing yards.

MIKE SALMON: They ran the wishbone, and we had no idea they would be running the wishbone. All the film we had seen, they had run a pro-style set. We were stunned. I think when that game ended, we still didn't know who was getting their pitch guy.

The Trojans were no longer ranked and only 4–3 when they faced the 7–0 and second-ranked Irish in South Bend. It had somehow been ten years since USC had beaten Notre Dame, the longest futility streak for either team in a series dating back to 1926. Robinson had been the coach in that USC victory ten years earlier, and now his matchup with Holtz rebooted the rivalry. The Trojans even bought billboards in Los Angeles, implying that a win over Notre Dame was part of the package that came with season tickets. Robinson, after all, had gone 6–1 against the Irish.

The billboards stayed up, but USC went down for the 11th straight time, 31–13. The Irish gained 418 total yards, 305 on the ground, a graphic illustration of their physical superiority. Four days later, the *Los Angeles Times* ran the headline USC SEEKING PLAYERS WHO CAN MATCH UP. Robinson told the *Times,* "The teams we've lost to were all top-15 teams, and we've not done very well against them. It's very clear to me we have to have the same kind of athlete here, who can compete at that level."

The university heard his pointed message. Robinson soon received from Garrett and Sample the type of leniency Smith had never received from McGee and Sample. In particular, USC began accepting more "special admits": high school recruits who met NCAA academic requirements but not the higher bar set by USC in recent years.

STEPHON PACE: When Robinson came back, the school started easing up on the admissions standards. Because this was John Robinson asking the school. He had already won a lot of games there. But none of the games he had won at USC and the things he accomplished there had been done with the 3.8 guys.

DARYL GROSS: We ended John's first year with an 8–5 record, but a lot of people forget that we almost went to the Rose Bowl. We were at the one-yard line in the final game, against UCLA. It was first and one, and if we score a touchdown, we win and go to the Rose Bowl. We threw an interception in the end zone.

JOHN ROBINSON: We did what Pete Carroll did in the Super Bowl. Second down on their one-yard line, we threw the ball. Our quarterback threw an interception. When Pete Carroll did that in the Super Bowl, I said, "Oh, my God, I've done that."

For the second straight year, the program accepted the bid to the lower-tier Freedom Bowl in Anaheim, where both USC and Utah came into the game 7–5 and unranked.

JEREMY HOGUE: To me it felt a lot different from the year before. When we played in the Freedom Bowl in '92, we stayed in Los Angeles while we prepared. So it didn't really feel like a bowl game. Whereas with Robinson, USC spent the money and we stayed at a hotel in Newport Beach. We did some bowl activities and we got some Freedom Bowl gear, which is not what you aim for, but we had a good time together as a team. Part of that may have been bigger than Larry Smith. I'm not sure in '92 that it was his decision not to go to Newport. That may have been an athletic department's decision, trying to save money. But certainly between Mike Garrett and John Robinson, who at least in the fall of '93 were getting along and seeing things the same way, we went down to Newport and had a real bowl game experience.

When the Trojans defeated the Utes, 28–21, Robinson's postseason record moved to an impressive 5–1. It was also USC's first postseason win since losing at the Freedom and John Hancock bowls. There was still much work remaining, but the national consensus was that Robinson did pretty well to finish 8–5 with Larry Smith's recruits.

JEREMY HOGUE: That was a transition year, and you see that with a lot of different coaches. Pete Carroll had a bad first year at USC. It takes the coaches a while to understand their roster and get their own recruits in and get everyone moving in the same direction. But even though we didn't win as many games as we wanted to that season, there was still optimism around the team. I also think USC started to be in the conversation with recruits that it wasn't in before Robinson arrived there.

One of the key recruits after Robinson's first season would turn out to be perhaps the best wide receiver in school history: junior college transfer Keyshawn Johnson. Shelley Smith at the time was a Los Angeles–based reporter for *Sports Illustrated*. Since 1993, she has worked in LA for ESPN. In 1997, after Johnson's rookie season in the NFL, Smith cowrote his precocious book *Just Give Me the Damn Ball!*

SHELLEY SMITH: Keyshawn grew up in South Central. He grew up right around the corner from USC. He would go to watch practice, and USC made him a ball boy. Ronnie Lott and other guys would bring him food because he and his mother lived in a car for a while. They would sleep in the cemetery, he said, because people didn't shoot up the cemetery.

So he grew up around USC and he always wanted to go there, but he changed high schools so often because of sports—and they moved because of gangs—and so he never really got the education. He'd been a con artist all his life. He thought he could just scam his way into any college that he wanted to go to, and he found out he couldn't. He ended up at West Los Angeles College, a junior college. Then I remember he was trying to decide between Tennessee and

USC. I said, "Go to Tennessee because that'll get you out of this environment." He said, "No, you don't understand. USC is a family. I'll have USC forever." He understood the legacy and the way they take care of their alums. So, you know, he was born to play there.

I asked Johnson to describe the neighborhood where he lived with his single mother and five siblings.

KEYSHAWN JOHNSON: My neighborhood was rough. It's South Central LA. It's bad. It's not south Beverly Hills. It's not Westwood. It's not Holmby Hills. It's not Malibu. I mean, it's south LA.

I've seen all sorts of stuff. I've seen guys murdered. I've been shot before. I've seen buildings burn down with people in it. I've seen guys, kids, blown up in the liquor store. I've seen people doing drugs right in front of you. Heavy drugs, whether crack cocaine or heroin. Right literally in front of you, where you were standing in line at McDonald's, and they were standing right there in line and they just decided, *Hey, I'm gonna smoke this crack right here like it was a cigarette on the bus stop.* I made a lot of mistakes myself. But you learn from them. And you learn from other people's mistakes.

Once I started playing high school football and junior college ball, I knew that USC was probably where I would wind up going. It just depended on who the coach was gonna be. I probably wouldn't have went there under Larry Smith. But once John Robinson got the job, it was not a question that I was going to USC.

SHELLEY SMITH: People knew he could play because he was a junior college All-American. But at West LA he didn't have a quarterback, so we never knew *how* good he was until he got to USC. I remember him saying, "See, I told you I was good." There had never been a receiver that big and that talented, and he's going up against DBs who are 5–7 and 5–8. He just always had an advantage.

In 1994, his first season at USC, the 6–4, 210-pound Johnson caught nine touchdown passes and had 66 receptions for 1,362 yards and a crazy average of 20.6 yards per catch. Led by steady senior quarterback Rob Johnson, the Trojans entered the season ranked No. 13, but after beating Washington in the opener, the next week they trailed, 35–0, at halftime at Penn State. The final was 38–14, and suddenly no one talked about the return to glory at USC.

Still, the Trojans hung in there. They were 7–2 and ranked 13th heading into their apparently easy game against the 4–6 Bruins. When UCLA won, 31–19, it was its fourth straight victory over the Trojans. That had never happened before in a rivalry that started in 1929.

JEREMY HOGUE: I think part of USC's difficulties with UCLA was that you thought you were better than their program. You sort of thought: *We're the ones with the national championships and the Heisman trophies. They're a basketball school. They don't aspire to what we aspire to.*

The reality is that UCLA has great players and great coaches and they recruit from Southern California just like we recruit from Southern California. But I don't think I really viewed it that way until after I graduated. One time I volunteered at a camp for at-risk high school kids between my junior and senior years. The camp was at UCLA, and they beat us that season. I walked into the locker room, and they had a huge banner up that said "City Champs." I remember thinking: *That's something you'd put up in a high school locker room. We want to be Pac-10 champs or national champs. We NEVER talk about being the city champs.*

But that was UCLA, especially under Terry Donahue. If they beat USC and had a marginal season, that was still a successful year. When you're playing a team with that mind-set—their game against you is their *season*—you better be prepared or you may be disappointed.

KEYSHAWN JOHNSON: Solid program. Solid university. But they'll never be USC. They'll just never be us. And I would have never fit the culture of UCLA. UCLA didn't even offer me a scholarship. They didn't even recruit me. And I was the number one junior college player in America. I was also roommates in college with Karim Abdul-Jabbar. He was our star running back, and I was the star receiver. So they had 24/7 access to me because they were recruiting Karim and I was his roommate. But I was a little too edgy for UCLA. I'm an inner-city-type kid. Urban. I wore an earring. I just didn't fit what they probably were looking for.

After losing the fourth straight time to UCLA, the Trojans semi-bounced back in the regular-season finale, tying Notre Dame, 17–17, to end their 11-game losing streak against the Irish. On January 2, 1995, USC was 7–3–1 and ranked No. 21 when it faced 6–5 and unranked Texas Tech in the Cotton Bowl.

KEYSHAWN JOHNSON: I was born and raised in Los Angeles. But my mom was born and raised in Dallas, and then she moved here. So that was the first time for me going back to Dallas as a football player and having my family, her family, come to the game. That was pretty cool.

Before the dinner banquet, the Texas Tech people said to come casual. So we were like, *Okay. We'll come casual.* Then they show up in sports coats, and we're in sweats. It's funny now, but I think that kind of ticked off Coach Robinson. We looked like a bunch of college bums, and Texas Tech looked neat. Their team was also talking during the buildup, how they were gonna stop me. But that didn't work out so well for them.

Johnson caught three touchdown passes and broke a Cotton Bowl record with 222 yards receiving. The Trojans crushed the Red Raiders, 55–14, but if Robinson was angry about the banquet, he also had no interest in humiliating Texas Tech coach Spike Dykes. Robinson pulled his quarterback Rob Johnson early in the third quarter or USC might have scored 80.

The following fall, the 1995 season seemed to be lining up as Robinson's best one yet in his second stint at USC. Keyshawn Johnson stayed for his senior year despite the NFL agents urging him to leave early. Rob Johnson graduated, but quarterbacks Brad Otton and Kyle Wachholtz were both capable. Overall, the Trojans returned 13 starters from the 8–3–1 team that ran wild at the Cotton Bowl.

USC started the season ranked No. 7, but *Sports Illustrated* saw the 1995 Trojans differently. *SI* put Keyshawn Johnson on its college preview cover and predicted that he would "lead storied Southern Cal back to No. 1." Robinson did nothing to discourage the high expectations, saying, "This is my third year. My first time here, we won the national championship in my third year. My third year with the Rams, we went to the NFC championship game. Good things happen in my third year."

By October 21, the Trojans were 6–0 and ranked No. 5 when they arrived in South Bend to face the 5–2 and 17th-ranked Irish. The previous season the teams had tied, 17–17, with Johnson catching six passes for 114 yards. When asked now for his comments on USC's star receiver, Lou Holtz called him "Keyshawn Jones."

"It doesn't bother me," Johnson said when the writers told him. "Coach Holtz has a lot on his mind. He's seen a lot of players come and go. He probably called Charlie Ward something else too. Maybe I remind him of Deacon Jones."

Johnson then produced his 14th 100-yard receiving game despite the double coverage Holtz assigned to him. But USC committed four turnovers in a 38–10 debacle that probably ended its hopes for a national championship in Robinson's third year.

I asked senior offensive tackle John Michels, who would now have to leave USC without ever beating Notre Dame, if the Irish were loaded with talent despite their 5–2 record going into that game.

JOHN MICHELS: No. I remember we were driving from the airport into South Bend, and there were conversations on the bus where guys were talking about what our national championship rings would look like. Our offensive line coach, Mike Perry, tore into us on the bus. He had won a national championship at Colorado. He knew how hard it was. He said, "Knock that crap off. You guys need to stay focused on the task at hand."

But we were still expecting to walk in there and end the streak. It was a cold, gray, rainy day, and things started going wrong. It was a good lesson for us. Our confidence had turned to cockiness, and that's a bad line to cross.

The next week USC trailed, 21–0, at halftime against a solid Washington team in Seattle. Robinson made exactly the right locker room speech, reminding his players that they were still 4–0 in the Pac-10 and still could play in the Rose Bowl. The Trojans fought back on the road with 21 unanswered points to earn a 21–21 tie. But after two more Pac-10 wins to clinch the Rose Bowl bid, they lost their fifth in a row to UCLA, 24–20, at the Coliseum.

Robinson, the onetime USC deity, suddenly found himself under fire. A columnist for the student paper, the *Daily Trojan*, even called for his dismissal, citing his recent 0–5–1 record against Notre Dame and UCLA. Other media questioned why Robinson chose to play both Otton and Wachholtz rather than settle on one quarterback. When asked about Robinson's status, athletic direc-tor Mike Garrett said, "I'm a big John Robinson fan." But when asked if Robinson, then in the third year of his four-year contract, was likely to get an extension, Garrett said only, "John and I will talk."

Six pressurized weeks later, on January 1, 1996, the 8–2–1 and

17th-ranked Trojans faced 10–1 and third-ranked Northwestern in the Rose Bowl. For decades the Big Ten school in suburban Chicago was known for its academics, not for football, but third-year coach Gary Barnett had transformed the program. The Wildcats were now the darlings of college football, if not the oddsmakers, who established USC as three-point favorites.

KEYSHAWN JOHNSON: Everybody said how good they were, the Cinderella football team wearing purple. And then a couple of their DBs said at the press conference, "We don't care about Keyshawn Johnson. He's not that good. We played against Amani Toomer. We played all the Big Ten teams." Just running their mouths. I said something like, "When I get a hold of y'all, y'all gonna remember. But I don't even know who you are."

JOHN ROBINSON: They captured everybody's imagination. And they were really good. Gary Barnett had done one of the better coaching jobs there. I remember phoning Bo Schembechler—Bo and I were really good friends—and I said, "Tell me about them." Bo said, "These guys can *really* play defense." They had lost one game all year, and that was early and they had had two punts blocked that game. But the rest of the time you couldn't score on them. They were dominant. We looked at the films and said, "Oh, my God, we better do something." Mike Riley was coaching with us at that time. Mike came up with the idea of going with the shotgun and no huddle. Seems kind of funny now, when you think about it, because everyone is doing it. But not back then. We came out and lined up on the ball with no huddle, and we went right down and scored. That was one of the better coaching efforts that I remember anyone on my staff making.

Otton passed for 391 yards behind excellent protection from Michels and Hogue and their fellow offensive linemen. Keyshawn

Johnson capped a prolific senior year (102 receptions and 17 touchdowns) with 12 catches for a Rose Bowl–record 216 yards. USC defeated Northwestern, 41–32, in front of a sellout crowd of 100,102 in Pasadena and a national audience on ABC.

JEREMEY HOGUE: The number one question I got asked going into that Rose Bowl was "Do you really want to beat Northwestern? Aren't they such a great story? Everyone in the country is rooting for them." What are you supposed to say? I mean, the only thing worse than beating them would be losing to them.

I have an overhead shot of the Rose Bowl from that day. It's maybe 25 percent maroon, and the rest of it is purple. They hadn't been to the Rose Bowl since 1949, and every wealthy Northwestern alumnus in the country flew into Los Angeles. It was a great game, a lot of back-and-forth, and we finally got a lead and held on to it.

That was clearly the peak of John Robinson's second coming at USC. That was my own personal career highlight as well. I was team captain for that game. My first game at USC was that loss to Memphis State in the 1991 opener. My last game was winning the Rose Bowl. Being part of a group of guys who came in under Larry Smith and those circumstances and stayed with it and were persistent and then left on such a high note made me feel very proud. I remember standing right next to John Robinson when the clock wound down. I turned to him as we started to jog across the field to shake hands with Northwestern. I hugged him and I said, "Thanks for coming back." I really meant that. People could argue later that he wasn't as big a success as he was in his first go-around, when he won a national championship. But he came back and changed the tone and put the program on the right trajectory. I've got a sense of loyalty to John that a lot of players from that era do.

KEYSHAWN JOHNSON: He was a player's coach. He understood that the players were the ones who got him to *be* John Robinson.

He was great in his own right, but he did understand that you're no good if you ain't got no players. John Robinson knew that, and he treated his players well.

That was also a great way for me to leave USC. I think that solidified to the world what type of football player I could be or already was. I'm Rose Bowl MVP, win the granddaddy of them all, beat the team the nation is pulling for. Then I graduate and walk off into the sunset and become the number one pick in the draft.

The 1995 Trojans ended the season at 9–2–1. Robinson's Rose Bowl record was 4–0. The *New York Times* headline was perfect: U.S.C. REWRITES NORTHWESTERN'S STORYBOOK ENDING. But the Trojans' next chapter would be turbulent.

11

THE JOHN ROBINSON-MIKE GARRETT RIFT:

1996–1997

The Pac-10 championship and Rose Bowl victory seemed to reassure Robinson's employers. In June 1996, with one year left on his original contract, he received a five-year extension at a reported $500,000 per year. His next team was young, though, and Keyshawn Johnson was irreplaceable. Still, the pollsters considered the Trojans' youthful talent and ranked them No. 7 before their opener with 11th-ranked Penn State.

USC lost, 24–7, in the Kickoff Classic at Giants Stadium in New Jersey. By mid-November, the overrated Trojans had lost two straight Pac-10 games while dropping to 5–5. The next week against the Bruins, USC fans exhaled when their team led, 41–24, with 6:12 remaining in the fourth quarter. Then USC fans freaked out when the Trojans lost, 48–41, in overtime. Bad enough that they coughed up a late 17-point lead; they also lost for the sixth straight time to UCLA.

USC's season ended with a 27–20 upset over tenth-ranked Notre Dame in Lou Holtz's farewell game as the Irish coach. It had taken 14 years to beat Notre Dame, and it may have saved Robinson's job as USC went 6–6 and 3-5 in the Pac-10. Two days after the Notre Dame game, the university confirmed that Robinson would return in 1997, a somewhat odd announcement given the fact that he had signed a new five-year deal that summer.

BILLY MILLER: John Robinson was a father figure to me. But I think what I started to see in him was fatigue, and I'm not saying this in a negative way. You're looking at him and you're thinking: *He's working himself to death, trying to get it right.* But I think that came with a cost. Mental fatigue. Physical fatigue. Coaching is a drain, especially at such a prestigious university.

I asked Robinson why the 1996 team collapsed and how much he was affected by the subsequent talk about his job security.

JOHN ROBINSON: Maybe we just weren't coaching very well, or maybe we just didn't put it together very well. I don't have a real clear feeling about it. It just wasn't going very well. But as a football coach, I don't know how much attention you pay. It's always out there, what I call "white noise." But I don't ever remember being affected that much one way or the other. You know, when we had a huge win, I would still get 50 letters, 20 of them calling me an idiot or saying I ran the wrong play. You had that same guy, who said the same thing, whether you won or lost.

In 1997, the Trojans returned 19 of 22 starters but also had quarterback issues, with neither Mike Van Raaphorst nor John Fox taking charge. They were 1–2 and already unranked when they hosted 25-point underdog UNLV.

Somehow USC trailed, 21–14, in the fourth quarter before fighting back to win, 35–21, in Robinson's 100th collegiate victory. On the Coliseum field afterward, Mike Garrett and Steven Sample presented Robinson with a Tiffany bust of the USC mascot, Traveler. But behind the scenes, the Robinson-Garrett rift had already heated up.

BILLY MILLER: Mike Garrett was coming into our locker room during games. In fact, I remember Mike Garrett just being all over the place. Almost trying to impose his will on every situation. So Coach Robinson and Mike Garrett did not get along.

This is not the NFL. You are not Jerry Jones. You don't own the team. You're an athletic director. Jerry Jones pays for every single player. He pays for every jersey, every football pad. It's different in the pros. But Mike Garrett had that approach, and quite honestly, it lost him a lot of respect from the players and it lost him a lot of respect from the coaches. We would see Mike Garrett come into the locker room and almost tune him out. Not from a lack of respect for who Mike Garrett had been as a football player, but as an athletic director, it wasn't the right time. It wasn't the right place.

JEREMY HOGUE: I saw some tension between them in '95, my last season. I hadn't really seen it before then. Until then it was more stylistic. Mike Garrett is a hard-ass disciplinarian. John Robinson is a players' coach. He could be an old-school hard-ass to the guys who *needed* that. But he could also be a more free-spirited, let-it-happen guy with the players who *that* resonated with. I think Mike Garrett expected every single guy to behave the way he did when he was a player: be a workaholic, live, eat, and breathe football. But I think you need to know your audience. I don't think Mike Garrett was that guy.

I'm sure the rubs started before they were visible to the players. But certainly by '95, it was pretty clear. Mike would come into the locker room at halftime, and if some guy wasn't playing well, he'd go over and light him up. If you're not playing well, you expect the coaches to be busting some people's butts and encouraging some people. There's going to be a whole range of things happening at halftime. But you don't expect for the athletic director to be walking in and cussing people out.

KEYSHAWN JOHNSON: I remember one time at halftime, we were losing to somebody and we were not playing great. Mike Garrett came in. He was trying to tell Coach Robinson stuff and like trying to coach the team at halftime. Coach Robinson told him to get the fuck out of the locker room. And you know, I was with Coach Rob 100 percent.

Sometimes Garrett would talk to me on the sideline. He would literally be trying to tell me what I should be doing as a player. And I would be like, *Who is this dude?* It's not even because I'm an accomplished player. He's accomplished in his own right. But he's not my coach.

Their relationship started to go south while I was still there and then especially as Robinson started to lose games. Now Garrett had the upper hand. Remember, there were only two things that mattered at USC. It was either go to play for the national championship or play in the Rose Bowl. So it became one of those things where Garrett was like, *You're losing now. So I'm gonna treat you like this.*

DARYL GROSS: I would say Mike was pretty consistent in how he went about his business. He was not going to be this warm and fuzzy administrator. My style was more like that. Mike's style wasn't like that all. Mike was pretty much the same with everyone, whether it was Pete Carroll or John Robinson or Paul Hackett. Whether you liked it or not, Mike was always going to be consistent.

Everyone understands the dynamics of locker rooms. But at the same time, a guy like Mike coming into the locker room makes sense. Mike played the game at the highest level: a Heisman Trophy winner, a longtime NFL player, and a Pro Bowler.

There was one situation, at the Washington game, where Mike

went in there. He wasn't going in there with bad intent because he didn't like the coach or something. He was going in there to help fire up the guys. He wanted to be helpful, and one can interpret that as being a distraction more than helpful. Some of the players took it very well and understood where he was coming from. Some of them didn't take it very well. He made a rah-rah speech. He did it rather passionately, and you can't blame a man for that. But it is unorthodox, and if it's not scripted by the coaches, it can make for a situation. John Robinson was a great coach, and Mike had a lot of passion, and everyone had good intent. But the execution of it was awkward.

TIM TESSALONE: Mike Garrett was not only a former USC player and not only a former Heisman Trophy winner. Mike was the embodiment of that tough Trojan: Iron Mike. He was passionate as a player and certainly as an athletic director. So he would talk to players in the hallways and on the practice field and in the locker rooms in a very passionate manner. You would have to ask John how he took to that, but it wasn't just some dude talking to you. It was Mike Garrett talking to you: USC's original Heisman Trophy winner.

I asked Robinson if it irritated him when Garrett came in the locker room and made statements to the players.

JOHN ROBINSON: Yeah. Oh, yeah. He had a couple times when he was angry. I think he wanted to be kind of like a general manager or something. He wanted to have influence over the team. And you know, he was a great football player, and I think he knew some things about football, which, when things weren't going right, he would express. That was unfortunate for everybody, because the team resented it and such. But when you're passionate about something, that kind of stuff happens.

In October 1997, one week after winning his 100th college game against UNLV, Robinson and his 2–2 Trojans made the short trip to Tempe to face 3–2 Arizona State. After USC lost, 35–7, Robinson called it "a disgrace to everyone involved."

On November 22, the season ended with a seventh straight loss (31–24) to UCLA. The Trojans at 6–5 were barely eligible for the postseason but reportedly were passed over by the Aloha Bowl. Then, amid constant rumors that Robinson would be fired, USC let him dangle for nearly a month.

BILLY MILLER: We heard about it. We felt it. You're too young to understand all the politics of it, but you could feel it happening. To this day Coach Robinson is my all-time favorite coach. I'm talking about any level, any man who ever coached me from Pop Warner to the NFL. And we blamed us that season. We felt like *we* let *him* down. We didn't do enough to let him keep his job. We didn't do enough to rejuvenate this historically great coach's name. And once you heard people saying *he* should be fired, the players at USC took it personally.

With Robinson still in limbo in mid-December, Trojans fans were stunned when two local papers reported that USC had offered the job to its former nemesis, Lou Holtz. Billy Miller said at the time, "You play at USC, you learn to hate that guy. Now he's going to be your coach?"

Holtz denied the reports, saying, "Absolutely not. Nothing could be further from the truth. I've never been offered the job at USC."

Robinson had not been fired yet, so what could Holtz really say? I asked Daryl Gross, the associate athletic director who was directly involved with every head-coaching hire, if USC ever flat-out offered the job to Holtz.

DARYL GROSS: Yes. You're talking to the horse's mouth on that one. What I learned from my scouting days, whether a coach is at

Notre Dame or UCLA or wherever, you have to quantify it metrically. Is the guy a great coach or not? If you take Notre Dame out of the equation, is Lou Holtz a great coach? The answer is yes. Of course, there's a subjective factor: *Wait a minute. We're at USC. You're gonna hire the Notre Dame coach?*

But at the time it wasn't about that. It was about: How do we get someone who can come in and get this program going in the right direction? Would England have wanted Patton even though he was from the United States? Yeah, he's a great general. He knows tactics and strategy. Lou Holtz obviously had a track record that was amazing. He was part of that long winning streak against USC. They could really run the ball at Notre Dame. They always ran it very well against us. They always made us look like a finesse team.

And the beautiful thing about it, Holtz was really interested in the job. He was *all* into it. We would probably spend a half hour to an hour on the phone for four or five nights in a row just talking about every element of the program. We hadn't even got to the PR part of it: How do you explain the Notre Dame coach coming into USC? It would be like Ara Parseghian coming in to coach USC.

But we never got that far because it fell apart for various reasons. His wife had some medical issues at the time, and that's mostly what stopped the momentum. Because we were going down a pretty fast track on that Lou Holtz hire.

On December 17, when USC finally fired Robinson, it all turned very messy. Scott Wolf is a USC alum who has covered the school's athletic programs for the *Los Angeles Daily News* since 1990. His current website is called *Inside USC with Scott Wolf.*

SCOTT WOLF: They had won the Rose Bowl with Keyshawn Johnson, and then they kind of lived off that for the next two years. Maybe Robinson lost his fire a little after winning that Rose Bowl. And that's how those two next seasons were viewed: Robinson was older, and maybe he didn't have the hunger and the energy he had before. There was just a lack of attitude in the whole program. I remember games where their conditioning was an issue. Then it became a question of whether the team was in shape.

Garrett had wanted to fire Robinson the year before, but Robinson had really good relationships with the alumni and boosters. Pat Haden was on the board of trustees, and he told me he didn't think Robinson should be fired. The president, Steven Sample, didn't want to fire him either. So I think they kind of agreed, *Well, we'll give it one more season.* Then they struggled again in '97, and I think there was less resistance this time.

TIM TESSALONE: Early on, things were going okay. We had Keyshawn Johnson, and we won a Cotton Bowl and a Rose Bowl. But then there were a couple of .500 teams. And you have a fan base and an athletic director who wants success right away. So another coaching change was made. And the parting did not come off well in the eyes of the public.

The public took its cue from the Los Angeles media, which reported that Mike Garrett had fired John Robinson in a voice mail.

DARYL GROSS: Sometimes when things get reported, a good story beats accuracy, and I think that's a bad postulate. All this stuff talked about how John got fired on an answering machine? I was around Mike that night, and he was trying to reach John to have a conversation and left him a message saying to call him back. That's the only thing that ever happened on the message machine, because I was sitting there when Mike made the call.

Coach Robinson was probably asked, "Did you talk to Mike?" He probably said, "Well, he left me a message on my voice mail." The press took that and made it that Garrett fired Robinson on his voice mail. They just ran with it. It sounds good, but it's not true.

SCOTT WOLF: They asked *me* for Robinson's home number, which I thought was hilarious at the time. Garrett definitely called him, but Robinson didn't answer, and Garrett fired him by message. Also, they hired Paul Hackett before they fired Robinson. I was actually the one who found out they were interviewing Hackett. USC had a couple guys in Kansas City, where Hackett was an assistant coach with the Chiefs. I called Robinson, and I said, "Hey, you heard anything about Paul Hackett?" He said, "Oh, no, I know Paul. He would have told me if they offered him the job. He hasn't talked to me about that, so I know they haven't talked to him." But they had already sewn up the deal that night in Kansas City.

KEYSHAWN JOHNSON: He fired him on a voice mail. It was so stupid, though. I mean, then you hire Paul Hackett? Why would you do that? Robinson had only been there for four years. Two of the four years he goes to a major bowl game. I don't understand why it's time for him to go. That's crazy.

BILLY MILLER: When they fired Coach Robinson, we had a meeting. It was guys who were juniors but were going to come back as seniors. We really wanted to leave. All of us did. We heard that Coach Robinson got fired on a voice mail. When you're a kid, you don't understand business. But you understand respect. He deserved a celebratory send-off even if he was at the end of his rope. So that left a lot of USC people angry. When you fire a guy over voice mail, a guy that means so much to so many people, that just comes off so wrong.

Here is how Mike Downey at the *Los Angeles Times* saw it: "The guillotining of John Robinson did not go smoothly. Mike Garrett gets rid of the help with all the tact of Leona Helmsley."

JOHN ROBINSON: Mike and I were never very close. He and I had been friends prior, but now the situation was strained a little bit.

Besides, when it is over, you're not going to be friends when you fire somebody.

I don't think he was out of line in doing it. We had lost a couple years in a row. I do think we could have gotten together and worked out a plan to fix what wasn't right in the program. I think I had enough of a résumé where you would say, "Let's see if we can change things." But we weren't about to get together and work it out. That was not gonna be. And that was not gonna be with any of the coaches that succeeded me either.

I asked Robinson if he was fired by voice mail.

JOHN ROBINSON: That was how I got the information. At the time, he kind of came off looking bad doing that. It's just one of those things. When you have a breakup, it's never done well. It just kind of happens.

I didn't feel *good* about the way things were handled. And a lot of people were upset about it. But I think it's important to recognize that I got fired because our team wasn't doing very well. Whether it's done clumsily or not, when I sat back and looked at it later, I said, "Okay, I don't think we deserved to be fired." But it was certainly one of the options that a guy in his position would have.

In his two head-coaching stints at USC, Robinson won seven of his eight bowl games, including all four Rose Bowls. His 1978 team split the national championship with Alabama, but should have won it alone since it had defeated the Crimson Tide that season. Over his 12 seasons, Robinson went an impressive 104–35–4. But in his last two years, he was 12–11.

JOHN ROBINSON: Coaching at USC was a good time in my life. I think the people loved our program. When you lost, it wasn't good. I had about four games that I look at and say, "Damn, you screwed that up" or "You should have done that" or "You should have done this." Those moments are still vivid. It's mostly the losses that you recall.

But from an overall standpoint, I feel really good about the time I coached there. I'm helping USC fund-raise now, and the people I meet seem to remember it as a great era. I kind of have that feeling too. There were a lot of great times.

12

THE STEEP DESCENT:

1998–2000

Even the opening moments of the Paul Hackett era felt odd, disjointed, and awkward. On December 17, 1997, the day of the messy Robinson firing, USC announced Hackett as his successor. But Hackett didn't attend his own introductory news conference. He stayed in Kansas City and prepared for the NFL playoffs in his role as the Chiefs' offensive coordinator. He spoke to reporters by phone in a conference call the next day, and through no fault of his own, the connection was so poor that at one point he said, "This is really bad. I don't know. Can you even hear me?"

As a longtime NFL assistant in Dallas, San Francisco, and Kansas City, Hackett made his reputation by working with Joe Montana on both the 49ers and the Chiefs, but before that Hackett received his first break from Robinson, who brought him in to coach the USC quarterbacks in 1976. Over the next five years, Robinson put him in charge of the passing game, and USC won three Rose Bowls and a national championship. In 1998, when Hackett returned to the Trojans, it was only his second head-coaching job. In his first he had lasted three seasons, going 13–20–1 at the University of Pittsburgh before his dismissal in 1992.

The 50-year-old Hackett was often called one of the gurus of the West Coast offense. Unfortunately, his version was overly complicated. Unlike some of the best coaches of all time—Vince Lombardi, Red Auerbach, John Wooden, and John McKay come to mind—Hackett did not believe in having his teams run a finite number of things exceptionally well. He seemed to conclude that more was more, which was evident from his large and jargon-heavy playbook.

In 1998, Petros Papadakis was a sophomore tailback and the team's best power runner in short-yardage situations. His father, John, was a starting linebacker at USC for McKay, and his older brother Taso played linebacker for Robinson. Petros was named a team captain as a senior in 2000. He later became a Los Angeles radio and TV commentator, at times irking his alma mater with his blunt observations.

PETROS PAPADAKIS: I went right from the UCLA game—John Robinson's last game—to Mexico. By the time I got back to school, he was fired and Hackett was hired. I did a lot of interviews at that time, and the media would ask me what I thought about the coaching change. I would say, "They fired John Robinson!" I grew up looking at JR as a football god, because I grew up around USC.

SCOTT WOLF: Lou Holtz already had turned USC down. So Hackett was not their first choice. But they wanted to get rid of Robinson and they didn't want to do a search, and they wanted to announce a new coach the same day they fired Robinson.

The big thing about Hackett was that he was there for the glory years during the late 1970s. I think they saw him as a way to return to that era of success, but I don't think they really did their homework. He was hard to get along with. He also had that really bad stint at Pittsburgh.

BILLY MILLER: You fire Coach Robinson, who we all love and adore. You could have brought in Moses, for God's sake, and everyone would have looked at him sideways for a minute.

I do think Coach Hackett was a smart football coach. I think he understood offense. Coach Hackett did not understand—very clearly did not understand—that a college coach is dealing with college *kids.* If you can get them to love the game of football and have fun playing it, then the players see you as a father figure instead of a CEO. Pete Carroll understood that. John Robinson understood that. Paul Hackett did not understand that even 1 percent.

Bobby DeMars was a freshman defensive lineman who spent most of his career as a dedicated backup. Maybe too dedicated: DeMars says he once lost 35 pounds in five days during one hellish stretch of summer camp. At the end of the seventh day, he passed out in the shower from exhaustion and dehydration. A 96-year-old man who swam in the USC pool was standing over him when he woke up.

DeMars is now a Los Angeles–based filmmaker. His 2015 documentary, *The Business of Amateurs,* examines the NCAA and big-time college sports at a time when college athletes are finding their voices like never before.

BOBBY DEMARS: John Robinson was a player's coach. He was a guy who always had his office open; it didn't matter the time of the day. Hackett was a totally different situation. The open-door policy went out the window. If you wanted to talk to Hackett, you literally had to set an appointment.

I was a redshirt freshman for Robinson. At the end of my freshman year I was told Hackett wanted to meet with me. I made an appointment with Hackett, and I went in there. I waited two hours, and he was a no-show, so I had to reschedule. That happened twice; the third time he showed up. He came in and he said, "So I hear you're transferring." I said, "No. I'm not transferring."

I was blown away that he said that because I was in the business school as a true freshman. I was part of the business scholars group. I went to USC for a lot of reasons, and having an off year in football with my coach being fired didn't make me want to transfer. It was something I hadn't even thought about, let alone breathed to anybody, and I didn't understand what he was doing.

I said, "I plan on staying here until I graduate," and he kept going down the path. He said, "Well, if you're gonna transfer, now is the time when you want to. If you wait until fall camp starts, you not only have to sit out that year, but another year, and even another year if you go within the Pac-10." I said, "Well, I'm not transferring."

I later found out he had this talk with some other guys, and some actually did transfer. That's how it happens. When a new coach comes in, they try to get rid of some of the old bodies that they don't think will pan out, and he just didn't see me fitting into the scheme. So that was my first taste of Paul Hackett.

PETROS PAPADAKIS: You could tell pretty quickly that Hackett was a pretty angry guy, but I responded to that because I was a pretty fucking angry guy too. But I don't think he related very well with most of the guys on the team. He was not a communicator. He was a dark room, offensive coordinator type of guy.

When he got to USC, he tried to kill us during spring workouts. He made us get up every morning at five a.m., and he tried to run people off the team. He put us in a gym where they closed the windows and turned the heaters on and made people run till they threw up. It was a typical coaching move. Every coach who takes over thinks the previous coach didn't know shit and didn't work the players hard enough.

So he basically ran the shit out of us in the morning and tried to kill us later that day in practice. It was the bloodiest spring I've ever been a part of. This was before they changed the rules about camp and what you could do. We had several *three*-a-days, and it was a bloodbath. But that was how I became noticed as a player in that era. I would take seven, eight, or nine carries in a row and get in a fight at the end. He liked that.

After two subpar years (6–6 and 6–5) under Robinson, the 1998 Trojans entered the season unranked, the same place they would end it. Still, Hackett did a credible job in the regular season, finishing 8–4 despite a tough schedule.

In the opener against Purdue at the Coliseum, a true freshman named Carson Palmer came off the bench in the third quarter and suddenly USC had a quarterback controversy. Replacing the sophomore starter Mike Van Raaphorst, Palmer guided the Trojans to 17 second-half points in a 27–17 win. A traditional dropback passer, Palmer would alternate between flashes of brilliance and bad decisions in an up-and-down freshman season.

In late November, UCLA sacked Palmer six times in its 34–17 victory, the embarrassing eighth straight loss for the Trojans to the Bruins. One week later in the regular-season finale, USC's signature win came against Notre Dame at the Coliseum. The Irish were 9–2 and ranked No. 8 when the 7–4 and unranked Trojans upset them, 10–0. The last time USC had shut out Notre Dame was in 1962, when it went on to win the Rose Bowl and the first of McKay's four national championships.

But teams that go 8–4 and 5–3 in the Pac-10 aren't allowed in the Rose Bowl. They play in second-tier games such as the Sun Bowl in El Paso, where the Trojans found themselves on December 31 against a TCU team that barely made the postseason with a 6–5 record—one year after finishing 1–10. No wonder the Trojans came in as 16-point favorites.

Earlier that December, USC had hired Chris Huston as an assistant sports information director. Huston remained there until March 2005.

CHRIS HUSTON: The key to the '98 season was the way it ended. TCU ran the precursor to the spread offense you see today. They made USC look pretty silly, but they did it by spreading the field and then running the ball.

That bowl game really showed that Hackett was out of his depth in the college game. He was very much focused on implementing a West Coast offense with an incredibly thick playbook and play calling that required a paragraph to call something in the huddle. At the same time he wasn't prepared to take on the new styles that were emerging in the college game. The Sun Bowl revealed that.

In the 28–19 loss to a 16-point underdog, USC trailed, 28–3, in the third quarter. It rushed for a school-record minus 23 yards. And it lost to a TCU team that had won its last bowl game in 1957, when the Dodgers were preparing to leave Brooklyn.

In 1999, the following season, Ed Orgeron was in his second year as USC's fiery defensive line coach. In their 2005 book *Conquest,* David Wharton and Gary Klein of the *Los Angeles Times* described Orgeron as "built like a cement truck, a wide load, with a voice to match." The *Times* reporters continued: "Whenever he grew excited, which was not at all unusual when it came to football, the defensive line coach could rattle windows, if not the confidence of freshmen."

The man known in college football as Coach O could also be funny and charming, particularly with high school recruits and their families. But he also had a troubled past, with two arrests for bar fights, one of which led to his resignation from an assistant coaching position at the University of Miami. In that incident in Baton Rouge, according to several media reports, the police affidavit said, "Orgeron head-butted the manager in the face." Police reports also said the manager was bleeding from his face. The charges wound up getting dropped, but Orgeron later told the *Orange County Register,* "I head-butted a guy, yeah. I was intoxicated."

That incident took place in 1992, six years before Hackett brought Orgeron with him to USC. In the intervening years, wrote Wharton and Klein, "Orgeron took some time off to put his life in order before returning to football." He resumed his career at Nicholls State and Syracuse before Hackett brought him to USC. But according to DeMars, his position coach could still intimidate.

BOBBY DEMARS: I was the only player in the business school at the time. I was also in the film school, and I had a pretty demanding schedule. I still had one of the highest GPAs on the team. I had been in the top 10 percent of my whole class, not just the football players, when I had first come into USC. I could have gone to Stanford or Harvard, and I chose USC because I grew up here and because I knew the value of having that degree. Orgeron thought I cared more about school than football. The reality is, I cared about both equally, and I tried just as hard at both equally.

I took advanced business statistics, and not only was it a heavy class, but the teacher was hard-core. So I had to leave practice twice a week—with maybe ten minutes left—and then sprint to the locker room, sometimes without showering. Then I would run to class and barely make it. When I had to leave early on those Tuesdays and Thursdays, Orgeron would tear me up. He'd call me a motherfucker or a pussy. But the thing is, he wouldn't shout it for everybody to hear. He would say it to me on my way out.

Orgeron had a huge temper. He was always in the weight room at like five in the morning, benching 300. In the weight room one time, he's screaming at me, and it's a huge scene; everybody's standing around, going "Jesus." He keeps getting closer to me, and then he pushes his head up into mine. He shouts as loud as he can with his head pushed into my forehead, "Stop fucking looking at me like that, Bobby!" It seemed like he was about to get physical, so the other guys came in and pulled him off. He just kind of threw them off and then stormed out.

He would also push his chest into yours and say, "You wanna fight me right now? Let's do it." You don't know whether he's joking or serious, but most of the time it seemed like he was dead-on serious. Look, everyone's been yelled at. But there's a difference between being yelled at and feeling like you're being threatened. You saw that kind of thing with the basketball coach, Mike Rice, at Rutgers. I don't go for that style.

In the 1999 season, the 21st-ranked Trojans moved to No. 16 with non-conference wins over Hawaii and San Diego State. Then Carson Palmer's sophomore season ended painfully in game three when he broke his right collarbone in a 33–30 triple-overtime loss at Oregon. In that same gut-wrenching defeat, the undisciplined Trojans committed a school-record 21 penalties.

The next Saturday, now-unranked USC beat unranked Oregon State, 37–29, but not before nearly wasting a 37–7 fourth-quarter lead. The Trojans also had 11 more penalties for a mind-bending total of 33 in two weeks.

Then the Los Angeles version of the Bad News Bears lost five straight games in one season for only the third time in USC history. Two of those five defeats were truly awful. Against Notre Dame at South Bend, the Trojans blew a 21-point lead in the third quarter and lost, 25–24. Against Stanford at the Coliseum, they led, 21–0, in the first quarter before surrendering, 38–35.

USC recovered to win three of its last four games, including a 17–7 victory that finally ended the eight-game losing streak against the Bruins. But even that drew criticism when Hackett and some players celebrated on the field as if they had just won the California lottery.

That season had begun with the 21st-ranked Trojans expected

to contend for a conference championship. They wound up 6–6 and 3–5 in the Pac-10.

CHRIS HUSTON: The most important thing that happened in 1999 was Carson Palmer breaking his collarbone just before halftime in the third game. He was able to redshirt that year. If he doesn't redshirt that year, his senior year is 2001 instead of 2002. That changed the trajectory of USC football. Instead of Norm Chow and Pete Carroll getting Palmer for two years—the way they did—they would have gotten him for one.

Even with the return of a healthy Palmer, the 2000 Trojans probably didn't deserve their preseason No. 15 ranking. But when they went 3–0 before Pac-10 play began, they rose all the way to No. 8. Then, for the second straight season, they lost five games in a row. This time all five defeats were within their own conference.

Plagued by penalties, turnovers, missed field goal attempts, and questionable clock management, USC lost to Oregon State for the first time since 1967; led Stanford, 30–20, in the final 5:22 before losing, 32–30; and lost at home to Cal to drop to 0–5 in the Pac-10 for the first time ever.

PETROS PAPADAKIS: I was the captain of that team in 2000. We weren't a bad-looking team. We had Carson at QB and Troy Polamalu at safety. We were No. 8 in the country after we won our first three. Then we went on a five-game losing streak, and the team just went in the tank.

Carson threw a lot of picks. And there was a giant rift between Hackett and Hugh Jackson, his offensive coordinator. Jackson was a holdover from the John Robinson era and was kept on the staff by Mike Garrett. So Hackett and Jackson was basically a forced marriage that never worked. By the time the year 2000 came along, they were openly fighting each other.

Hackett called me in during the losing streak. They were trying to root through the team and find out what was wrong with everybody. This is what happens when a coach is about to get fired: Everybody starts to splinter. The assistants and the head coach start looking to blame somebody, and they all start trying to line up their next jobs. I don't think that's a rare thing, but when things go wrong at USC, they go wrong pretty fast and probably in a worse way than they do anywhere else.

The fractured communication between Hackett and Jackson might have contributed to the numerous times Palmer waited too long for the play to be signaled in and the Trojans were called for delay of game. Palmer would end this tumultuous season with 16 touchdown passes and a single-season school-record 18 interceptions.

As their coaches feuded and malfunctioned, the USC players divided into cliques, which is hardly unusual for a losing team under enormous pressure in a large media market. Lenny Vandermade was a freshman offensive lineman who became a three-year starter despite shifting from center to guard in midcareer.

LENNY VANDERMADE: I was a young guy, so I wasn't totally sure what was going on. But the culture in 2000, it seemed almost like everyone was out for himself. Everybody worried more about the NFL, about the next level, than about their time at USC. I also don't think the players ever really bought into Paul Hackett. Most were recruited by John Robinson, and Hackett could never quite shake that. You would hear it a lot in the locker room: "When John Robinson was here . . ."

After we lost to Stanford in October, you heard a lot of different things going around. We blew another lead, and Stanford beat us on the last play of the game. After that the feeling was that Hackett was going to be fired.

PETROS PAPADAKIS: Mike Garrret was getting grief from the alumni and the media. Before he had hired Hackett, he had fired a very popular guy on an answering machine. Garrett and Robinson didn't like each other from way back. They got in a couple of fights in front of me. Garrett would stop me and try to talk to me about running the ball, and JR would say, "Those are my players. Don't talk to my players."

Garrett was a bit less hands-on in the Hackett era, but he was still ultra-involved and the coaches put on a show for him whenever he showed up at practice and they'd make us do more shit. But with the alumni and the media, Garrett was taking the heat for hiring Hackett. Then Garrett would often not speak to the media. He wasn't a very comfortable public speaker at that time. He got better when USC started to win.

After their five straight defeats, the Trojans went 2–2 in their last four games but still finished 5–7 overall and 2–6 in the Pac-10. That left them tied for last place in the conference, which had never happened before at USC.

The Hackett years all but ended on November 25 with a 38–21 loss to 11th-ranked Notre Dame in the 2000 season finale. At the Coliseum on national television, USC continued to make too many crucial mistakes. Yet when asked after the game if he deserved to return, Hackett said, "Are you out of your mind? Of course I do."

USC dismissed him two days later with two years remaining on his five-year contract.

Hackett went 19–18 in his three seasons. His teams regressed each year—8–5, 6–6, and 5–7—and were never fundamentally sound. In his one postseason game, USC lost in the Sun Bowl to 16-point underdog TCU. The fault, of course, wasn't all Hackett's. His players and assistants also underperformed. But that fact wasn't enough to save his job.

PETROS PAPADAKIS: Hackett got fired unceremoniously. We lost to Notre Dame, and then he got fired the following Monday. First he gave a very awkward speech to the team. The tone was kind of self-righteous and relatively appropriate for how he felt he was treated. Some of the guys appreciated it; some of them didn't. There was a smattering of applause, and then he was chased to his car by the media. He didn't stop and give them a statement. He was chased by the media out of the fucking school.

LENNY VANDERMADE: I was bummed when he got fired. I had a good relationship with my offensive line coach, Steve Morton. At the same time I knew that there were high expectations at SC. And 5–7 is not gonna cut it. Even 8–4 is not gonna cut it for long at SC. So I understood, and life goes on.

CHRIS HUSTON: What the Hackett years proved was what you could do at USC even if you were an ineffective coach. You could still bring in talent. When you coach at USC, there will be 30 guys who are going to play for money one day. That's the base you're working with on your 85-man roster.

   The talent that Hackett brought in ended up being very important to the revival of USC football. He brought in Carson Palmer. He brought in Troy Polamalu. He brought in most of the good offensive linemen who would start for Pete Carroll and start winning bowl games.

PETROS PAPADAKIS: When people ask who I played for and I say "Hackett," they kind of roll their eyes. But he did not leave a bare cupboard. No one does at USC. The place recruits itself.

13

A NEW MESSIAH NAMED PETE:

2001–2002

By 2001, the negative numbers were undeniable. They were also, at the same time, hard to believe.

It had been five years since the Trojans had won the Pac-10, 11 years since they had finished in the national top ten, and 23 years since John Robinson's 1978 team had won the program's last national championship. Ted Tollner, Larry Smith, and Robinson during his second stint all had contributed to the once-mighty program's decline, but Hackett was perceived to be the worst hire by far.

LENNY VANDERMADE: Before he brought in Pete Carroll, I don't think Mike Garrett's position was very secure at all. He kind of got rid of J. Rob, a beloved guy at USC. Then he hired Hackett, and he didn't pan out. I think that reflected badly on Mike. So I think his next hire had to be a great one.

DARYL GROSS: Mike had a great relationship with Steve Sample and some of the trustees. Mike wanted to win more than anybody.

And I think people recognized and respected that. But we *were* getting to a point where we really needed the next coach to do well. It wasn't like the previous coaches were doing horrible. But seasons like 6–6 and 6–5 and 5–7 do not meet USC's standards.

ARTIE GIGANTINO: Mike McGee had hired John Robinson the second time. Then immediately Garrett replaced McGee as the AD. Garrett later brings in Hackett, and that was a farce. Pete Carroll came after Hackett. Before they decided on Pete, I talked to Garrett one night. He did not know what to do. But then he said, "Fuck it, I'm gonna go with the guy with the energy." Because he was thinking of bringing in Mike Riley or maybe Sonny Lubick to just stop the bleeding for a couple years. But he went with Pete, and obviously the rest is history.

That history might have been altered if not for the Daryl Gross-Pete Carroll connection. Gross, USC's senior associate athletic director, had scouted for the New York Jets from 1989 to 1991, Carroll's first season as New York's defensive coordinator. In 1994 the Jets promoted Carroll to his first head-coaching position. But when they started 6–5 and finished 6–10, he was abruptly and perhaps unfairly fired. Carroll spent the two next years as defensive coordinator for the San Francisco 49ers, whose defense he helped elevate to No. 1 in the league in 1995.

In 1997, Carroll replaced the autocratic Bill Parcells as head coach of the New England Patriots. Over the next three years, the more congenial Carroll went 27–21 and made the playoffs twice, but owner Robert Kraft fired him after the 1999 season. "Last year we barely made the playoffs, and this year we're 8–8 with a fifth-place schedule," said Kraft. "We need a momentum change." Kraft didn't say so, but he was already smitten with Bill Belichick, who was much more in the Parcells mode. Kraft hired Belichick three weeks after dismissing Carroll.

Carroll had been out of coaching for one year, doing media work and consulting, when USC fired Hackett. During the subsequent 18-day coaching search, Gross suggested that Garrett consider Carroll. On December 15, 2000, Carroll signed a five-year deal reportedly worth close to $1.2 million per year. But as the iconic story goes, Carroll was not the first choice to replace Hackett. He was not even the second or third choice.

DARYL GROSS: We wanted to get a guy who was a sitting college head coach who had been successful. Given that model, we were interested in Mike Bellotti at Oregon and Dennis Erickson at Oregon State. We also looked at Mike Riley, who was not a sitting head coach but had been at Oregon State before Erickson went there.

Erickson had the most significant success. He was a terrific coach, and we really went hard after Dennis. Oregon State was getting ready to go to the Fiesta Bowl and play Notre Dame when we started talking. I remember being on the phone with his agent, Tom Condon, and the numbers were astronomical at the time. The deal almost reached $2 million, and that was just out of sight.

Then Dennis called me when I was at a USC basketball game. I went into the parking lot and was trying to talk him into not dropping out of this process. He kept telling me that it was too tough to tell his players that he was leaving. When we got off the phone, I said, "Well, he's not it."

We interviewed Mike Bellotti and Mike Riley. Then I said to Mike Garrett, "Pete Carroll is still there. I know he doesn't fit our prerequisites, but we gotta bring him in. He's gonna interview well, and you're gonna love the guy." So then we interviewed Pete after the other guys, and Pete was by far the most dynamic interview.

One more thing that a lot of people don't know: I went after Pete once before, with Mike Garrett's blessing, back when we were talking to Lou Holtz. Pete just had a 10–6 season at New England. I offered him a million dollars a year, which was nuts at the time. Pete said,

"Golly, I really appreciate it. But we're doing too good right now. We got so many great things going, and we want to win a Super Bowl."

Now we're here three or four years later. Pete had gone 10–6, 9–7, and 8–8 at New England, and that wasn't good enough. And the year he went 8–8, his field goal kicker, Adam Vinatieri, who is one of the greatest ever, missed two or three game-winning field goals that season. New England could have been 10–6 or 11–5. So everyone who said, "Pete Carroll? He's been fired twice in the NFL"—that was just perception, bad data, and noise. Pete Carroll could *coach.*

Him getting fired at the New York Jets? The owner, Leon Hess, had wanted Richie Kotite to be the head coach, not Pete. But the GM had pushed for Pete. Pete starts out hot with the Jets, and then it goes sour and they fire him after one year. Well, who does *that?* Then Richie Kotite comes in and wins one game with the Jets. So that firing shouldn't have happened, and I would argue that the New England firing shouldn't have happened. The guy was a brilliant coach, and we were convinced of that.

Nobody else was convinced, though. Carroll had never been a college head coach. He had last coached in college, as an assistant, 17 years before at unheralded Pacific. Since then he'd become an NFL veteran, which reminded people of Hackett when *he* had come to USC. Carroll, unlike Hackett, had NFL head-coaching experience, but his 33–31 record completely underwhelmed Los Angeles. "I'm not mad at Pete Carroll," wrote Bill Plaschke in the *Times.* "I'm mad at USC for hiring him."

SCOTT WOLF: Mike Riley couldn't get out of his contract with the Chargers. They wanted Dennis Erickson, and he wound up signing a new deal at Oregon State. They talked to Mike Bellotti, who was kind of a hot name at the time at Oregon. I remember when they did interview Carroll. One of the guys in the athletic department told me not to make a big deal out of it because it was a courtesy. Carroll was just that NFL guy who had been fired twice, and I think he was kind of pestering USC to give him an interview. He knew the USC people because his daughter played volleyball there.

CHRIS HUSTON: We had three press releases written. One was announcing the hiring of Mike Riley. One was announcing the hiring of Sonny Lubick. And one was announcing the hiring of Pete Carroll. These press releases were ready the night before. In the morning we got the call, and my boss, Tim Tessalone, said, "Pete Carroll."

There was a lot of consternation once the word trickled out. There was a lot of faxing and letter writing and calling into Heritage Hall protesting the hiring of Pete Carroll. It seemed like another bungled hiring, just the same way Hackett was bungled.

TIM TESSALONE: He was certainly not a name. He was certainly not the first choice. Then he did a great job at the presser, but I still recall standing around with Daryl Gross after everybody had pretty much left. T. J. Simers was still there from the *LA Times*. T.J. goes, "Well, we'll see you next year, at your next press conference."

SCOTT WOLF: They had security guards at his press conference. I had never seen that at a USC press conference, but people were furious. They were calling him a retread. He had no college background. How's he gonna recruit? He's not used to college football. He's not a USC guy. There was a long list of complaints about him. He didn't excite anybody.

DARYL GROSS: Oh, my God, that's an understatement. People were going nuts about it. There was one columnist in Orange County, named Steve Bisheff, who wrote a story about me. He said, "Who is this shadow AD? He's the guy who suggested Pete Carroll. If Pete Carroll is what Daryl Gross says he is, he'll get an AD job somewhere. If he isn't, he'll be the goat."

SCOTT WOLF: I used to constantly needle Carroll. I used to tell him what little shoes he had to fill, following Hackett. But the first time I met him, I could see why they hired him. In a one-on-one situation, he can be very charismatic. Hackett was the kind of guy everyone hated in the athletic department. Carroll would talk to the lowest-rung person on the totem pole. Hackett had never been a player's coach, so it was a total 180 from what they had. Carroll was not a disciplinarian. He was more of a fun guy. So the biggest change was Carroll's enthusiasm. He was such a boyish character.

BOBBY DEMARS: I committed to USC after they won the Rose Bowl in 1996. So technically I was the only player involved in those entire six years. I saw a lot during that time. John Robinson signed a five-year extension the month before I committed, and I was like, *Wow, he's gonna be my coach for the whole time through.* He was gone three months into my first season. Then I played for Paul Hackett. By the time Pete Carroll came in, I was going to maybe just graduate and not come back for my last season because I was pretty disillusioned with football. But I could see that Pete Carroll would be something special.

LENNY VANDERMADE: Not too long after they hired him, he did this thing with us at the Coliseum. It was a tug-of-war. He had 11 defensive guys on one side of the rope and 11 offensive guys on the other side of the rope. This is the 50-yard line of the Coliseum, so everyone's kind of juiced up. Guys were taking their shirts off; everyone's yelling and screaming. Eventually people start cheating and grabbing the rope, and at one point everyone kind of fell into this pile. We all stand back up, and he kind of broke it down. He said, "What just happened there?" We said, "We're playing-tug-of war." He said, "If we pull in different directions, we're gonna end up in a pile and we are going nowhere. We all have to pull in the same direction." Then he made us all stand back to back, facing out, toward the stadium. He said, "Nothing can come between us right now. If we can establish that, we'll be unbeatable."

Carroll was also pragmatic. A defensive specialist, he brought in Norm Chow to run the offense. They would later part ways after four seasons amid some tension between them during a dynastic run. For now, Chow's hiring was met with much greater local fanfare than when Carroll had signed on.

Chow built his reputation as an offensive coordinator and quarterback guru by teaching Steve Young, Robbie Bosco, and Ty Detmer during his 27 years as an assistant coach at BYU. In 2000, after getting passed over for the BYU head-coaching job, Chow spent one season as offensive coordinator at North Carolina State, where the Wolfpack averaged 31 points a game with a freshman quarterback named Philip Rivers.

NORM CHOW: USC was down at the time, but USC's always USC. I knew if you turn that opportunity down, you're not gonna get another shot to coach there.

Pete Carroll, as you know, was not a popular choice and not the first choice, either. When they settled on Pete, he realized quickly that he better get some college guys rather than NFL assistants. But then I was shocked when I got there. They give you an office, and the chairs are broken and the desks are all beat up. I kept thinking, *Holy mackerel. This is supposed to be USC.* The morale also wasn't so hot. The first two players I met were Carson Palmer and Matt Cassel. They were very discouraged at what happened in the past and were very eager to try to get it going.

I didn't know Pete Carroll at the time. As I got to know him, it was very obvious that he's an awfully bright football coach. He's a guy who is very willing, almost to a fault maybe, to try things, and it proved to be a little bit of a . . . later on, he tinkered so much. But that first year we were there, we just didn't have the players to do some of those things he wanted to do. But Pete put together a good coaching staff. Ed Orgeron and Kennedy Pola, and those guys deserve a ton of credit for the recruiting they did there at the beginning. It started with guys like Shaun Cody. I think he was the big breakthrough, recruiting-wise.

An athletic defensive lineman, Cody went on to become a consensus first-team All-American for the Trojans. Before then he was pursued by hundreds of colleges, finally trimming the field to USC, Notre Dame, and Washington.

SHAUN CODY: I was doing all those high school All-American events with all the best high school players around the nation. These guys were going to Oklahoma and Texas and Miami and Florida State. People were asking me, "Shaun, where you going?" I said, "I'm going to USC." They would say, "Why the hell would you go to USC? They're terrible right now."

USC was close to home, but it was still kind of a leap of faith for me. Coach Carroll was preaching to me, "It's easy to jump on a ship that is sailing smooth. If you want to be part of something that hasn't been done here at USC for a while, let's get this program back where it was. Let's turn this thing around."

Something about that really stuck with me. And he's pretty charismatic when he's trying to convince you. He's a salesman. For all his great qualities as a football coach, his psychology and getting into people's brains is one of his main attributes. He also had this aura of enthusiasm. He was always working on something, trying to get better at something, crafting something. He was *very* high energy.

Still, the fast-talking, fast-walking Carroll got off to a plodding start at USC. With the memory of the 2000 Trojans (5–7 overall and 2–6 in the Pac-10) still fresh in the minds of the pollsters,

John Robinson, talking with quarterback Sean Salisbury, had become USC's head coach in 1976. Robinson replaced the iconic John McKay and then proved a worthy successor by winning a national title in his third season. TOM SIROTNAK

Running back Marcus Allen won the Heisman Trophy in 1981 and gained a collegiate-record 2,342 yards in a single season. No one dreamt it at the time, but it would be 21 years before another Trojan would win the Heisman. TOM SIROTNAK

Marv Goux was a fiery and beloved USC assistant for 26 seasons before he was implicated in a ticket selling scandal that led to stiff NCAA sanctions in the early 1980s. TOM SIROTNAK

Larry Smith started fast at USC, taking the Trojans to three straight Rose Bowls in the late 1980s, but his entire tenure was plagued by his almost constant conflicts with his players. TOM SIROTNAK

It was never boring when Todd Marinovich played quarterback for the Trojans. After feuding with Smith, however, he left USC following his sophomore year and was drafted by the Los Angeles Raiders. TOM SIROTNAK

Leroy Holt was a team captain, a bruising blocker and runner, and the first USC fullback to start all four of his seasons. TOM SIROTNAK

Linebacker Junior Seau was an All-American in 1989 and the Pac-10 Defensive Player of the Year. When he, Mark Carrier, and Todd Marinovich all left USC early within a two-year span, it raised questions about Larry Smith's ability to keep his stars on campus. TOM SIROTNAK

For over 45 years, the world-famous USC Song Girls have displayed their spirit and athleticism. TOM SIROTNAK

Keyshawn Johnson, perhaps the best wide receiver in school history, celebrates after winning the 1996 Rose Bowl MVP. USC beat that season's Cinderella team, Northwestern, 41–32. DAN AVILA

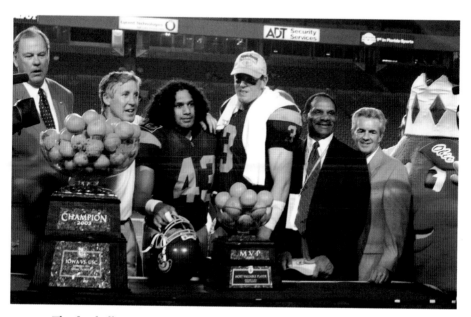

The football program returned to national prominence with its 38–17 win over Iowa in the 2003 Orange Bowl. Head coach Pete Carroll stands next to two USC greats—Troy Polamalu (43) and Carson Palmer (3)—and to their right is athletic director Mike Garrett. DAN AVILA

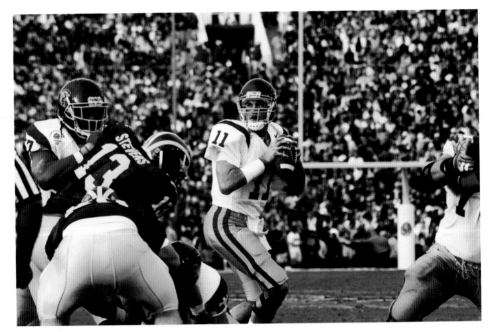

Matt Leinart began the 2003 season as an unknown redshirt sophomore who had never thrown a collegiate pass. He ended that season by throwing three touchdown passes and winning MVP in this 28–14 win over Michigan. USC won the AP national title, but had to share the crowd with the BCS champions, LSU. DAN AVILA

Reggie Bush (5) and LenDale White (21) gave the Trojans a dynamic tailback tandem. The more powerful White and the more electric Bush were nicknamed Thunder and Lightning. DAN AVILA

Pete Carroll leaves the field after the victorious 2009 Emerald Bowl. Sixteen days later, he left the USC program that he had returned to greatness to become head coach of the Seattle Seahawks. DAN AVILA

Carroll's replacement, Lane Kiffin, confers with his freshman quarterback Matt Barkley. They would later clash, especially in the disastrous 2012 season, one of the most disappointing in the history of college football. DAN AVILA

Steve Sarkisian became the Trojans head coach in December 2013. He was fired in the middle of the 2015 season, just 18 games into his tenure, amid controversial circumstances. DAN AVILA

In 1923, the year the Los Angeles Coliseum was built, USC played its first varsity football game there. The venue is still synonymous with the storied team in cardinal and gold. DAN AVILA

the 2001 team entered the season unranked. When USC defeated San Jose State, 21–10, in Carroll's debut, only 45,568 fans showed up at the Coliseum, a graphic illustration of the program's deep malaise.

Then came four straight losses—all by five points or less—to Kansas State, Oregon, Stanford, and Washington. The last time USC had started 1–4 was in 1958, in the short-lived Don Clark era that preceded John McKay's iconic reign.

SCOTT WOLF: I remember telling Carroll, "The last guy who started 1–4 got fired at SC." He knew he wasn't going to get fired, but he was frustrated. And people were skeptical because of the 1–4 record.

But even though they were losing, they were in those games and showing a lot of fight. They lost to Washington on a last-second field goal. Then Carroll stormed out on the field and told Rick Neuheisel something like "We're not gonna lose to you again." It was some kind of brash or arrogant comment. Carroll had a tendency after games—and sometimes before games—to say things to other coaches.

CHRIS HUSTON: When we played at Washington, I was on the field before the game, and then I had to go inside to take a piss in the locker room. Then the team came in, and I couldn't leave the locker room again until they went back out to play. So I got stuck in there for the pregame speech. Now, the later Carroll pregame speeches would be very flowery and full of New Age stuff and all that "one heartbeat" stuff. This Carroll pregame speech was laced with "fuck" and "shit" and "kick the shit out of them" and "hurt them." The line I remember the most is "I want you to hit them so hard, they will dread wanting to play you again."

He could hardly contain himself. I would compare it to some of the things you hear Jim Harbaugh say before a game. I remember thinking, *Wow, this is not the guy who's projected to the public. This is red meat, fire and brimstone.*

DARYL GROSS: We beat Arizona State, and then we lost to Notre Dame. So we started that year 2–5! I remember Mike Garrett calling me into the office. He said, "We're 2–5. What do you think now?" I said, "Mike, everybody we're losing to is in the top 25. They're beating us by a field goal. What are we worried about? This thing is going to turn around eventually."

Pete had this talk with the team after one of the losses. He said, "I'm not a negative person. I wasn't going to bring this up. But whatever you guys had from the last regime, I don't know what it is, but we gotta get over it."

After his graduation from USC, Petros Papadakis went straight into broadcasting as a radio host and sideline reporter. He has covered Trojan football ever since, primarily for Fox Sports. He is also one of the hosts of the popular *Petros and Money* radio show.

PETROS PAPADAKIS: USC fans were frustrated. Pete Carroll had spent a lot of money on Norm Chow, and Carson Palmer looked a lot like he had the year before. He was throwing interceptions, and he wasn't making great decisions. They obviously had a lot of talent, but it looked like the same old story.

NORM CHOW: People said, "Holy mackerel, they're 2–5." And it wasn't really anybody's fault. There weren't enough offensive linemen. I remember when I first got there, I went to Pete one day and I said, "Hey, where are the offensive linemen?" And we kind of chuckled about that.

There was also a lot of talk about changing quarterbacks. Pete and I had some very—what's the right word?—heated conversations if you will. After we lost at Notre Dame, Pete wanted to make a change at quarterback. I said, "Hey, you're the head coach, but I don't think we should do this. I think we should give Carson another shot."

But Pete was very ready to make the change. So the agreement was that if Carson didn't play well that next game against Arizona, there would be a change made. Then Carson did very well against Arizona. That was a very pivotal game for us and a very pivotal game in Carson Palmer's career.

It happened against a struggling 3–4 team and only raised USC's record to 3–5. Still, the 41–34 victory in Tucson on October 27, 2001, often gets cited as the turning point for the entire Pete Carroll era.

Palmer threw for two touchdowns and 249 yards, but the Trojans blew a 31–13 halftime lead and were tied 34–34 in the final two minutes. Arizona had the ball at its own 42 when cornerback Kris Richard intercepted a pass and ran it back 58 yards for the game-winning touchdown.

TIM TESSALONE: We were 2–5 and about to go 2–6. We ended up winning the next four and going to the Las Vegas Bowl. It went from "year one is a disaster" to "year one is done and we got through it. Let's move on to year two."

DARYL GROSS: We ended the regular season against UCLA at the Coliseum. We were 5–5, so if we win that game, we're eligible for a bowl game. We shut them out, 27–0. We beat the hell out of them.

With a four-game winning streak but a still-modest 6–5 record, the 2001 Trojans spent their Christmas Day playing 7–4 Utah at the Las Vegas Bowl. Both teams came in unranked, and only 22,385 fans watched USC lose a 10–6 snoozer.

Alex Holmes was a sophomore tight end who became a starter the next season. The outgoing, straightforward Holmes also became a de facto recruiter for USC. Shaun Cody, Matt Leinart, Mike Williams, Reggie Bush, LenDale White, and Dwayne Jarrett all were hosted by Holmes on their campus visits.

ALEX HOLMES: Everyone was disappointed in the season we just had. And then playing in a bowl game in Las Vegas, I don't think we were as focused as we needed to be.

I asked Holmes if that meant the players partied in Vegas.

ALEX HOLMES: Yeah, that's one way to say it. Look, I wound up playing in the Orange Bowl and the Rose Bowl. I don't even think about the Las Vegas Bowl.

NORM CHOW: Utah, at the time, was trying to make its mark, and you knew they would come in ready to play. And with our guys you could tell they were just going through the motions during the practices. We also had a rule that you don't gamble in your hotel and you don't hang out in the bars and all that stuff. So the coaches would go across the street, have some fun, and play some cards for a little bit. The night before the ball game, we went across the street, and half our team was in there doing the same thing. So I knew we were in trouble.

PETROS PAPADAKIS: It's hard to motivate a USC team to play in the Vegas Bowl. You just don't know what you're gonna get. And the truth is, we didn't have a running back that game. We had a junior college guy who was really a fullback. USC had one yard rushing in that game! The Utah guys played lights out and hit them in the mouth, and I don't think they were ready for that.

LENNY VANDERMADE: Utah won their conference, but we lost to a team we had no business losing to. So I think we were seen as just a mediocre football team, an underachieving team, because we had talent. At that moment, there was nothing that suggested to the outside world that USC was about to go on this run.

DARYL GROSS: Norm Chow was important to USC's success. And symbolically he was really important because he had a reputation. But when we lost 10–6 in the Las Vegas Bowl, Coach Carroll wasn't all that excited about our offense. And Pete was going to fix things. What he did I thought was really smart. He got his other assistants, Lane Kiffin and Steve Sarkisian, more involved in the offense. I think that was helpful to Norm. They all worked on it together, and if you look at that offensive staff, you got Norm, Lane, and Sark, and that's a pretty good recipe to score a lot of points. And that's what started to happen.

CHRIS HUSTON: There's been a lot of revisionism about the early Carroll years. And a lot of that revisionism came from Carroll. You saw him later trying to claim that he basically rebuilt the offense. Carroll said, "I turned it into the *USC* offense." But if you talk to players, they will tell you it was Chow's offense and Chow was calling the plays. I think Carroll was trying to downplay the influence Chow had on the program.

I asked Chow if the rumors were true. After the offense sputtered in the Las Vegas Bowl, did Carroll take away some of his play-calling responsibilities?

NORM CHOW: That's what seems to be going around. But it wasn't the play calling, and it wasn't Kiffin or Sark. It was more, "We gotta do some stuff. We have to get better at the run game." That's when Pete brought in Alex Gibbs, the offensive line coach for the Denver Broncos, to help us with the run game. Alex was more of a pro run game guy than I was, and Pete wanted improvement in that area. At that point in time, play calling had never come up.

Coming off the 6–6 record in Carroll's first year, the 2002 season started with the Trojans ranked No. 18 and the same lingering questions about their senior quarterback, Carson Palmer. With 39 career touchdown passes, 39 interceptions, and a 16–16 record in the games he started, Palmer seemed by definition to be average.

TIM TESSALONE: He wasn't even on the cover of our media guide. Troy Polamalu was.

CHRIS HUSTON: Carson had to kind of unlearn a lot of bad habits. The first time he was on the field with Norm Chow, Chow said, "I want to see you drop back and throw a pass." Carson said, "How many steps do you want me to take?" Chow said, "I don't care; I just want to see you throw."

Paul Hackett was a master of getting lost in the details: "If you have your feet at certain angles while you're making your seven-step drop . . ." So Hackett had Palmer and the other quarterbacks thinking more about their perfect seven-step drop than just throwing the ball into someone's hands.

ALEX HOLMES: By then our recruiting picked up with the new coaching staff, and we had more weapons on offense. We had Mike Williams come in as a freshman receiver. Justin Fargas came in at running back. Carson looked super comfortable in the offense that spring, which I don't think he ever felt before. It was his second season with Norm Chow. The offensive line had played together. We were optimistic.

DARYL GROSS: We open against Auburn. Auburn is favored. We beat them, 24–7, at the Coliseum. Then we go to Colorado, and they are favored. We beat them, 40–3. After that second game, we said, *We might be pretty good.*

Not necessarily. In the next three games, USC lost at Kansas State, beat Oregon State at home, and then lost at Washington State.

PETROS PAPADAKIS: When they lost to Washington State, they were 3–2, and that's when you heard the murmurs. I was with them that game. It was a great game, and Washington State was pretty good that year. USC lost in overtime because Carson was still making a lot of mistakes. I remember Sarkisian coming into the locker room. It was kind of a weight room for some ancillary sport at Wazoo, and I remember him punching an incline machine or something like it. He was really frustrated. He was chair-throwing frustrated.

I think they all felt like they would get fired. Garrett was crying in the locker room, and this is a grown man, Mike Garrett. But they *all* felt like that was it. They would go 6–6 again, and they would get fired, and Garrett would never be able to hire anybody ever again, and Carroll would just be another forgotten coach like Hackett was.

From that point on, they didn't lose again for quite some time. They lost at Cal in 2003, and then they didn't lose until Texas in 2005.

After the overtime loss at Washington State, a good USC offense became a great one and the Trojans won their last seven regular-season games. Palmer ended up throwing for 3,942 yards and 33 touchdowns. At Oregon he set two USC passing records with 448 yards and five touchdowns. He shredded Notre Dame for 425 yards and four TD passes in a national TV game that clinched the school's fifth Heisman Trophy and the first since Marcus Allen's back in 1981. The Trojans averaged 36 points a game while totaling 465. The last time USC had scored that many points (467) was in 1972 when John Robinson debuted as offensive coordinator and John McKay won his third national championship.

Junior tight end Alex Holmes caught 29 passes that season, the most for a Trojans' tight end in ten years. I asked Holmes, an admirer of both Carroll and Chow, how important Chow was to the offensive surge that began in 2002 and continued the next two seasons.

ALEX HOLMES: I think the argument could be made that he was the most important part. Norm's offense is not super complicated. It's really a handful of plays, but they're run out of different sets and motions and movements. That let Carson Palmer feel comfortable.

Coach Chow was also unbelievable at utilizing talent and creating mismatches. He accomplished that with misdirection and putting guys in motion. If you can motion a guy out and get a running back on a linebacker, that's a win for us. If you can motion Mike Williams and get him on a slot defender, that's a win for us. That's what we were constantly doing, and I have to give that credit to Coach Chow. Also, we're now two years in with the always-compete stuff that Coach Carroll was preaching, and every single day we're going against guys like Troy Polamalu. So by that point we were competing at a very high level at every practice.

By late November 2002, USC had won five straight since losing to Washington State and had climbed to No. 7 with two big games left in the regular season: UCLA at the Rose Bowl and Notre Dame at the Coliseum. First the Trojans dismantled the 25th-ranked Bruins, 55–21. Then they crushed the seventh-ranked Irish, 44–13, while rolling up 610 yards on offense. Meanwhile, Carroll's physical, fast-playing defense held Notre Dame to 109 total yards.

NORM CHOW: They didn't seem to play like you expected a Notre Dame team to play. They didn't play very hard or for very long either. Pete Carroll, on the other hand, always had our guys emotionally prepared to play every week.

DARYL GROSS: The year before when we played Notre Dame, we were in South Bend. I remember Pete called Marv Goux, who was still alive but getting very sick, and Pete said, "Hey, Marv, I'm walking through that tunnel right now you were telling me about." It was a close, contested game, but we lost. So Pete in his first year wasn't the answer yet as far as the problems we had with Notre Dame.

In 2002, the week before we played Notre Dame, Steve Lopes and I flew out to New Orleans and Miami to talk about possibly playing in the Sugar Bowl or the Orange Bowl. That was when the Bowl Championship Series (BCS) was starting, and you had to be ranked a certain number for certain bowls. Our pitch to the Sugar Bowl and Orange Bowl guys was "We beat UCLA and we'll beat Notre Dame, and we'll be ranked so high, you're gonna want to take us."

The Miami guy said, "Why would we bring a Pac-10 team all the way out to the Orange Bowl?" I said, "We'll bring people. You don't understand USC. They've been waiting for this for a long time." The guy said, "Well, when's the last time you beat UCLA and Notre Dame in the same season?" And USC hadn't done that since 1981!

So then we play Notre Dame in the Coliseum. We beat the hell out of them, and that just sealed the deal. We played Iowa in the Orange Bowl.

During the buildup to USC's first major bowl game since John Robinson's 1995 team won the Rose Bowl, the national media gushed over Carroll while the Los Angeles media continued to concede that its gut reaction to him had been wrong. In Carroll's second season, he had returned the program to national relevance.

On January 2, 2003, the Trojans were 10–2 and ranked No. 5 when they faced 11–1 and third-ranked Iowa at Pro Player Stadium in Miami. The teams looked evenly matched when they went inside at halftime tied, 10–10. Then the Trojans scored 21 points on their first three second-half possessions. Mike Williams caught six passes for 99 yards and one touchdown. Palmer, the game's MVP, threw for 303 yards and one touchdown. USC won decisively at the Orange Bowl, 38–17, to finish 11–2 and No. 4 in the polls.

SCOTT WOLF: USC had never really gone to a game like that. They either went to the Rose Bowl or else some crappy bowl game. Then they blew out Iowa. The next morning their hotel was packed with people. Carroll was like a little kid. He was just enjoying all of that. He actually told me later that the 49ers offered him to be their head coach right after that season and he turned them down. He had always been a lifelong 49ers fan, and he was a big Bill Walsh guy. Everyone thought if he ever got offered that job, it would be a slam dunk. But he told me the organization wasn't the same as it was when he worked there in the past. And of course USC was rolling.

CHRIS HUSTON: That was probably the most special team of the Carroll era, and that was kind of the team that everyone loved. They played a really hard schedule. They had some of the players from the Hackett era, who remembered what it felt like not to win, and they got to experience winning. Carson Palmer became a great quarterback. The USC defense became a great defense. Pete Carroll became a great coach because he had command over all the weapons at his disposal. Pretty soon it wouldn't be, *Will USC win?* It would be, *By how much?*

LENNY VANDERMADE: We beat Iowa by three touchdowns, and they came into the Orange Bowl ranked number three. At that point we thought we could beat any team in the country. And we were just getting started.

14

RETURN TO GLORY:

2003–2004

On December 11, 2002, a few weeks before the Orange Bowl victory, Norm Chow had won the Broyles Award presented annually to the nation's top assistant coach. Three days later his pupil Carson Palmer became the school's fifth Heisman winner and its first quarterback to receive the coveted award. Then, on the day before Christmas, Chow turned down a head-coaching offer from Kentucky.

"Chow said he and his wife were moved by the ovation he received Monday night during the team's annual awards banquet," Gary Klein wrote in the *Los Angeles Times*. "A capacity crowd in the ballroom at the Regent Beverly Wilshire Hotel erupted in applause and gave Chow a prolonged ovation when he was introduced." Chow told Klein, "That was enough for my wife and I to say we're not leaving. We want to be Trojans. I want to work for Pete Carroll and help win a national championship."

It had been 25 years since USC's last one, back in 1978, when John Robinson's team shared the national title with Alabama. If the 2003 Trojans were going to end the drought, they would have to do it without Palmer and several running backs who also had graduated.

LenDale White and Reggie Bush, the two widely recruited freshman tailbacks, both looked ready for the college level, but there was no clear-cut choice at quarterback. Redshirt sophomore Matt Leinart had never thrown a collegiate pass. Neither had true freshman John David Booty, the nation's top quarterback recruit, who had impressed the coaches before hurting his back during the summer. The top two other options, juniors Matt Cassel and Brandon Hance, had thrown a total of four passes between them.

NORM CHOW: That spring, there was a very heated battle to replace Carson. The obvious choice was Matt Cassel, because he was Carson's backup the year before. But there was also Brandon Hance, a transfer from Purdue. Matt Cassel was 6–4 or 6–3, and Matt Leinart's the same size. Brandon Hance was about a six-footer and more of a run-around guy, a little like Russell Wilson, who is with Pete now in Seattle.

Pete had the foresight to know that those would be the quarterbacks of the future. But we had these heated discussions because I was in Matt Leinart's corner from the get-go and Pete kind of liked Brandon Hance. We opted to go with Matt, and he started to flourish. It wasn't any mechanical thing that we did with him. He was a bright guy, and I thought he had enough arm strength. I don't know what happened in the NFL, but Matt Leinart was as bright as the day is long. He understood what we were trying to do, and that's the advantage I thought he had over the others. And then the rest is history.

LENDALE WHITE: I committed to USC not knowing who our quarterback would be. Even when I got there, I figured: *We just lost Carson Palmer. Whoever's coming up behind him, maybe seeing a Heisman winner go to work will help make him be ready. But if we* *don't really have a quarterback, we can just run the crap out of the ball this season.*

And then we went down to Auburn.

On August 30, the eighth-ranked Trojans traveled to the Deep South to open the season against the sixth-ranked Tigers. On national television, in front of a raucous crowd of 86,083, Leinart threw for 192 yards and one touchdown while managing the offense almost flawlessly. The Trojans won, 23–0, in a national statement game over the team predicted to win the SEC.

TIM TESSALONE: We came into that season thinking: *We lost the Heisman winner. Now who's going to start at quarterback?* We ended up starting this semi-scrawny lefty, and then we go and play in a hostile stadium in steamy late August weather. When we shut them out, 23–0, I think everybody kind of looked at each other and said, "This season might be kind of cool."

LENNY VANDERMADE: We understood who Auburn was. We knew all about the SEC. But it didn't matter to us. I don't want to sound arrogant, but the mood in our locker room was: *Let's get on to the next one. This is just one game closer to the national championship.*

By late September the Trojans were 3–0 and ranked No. 3 when they faced 3–2 and unranked Cal at Berkeley. It had been 28 years since the Golden Bears had defeated a top five team, but they stunned USC, 34–31, in triple overtime. The loss ended the Trojans' 11-game winning streak while also giving the public a glimpse of the burgeoning friction between Carroll and Chow.

Cal scored 34 points and rolled up 469 yards against Carroll's defense, but afterward he singled out the running backs for their lack of focus. He appeared to be criticizing Hershel Dennis, who fumbled near Cal's goal line during the first overtime. Carroll also seemed to take a swipe at Chow's offensive game plan. "We need to run more," Carroll said. "I'm trying to stay with what we're doing." USC had passed 39 times and run only 24 times. When a local reporter noted that USC had trailed, 21–7, at halftime, Carroll said that didn't matter.

CHRIS HUSTON: That was the game where the training wheels sort of came off Leinart's bike. Cal was in a resurgence under Jeff Tedford, and this was the first real challenge of Leinart's young starting career. He was very carefully managed in that first game against Auburn. They put him in a lot of safe situations. But the Cal game was the first game where he sort of had to make plays, and he had three interceptions.

SHAUN CODY: That was a tough loss. You go up to Cal, and their stadium is shitty and falling apart. It was a rainy day and it was a battle, and we lost in triple overtime. That was a painful game for us.

Sophomore Brandon Hancock started at fullback that season. After starring on the field and in the classroom at his Fresno, California, high school, he had committed to Stanford before changing his mind once he and his father met Carroll.

BRANDON HANCOCK: The triple-overtime loss to Cal was super deflating because everyone thought we would run right through the Pac-10. Then we found ourselves in a dogfight the next week at Arizona State. Leinart got knocked out in the second quarter, and we were tied at halftime 10–10. Leinart came back out for the third quarter, and we won 37–17. Then we really never looked back.

SCOTT WOLF: After Leinart got hurt in the ASU game, they put in Matt Cassel, and he struggled. They were going to start Brandon

Hance in the third quarter, and then Leinart came out of the locker room late. He told them, "I'm playing." I didn't really like Leinart when he was there. He changed a lot when he got famous. But that was one of those legend of Matt Leinart stories.

It was also a coming-out moment for the powerful freshman tailback LenDale White. In the desert heat at Sun Devil Stadium, he carried 22 times for 140 yards and two second-half touchdowns. No other true freshman in USC history had rushed for that many yards in a single game.

Ben Malcolmson covered the football program from 2003 through 2005 for the *Daily Trojan.* In 2006, two months from his graduation, he tried out for the team as a walk-on purely so he could write a story about it. When Carroll put him on the roster, a shocked Malcolmson enrolled in grad school and spent one season on the team he'd been covering. He later moved with Carroll to Seattle, where he is Carroll's personal assistant.

BEN MALCOLMSON: USC caught fire after the loss to Cal. They were just killing teams by the end of that year. So you were watching something that you could sense was special, but you didn't know how special. You had no idea they'd win 34 straight games.

On December 6, 2003, torrid USC was 10–1 and ranked No. 2 in the BCS standings when it finished the regular season with a 52–28 win over Oregon State. Logically, the Trojans expected to play for the national championship in the Sugar Bowl. In reality, the BCS computers and complex formulas dropped them to No. 3 in the final BCS standings despite the glaring fact that the coaches' and writers' polls both had USC ranked No. 1. In short, the Trojans were shafted out of the chance to win an outright national title.

Still, USC was headed to the Rose Bowl for the first time in eight years, with a chance to win a share of the national championship. While going 11–1 in the regular season, the Trojans scored a Pac-10-record 506 points and the defense allowed just 225.

In the run-up to the Rose Bowl, the national media flooded Carroll with praise for returning a storied program to its rightful stature. Earlier in his career with the Jets and Patriots, Carroll had been perceived as perhaps *too* enthusiastic for the NFL. Some of his critics called him Pom Pom Pete. Now he was described in a *New York Times* headline as A PERFECT FIT AT U.S.C. *USA Today* proclaimed, CARROLL RE-ENERGIZES TROJANS.

JOHN DAVID BOOTY: To me, his enthusiasm always rang true. Everybody always asked me, "Is he really that way?" And he was. He was optimistic every day. He was intense every day. He had energy every day. When you see the same guy, day after day, the players start to buy in because he's not a fraud. That's really how he is and what he believes. I mean, if he *didn't* feel that way, then he sure fooled us. But I saw it as sincere. That's who he was. And it was infectious.

SCOTT WOLF: There was a controversy at the end of the 2003 season because they might have to split the national title. That was the talking point during the month before the Rose Bowl. People were saying, "You guys could win the Rose Bowl and not win the national title." Because Oklahoma and LSU were playing in the Sugar Bowl.

That month was an example of how good Carroll was at keeping the team focused on what he wanted it to be focused on. In this case it was winning the Rose Bowl. The players were almost brainwashed. They said to the media whatever he told them, and it seemed like they believed it. They thought he had the answers.

On January 1, 2004, the 11–1 and top-ranked Trojans played 10–1 and fourth-ranked Michigan before 92,849 at the Rose Bowl. Leinart threw three touchdown passes and was voted MVP. The defense sacked Michigan quarterback John Navarre nine times. After the Trojans won, 28–14, the final AP poll named them the 2003 national champs. The BCS crowned LSU, which defeated Oklahoma in the Sugar Bowl, but the slighting of USC was so egregious that the BCS made major changes and there were no more split champions after that season. Ten years later, in 2014, the BCS went to the four-team playoff system that college football fans and national TV networks seem to prefer.

In the five moribund years before Carroll arrived, the Trojans had gone 31–29. Now, in 2003, USC's 12–1 record was the program's best since 1978, which was also the same year the Trojans had last won a national championship. And like McKay and Robinson before him, Carroll won it all in his third season.

SCOTT WOLF: USC had a huge trophy presentation on campus. He had clearly achieved god status there. He could do whatever he wanted. Nobody questioned him on anything. Mike Garrett couldn't tell him anything. With Garrett, everyone basically irritates him at some point. And I think he enjoys flexing his muscles with coaches. But from that point forward, if Carroll wanted something done, they would just do it. And at that point Mike Garrett looked like a genius.

Justice Winston was a sophomore offensive tackle who had started since the second game of his freshman year. He later played seven seasons in the NFL.

I asked Winston where Carroll stood at that point in his USC career.

JUSTICE WINSTON: To us, he was still the same coach. But the more you win, the more you become a public figure, especially at a school in Los Angeles. He started doing Nike commercials. He started getting more five-star recruits. Later on he foreworded that book *The Inner Game of Tennis*. I really think his time at USC made

Pete Carroll a national figure, which led to the job in Seattle, which led to him also being successful there.

In the summer of 2004, there was preseason talk of a second straight national title, which seemed a bit problematic with a rebuilt offensive line and 11 starters lost to graduation. But with another top recruiting class, Shaun Cody and Mike Patterson leading the defensive line, Leinart a Heisman candidate as a junior, and the sophomores White and Bush ready to flourish at tailback, USC entered the season ranked No. 1.

The Trojans looked sloppy on national TV in their opener but still beat unranked Virginia Tech, 24–13, thanks mostly to Bush, who caught five of Leinart's passes and turned three of them into long touchdowns. Bush later cited Chow's well-designed plays, saying, "He got me into some fortunate situations where we had mismatches." Although that might have been true, Bush's vision, speed, and dynamic cuts had made defenders look silly since he had gained nearly 300 yards in his first Pop Warner game as a nine-year-old. Roughly ten years later, at Bush's very first practice at USC, offensive line coach Pat Ruel told him to sometimes slow down in order to let his linemen make their blocks. Carroll, who *always* wanted his team to play fast, told Ruel, "You do not tell a speeding bullet to slow down."

The week after Bush's big game in the 2004 opener, it was LenDale White's turn as he rushed for three touchdowns and 123 yards in a 49–0 romp over Colorado State. There were later two narrow wins over Stanford (31–28) and Cal (23–17), but then USC pounded its last eight regular-season opponents by a composite score of 272–72. That included a 41–10 thrashing of Notre Dame, with Leinart passing for a career-best five touchdowns and 400 yards. Then, in the regular-season finale, the top-ranked Trojans fought off unranked UCLA, 29–24, for their sixth consecutive win over the Bruins.

USC, at 12–0, had just produced its first perfect regular season since 1972. Then, on December 11 in New York, Leinart followed the path of Carson Palmer (two years earlier) and won the Heisman Trophy after passing for 2,990 yards and 28 touchdowns. Bush finished finishing fifth in the balloting. Two players from Oklahoma—tailback Adrian Peterson and quarterback Jason White—came in second and third.

The stars from the Trojans and Sooners reconvened three weeks later at the Orange Bowl in the BCS title game on January 4, 2005. In addition to each team having two of the top five Heisman candidates, they were both 12–0 and had been ranked No. 1 (USC) and No. 2 (Oklahoma) for the entire season. In Carroll and Bob Stoops, both had A-list college coaches who already had won a national championship.

The oddsmakers had the Trojans as a one-and-a-half-point favorite, while *Sports Illustrated* predicted, "Sooners by a field goal." But pretty much everyone agreed on one thing: this could be one of the best college football games ever.

So why did Larry Birdine talk so much pregame trash? Oklahoma's defensive end told the media that Leinart was "a good quarterback, but he's not a Heisman Trophy–winning quarterback." Birdine also said, "I want to respect them because I have to play them, but then I watch them on tape and everything, and I realize they're an average team." And then there was this: "The Pac-10 has no speed. Our receivers are bigger than their receivers. Our D-line is faster than their D-line." USC mostly kept quiet as it seethed, while liking what it saw in Oklahoma's game films.

LENDALE WHITE: We knew Adrian Peterson was their motor, period, and we knew if we stopped AP before he ever got going, we knew that we would win because we knew our offense. We knew we would score points. That wasn't an issue.

SHAUN CODY: We were confident from a defensive perspective. You give Pete Carroll a month to study any team and break them down, he's one of the best chess players in the game. They were also supposed to be the tougher, more physical team. So it was easy for our coaches to tell a bunch of young guys, "Oklahoma says they're tougher than you." That became our war cry. We wanted to show them how physical we were on the West Coast.

NORM CHOW: Emotionally, USC was hard to beat. I remember leaving the hotel to play Oklahoma, and my wife asked me how we were gonna do. I don't know why I remember this so vividly, but I told her, "I don't know if we're good enough to beat these guys, but they better darn well be ready because Pete has our guys ready to play." That was one of his greatest strengths: his ability to get guys ready and to also keep them loosened up. You want them ready to go, but you don't want them uptight.

BRANDON HANCOCK: I blew out my knee that season, but I was there in Miami and some people were saying we would get steamrolled. They had Adrian Peterson. Their defense was tough as nails. They had seven or eight guys on defense who were going to be drafted by the NFL. Then when we came out, they were talking smack, and there was almost a fight in the tunnel. Our defensive line coach, Ed Orgeron, was riling up the troops. Then it was go time.

Oklahoma scored on its first drive, and everybody thought, *Oh, shit, this game is going to be a bloodbath.* Then we just took over. It was a physical mismatch. It wasn't even a contest. For Oklahoma, that was about as low as low could get. They got caught with their pants down.

LENDALE WHITE: By halftime that game was over. We were up 38–10. And Oklahoma just quit. You could tell when you went in at halftime and you looked over at them. It was just mind-boggling. It's the national championship. You're ranked number two in the country, and you think you're gonna come in and put up a fight. Then you're down by 28 points at halftime against a team that just put 38 up on you in the first half. So what's gonna stop them in the second half? It's like what Keith Jackson said about our team: "USC is cocky, but they have a right to be."

ALEX HOLMES: They had this defensive guy who had really been talking crap, all this really crazy stuff, the week before the game. By the end of the third quarter, he was basically asking us to chill out. That was kind of fun.

SHAUN CODY: You could see their sideline deflate. That's when we knew to step on the gas. By the end of the game, that last quarter, they kind of seemed like: *Let's get out of here and make sure no one gets hurt.*

USC demolished Oklahoma, 55–19. Leinart won MVP after throwing for 332 yards and an Orange Bowl–record five touchdowns. Steve Smith caught an Orange Bowl–record three touchdowns. LenDale White rushed for 118 yards and two touchdowns on only 15 carries, and he did it on a sprained ankle that had mostly kept him from practicing. The physical USC defense held Adrian Peterson to 82 yards on 25 carries and intercepted Jason White three times.

TIM TESSALONE: I don't think anyone said before the game: "Hey, we're gonna win 55–19." But some things we hoped for actually happened, and it was over before it started. It was funny many years later, watching the Seahawks win the Super Bowl. I turned to my wife and said early in the game, "This is the Orange Bowl all over again." It was exactly the same. Boom, and it's over.

BEN MALCOLMSON: In the locker room, they weren't really crazy and over the top while they were celebrating. That was really weird to me because they just won the national championship. And this was coming off the year before, when they split it with LSU and there was a controversy. You'd think they'd be going crazy. But they kind of knew it was going to happen. It was just that confidence they had.

NORM CHOW: I remember the party at the hotel. Pete wouldn't let anybody leave. They had a party all night long, and we had to be on the plane the next morning. I couldn't do it. I snuck out and went back to my room.

As the jubilant Trojans won their second consecutive national title, they extended their winning streak to 22 games. Furthermore, in what was forecast to be one of the best college football games of all time, they turned Oklahoma into a high school team.

ALEX HOLMES: After winning a second national championship, after two Heisman Trophy winners in a three-year span and all the players that went to the NFL, people were like, *Holy crap, this is the best program in the country.*

BRANDON HANCOCK: The national public, not just the West Coast or the Pac-10, started tipping their hats to USC and saying, "These guys are legit. This is a dynasty in the making and next season may be the best college football team ever." That's when things really changed and started to ratchet up. Pete Carroll became a larger-than-life figure. The Lakers were doing their thing, winning championships with Phil Jackson. But there was no NFL team in Los Angeles, and going for a three-peat in college football was unprecedented. So Carroll had more swagger, but he also still had that likability factor, not just with the Hollywood celebrities but with all the power players in the town—the police chief, the mayor. And of course with the fan base.

He was probably the biggest thing in Los Angeles. He drew so much water and was such a big celebrity himself, he was even more so than his quarterback who was dating Paris Hilton and his running back who was on the cusp of hanging with Kim Kardashian.

For those who don't watch *TMZ*, Hancock means Leinart-Hilton and Bush-Kardashian.

SCOTT WOLF: A lot of egos were getting out of control because they were having such great success now. They were openly talking about being the best football program of all time. They were saying, "When will we ever lose a game? Nobody's better than us." And if you look at their team—LenDale White and Bush and Leinart were all coming back for another year—it did look like a potential dynasty.

15

HOLLYWOOD'S TEAM:

2005

On January 15, 2005, eleven days after winning the MVP at the Orange Bowl, Matt Leinart announced that he would return for his senior season rather than enter that spring's NFL draft. Projected to be a top ten pick, he was perceived as a young man forsaking instant wealth for the chance to spend more time in cardinal and gold.

"I went with my heart. I went with my gut," Leinart told the crowd packed into the lobby at Heritage Hall. "I think college football and this whole atmosphere here and being with my friends and my teammates is ultimately more satisfying and will make me happier than any amount of money could make someone happy."

Carroll said after hugging Leinart, "This is a wonderful statement about college football. For those guys, really, this is the time of their lives."

BEN MALCOLMSON: That was huge. That was earth-shattering. This was a Heisman Trophy winner whose record as a starter was 25–1.

BRANDON HANCOCK: I don't know how seriously he considered leaving. I know he tested the water. He was obviously a guy who could have been drafted high. But I think he looked at the grand scheme of things and he thought, *What's the rush to get out of here?* It's always a lot harder to walk away from something when it's going so damn good. We were going for a three-peat, trying to rewrite the history books.

PETROS PAPADAKIS: Leinart was hurt! That whole Leinart thing, where he said he wants to stay and he loves SC and what a great place and they did that whole press conference and he was humping Carroll, basically? A week later he had elbow surgery and hernia surgery. How was he gonna work out for anybody in the NFL? He wasn't gonna be able to go through the draft process. He had to stay. So that was all orchestrated. Leinart stayed because he had two surgeries—not one—to recover from. Then he didn't play that entire spring. So that whole press conference was a facade. I was too close to the program at that point, and I took it very personally. They made a real drama out of it.

Garry Paskwietz is a USC graduate and the publisher of the *WeAreSC* website. He's covered the football program since 1996.

GARRY PASKWIETZ: Part of his desire to return was the chance to accomplish some rare air in college football: three national titles, two Heismans, the winning streak. There were also some arm issues that may not have allowed him to work out for NFL teams at full strength during the draft process that contributed to his decision to stay. Of course, he made the decision to stay before Pete Carroll told him that Norm Chow wouldn't be coming back as the play caller. Leinart and Chow had a uniquely good relationship, as evidenced by the results they achieved on the field.

LENDALE WHITE: Losing Chow, for Matt, was like losing the guy who got you the Heisman. You know what I mean? He's the quarterback guru.

The news of Chow's departure came in February 2005, just two months after the news that Ed Orgeron was leaving to become head coach at Mississippi. Before Chow left USC, he had interviewed that January for the top job at Stanford. But rather than making Chow college football's first Asian American head coach, the Cardinal chose an angry white guy named Walt Harris. He went 5–6 and 1–11 before Stanford fired him.

Later in January 2005, Carroll, Lane Kiffin, and Steve Sarkisian held their now-famous meeting at the Senior Bowl in Alabama. Sarkisian had been the USC quarterbacks coach from 2001 to 2003 before spending 2004 in the same job for the Oakland Raiders. Kiffin had started at USC in 2001 as the tight ends coach and then coached the wide receivers the next two seasons. In 2004, Carrol promoted Kiffin to passing game coordinator.

At the Senior Bowl meeting, Carroll, Kiffin, and Sarkisian reportedly discussed the idea of keeping Chow on the staff as assistant head coach but taking away his play-calling responsibilities. Instead the USC offense would be run jointly by the 30-year-old Kiffin and the 31-year-old Sarkisian, who Carroll planned to rehire away from the Raiders. When Chow learned of the plan for the upcoming season, he left the USC program for his first NFL job as the offensive coordinator for the Tennessee Titans.

The Trojans had recently scored 55 points in the Orange Bowl, for their 22nd straight win and second consecutive national championship. Leinart had joined Palmer as a Heisman Trophy winner, and both had been unproven before being tutored by Chow. Thus the news of his exit created national headlines and rekindled the rumors about a rift with Carroll.

LENDALE WHITE: It was a whole bunch of tension between a lot of them coaches. Kiffin and Chow, Sark and Chow, Pete and Chow, but Chow is a certain individual, man, and he stands up for what he believes in. I don't know if it was a gang-up thing. That would be speculation for sure.

We were a little bit shocked when we heard, but being on that team, you knew certain in-house things were going to happen. You heard certain ripples. And we all kind of understood that it was two alpha males in the same room, in a sense, so somebody had to go before it turned into a big blowup. I think Norm Chow did the best thing he could do, and that was just move on. But I do believe that Norm still wanted to be there with us.

GARRY PASKWIETZ: It was not Chow's choice to leave. Pete was looking to take away his play-calling duties in order to turn them over to Sarkisian/Kiffin. Norm wanted to call plays, he realized it wasn't going to happen at USC, so he left and went to the Titans. It was never his desire to coach in the NFL. He had been a college coach all his life and loved coaching young men in that age range to help develop them.

BRANDON HANCOCK: I wasn't upstairs in those meetings. But there were whispers of a power struggle or an ego struggle. When there was a lot of praise in the media, a lot of that praise was directed at Chow. Maybe that started problems. Who was getting credit for what?

It may have been partly stylistic. If you look at how they operate, they're night and day. Norm Chow is a stoic, soft-spoken older dude who's not really hip to the things that make young people tick. Coach Carroll is a fiery guy who listens to rap music and knows who the hottest actors and musicians are. There was definitely some friction. I'm not sure why. But like any business, especially when you're surrounded by a bunch of men hopped up on testosterone, there's going to be egos and they are going to clash.

CHRIS HUSTON: There's a psychological thing with Carroll. He hadn't been all that successful in the NFL, and there were all these things he wanted to try. But when he got to USC, he couldn't try all those ideas because he first and foremost had to win or else he might be fired. This was probably his final chance.

So he brought in this excellent staff. Norm Chow won a national title at BYU and had been a hugely successful offensive coach. They had Ed Orgeron. They went through this process together, and they won all these games. Then I think Carroll was like: *Now I have the power to do everything my way.* That meant Norm Chow had to go, because Carroll wanted to have his handpicked guys running the offense: Kiffin and Sarkisian.

PETROS PAPADAKIS: USC has always had head coaches who people adored, like John McKay or John Robinson, who were in their own way charismatic people. Pete is charismatic in his way. But many great assistants in football history also came from USC— from Norv Turner, to Marv Goux, to Dave Levy, to Hudson Houck, to Joe Gibbs.

The great assistants on those first Carroll staffs were Kennedy Pola, Norm Chow, Tim Davis, Ed Orgeron. They were also adult voices, alongside Carroll, that pushed his message. Now, with success, you will lose assistant coaches. But it's the way that Pete lost them and how they felt after they left and who replaced them that really tells the story. I really think Pete wanted to be the only adult voice out there. So he pumped up these two young guys: Sarkisian and Kiffin.

But USC never won a championship without Norm Chow calling the plays. And the second Pete tried to say, "Hey, Lane's gonna call plays," Norm Chow left. They had gone undefeated the previous season. But you could see the vein in Carroll's head pop out when he was asked about Norm Chow's offense at halftime of the Oklahoma championship game. He was pissed. He didn't like that. And so after that season, he told Norm he would not be calling the plays. It was because he wanted Norm out.

And then, Lane is Lane. He's an abrasive guy who rubbed a lot of people the wrong way. Carroll set up this thing where he pitted Lane against Chow so he could get Chow out of there. As for Sarkisian, he played quarterback for Chow at BYU. Then Sarkisian was coaching fucking high school baseball at his alma mater. Then Carroll paid Norm all that money to come to USC, and Norm went and dug Sark out. But Sark later let Pete push Norm right out of the program, and Sark really sold his soul during that moment. Chow was the guy who started his coaching career. But Sark let Carroll throw him under the bus. Then Sark ended up with a head-coaching job at Washington and then the head job at USC. Sark got opportunities because of staying close to Carroll, and so has Lane.

SHELLEY SMITH: Pete was handing more of the play calling to Lane, and by that point Lane and Norm didn't get along. Norm was also getting a lot of attention, and Pete might have been jealous of that, but I don't know. I think it was out of respect for Monte Kiffin as well. Everybody knows Monte and Pete were close. I think out of respect to Monte, he wanted to give Lane a break.

CHRIS HUSTON: Lane Kiffin is basically Pete Carroll's godson. Monte Kiffin is Pete Carroll's mentor. Not only his personal mentor but also his football mentor. Monte Kiffin's defense is Pete Carroll's defense. That Monte Kiffin–Pete Carroll relationship is very important because it paved the way for Lane Kiffin at USC. Pete really wanted Monte to get an NFL head-coaching job for a long time, and he did his best to help. But Monte couldn't get one, and he had always done so much for Pete Carroll. So Pete wanted to do as much for Lane as possible.

By the way, everybody loved Monte Kiffin. He was a character. He was one of those guys who'd hang out in a coffee shop until two

a.m. and talk football. Lane is more like Paul Hackett. Lane would
rather watch film and wants nothing to do with people.

I asked Chow about his relationship with Lane Kiffin.

NORM CHOW: The same as he probably had with the other
coaches. How do you put it nicely? He was a good fellow. He was
a young guy who everyone knew was Pete's guy because of Lane's
dad, and he was able to do a lot of things real early in his career that
most people don't get a chance to do. And Lane is fine. He's a good
guy. But he struggled obviously with some relationships with the
other coaches because everybody knew he was Pete's little guy.

Here's what really happened. When I took the job at USC, Pete
didn't have a lot of ties in college. He told me, "I'll let you hire who
you want to hire as far as your staff is concerned." And I didn't
really feel real strongly about, *We should hire this guy or that guy.*
But then at the end, when we needed a tight ends coach, Pete said,
"Do me a favor. Just interview this guy. We don't need to hire him."
He was Monte's son, and Monte is Pete's guy that he looks up to.
Pete said, "Just interview him to help his career along." Lane was
a quality control coach at Tampa Bay, and an interview from USC
would be a good deal. We had no intention of hiring him. Pete
didn't seem to anyway, and I didn't know the guy. So we brought
him out. And as it wore on, Pete said, "Why don't we just bring him
on because we really don't have anybody else that we feel strongly
about."

So we did. Pete obviously gave him the break of a lifetime, and
then he's been in situations where he probably didn't belong. We all
know that. Everybody in the country knows that.

I asked Chow specifically about his 2005 departure from USC.

NORM CHOW: Sark, Kiffin, and Pete met at the Senior Bowl. And
like I said earlier, Pete loves to tinker, and I guess it was not good

enough what we had done. He wanted to give those guys a little bit more responsibility. Those are his guys, he wanted to take care of them, and I'm sure they were clamoring for more responsibility as well. I don't know if you've noticed Pete's career, but he really encourages guys to move up and better themselves. I think he looks at it as a feather in his cap that his guys are moving up. And then at that point in time, the NFL came calling.

I always wanted to give the NFL maybe a shot. I didn't sit around *aspiring* to the NFL, but a couple teams called after that season. And understanding what Pete was trying to get done with Sarkisian and Kiffin, I had a chance to make some money and set my family up for retirement for the rest of our lives. USC is top shelf, but it was time to move on professionally.

I asked Chow if he felt pushed out at all.

NORM CHOW: A little bit. A little bit. But I mean, when you say "pushed out," you double your wages, you get a shot to be a coordinator in the NFL. Not a position coach, a coordinator. There's only 32 of those guys.

A lot of people say that—"you got pushed out"—but in my mind and in my family's mind, Pete forced us to—not forced us, but what's the right word? Pete encouraged us to be financially solid. So I coached three years in the NFL, got paid, and got fired. I set my family up for our retirement. So I thank Pete for that. And I loved the time I had at USC. I have two children who graduated from there. I loved the people there. The school is terrific. And so, yes, it was very difficult to leave. It was very, very difficult because of the relationships that were made.

It has never been hard to find critics of Lane Kiffin, who later would become USC's head coach for approximately three and a half stormy seasons. On the other hand, here is what two of the best offensive players of the Carroll era say:

JOHN DAVID BOOTY: I loved working with Lane Kiffin. I think he's a great offensive mind. He'd been around USC for quite some time and had a great pedigree with his father and their whole family being around football. I don't think there was really much of a drop-off, outside of experience, with Kiffin and Chow. Obviously, the terminology didn't change. Nothing really changed. The only thing that it changed is really the experience of play calling over the years that Chow had.

LENDALE WHITE: Let me be real. My first connection with that school was Lane Kiffin. He was the first guy I ever spoke to. He was the first guy to get me to believe in USC. It was Lane Kiffin coming into my high school and sitting down with me and telling me they thought that I would be a great fit. I'd seen *Boyz N the Hood* growing up, and I remembered the guy coming into the house to get Ricky. He was a recruiter from USC. There's things that you just remember when you're growing up, and I remembered that. It was Lane who got me to visit USC in the first place.

By August 2005, Chow had moved on. So had offensive line coach Tim Davis, defensive line coach Ed Orgeron, and five defensive starters who had graduated. Still, USC was ranked No. 1 in every major preseason poll.

How could it be otherwise? In the last three years, the Trojans had won 36 of their last 39 games. Their last defeat had been at Cal way back in September 2003. Since then they had won 22 games in a row and back-to-back national titles. Now the defense was young but gifted due to the relentless Carroll recruiting machine. The offense returned a healthy-again Leinart, the electric tailbacks Bush and White, the dynamic receivers Steve Smith and Dwayne Jarrett, and four of five starting linemen. As the 2005 Trojans began their pursuit of a third straight national title, some were hailing them as one of the best college football teams of all time.

LENDALE WHITE: For us, it was three-peat or nothing. Yes, we focused on every game individually. But when you look at that offense? We knew damn well if the defense played like their normal self and got off the field, our offense would kick butt. Lane Kiffin was telling us, "I'm gonna put the pedal to the floor. We're gonna try to score as many points as we possibly can." At that point we were so well oiled, I don't think anyone doubted that we were gonna win a third championship.

BRANDON HANCOCK: It was us against the world. People hate us now because we are so stinking good. Everyone is trying to find the cracks. We're under a microscope.

JUSTICE WINSTON: People were saying we were maybe the best college football team ever. At the time, we thought so, too. Looking back on it, to be perfectly honest, we were probably a little overrated. Maybe because of the media atmosphere, being in Los Angeles; that kind of hyped things up. I think we had a really good group of players. But for us to be called the best ever that early, I think was blown out of proportion.

SHELLEY SMITH: We didn't really cover them until that season. We basically ignored the year Carson Palmer won the Heisman. We, meaning *College GameDay*. We did one thing with Carson—we did a talkback—and we never did any stories on USC. USC wasn't USC yet. It took that win in the Orange Bowl, and that's when ESPN jumped on the bandwagon. Then we sent a crew, including myself, to every game, and I was at almost every practice. That's when they were just becoming the rock stars of LA.

Ken Field was Smith's Los Angeles–based producer.

KEN FIELD: Our assignment was to follow the team until they lost because they would probably do something that was pretty unprecedented by winning three straight championships. There was a ton of buzz leading up to that season. Part of it was that LA didn't have an NFL team. USC filled that void, and this was maybe the greatest three-year stretch the school had ever seen.

The Trojans were 3–0 and hadn't been tested when they received their first scare at Arizona State. Trailing at halftime, 21–3, USC charged back to win, 38–28. As the Trojans outscored the Sun Devils, 35–7, in the final two quarters, the tailback tandem dubbed Thunder (White) and Lightning (Bush) rushed for a combined 264 yards.

Two weeks later, on October 15, Hollywood celebrities and NFL dignitaries flooded into South Bend, Indiana, for the regular season's most anticipated game. The Trojans were 5–0 and ranked No. 1 and the Irish were 4–1 and No. 9. In the three previous seasons, USC had shellacked Notre Dame by a combined score of 130–37. Yet when Charlie Weis had been hired before that 2005 season, the rookie Irish coach had said at his first news conference, "I sure hope when that team from California comes to town that they're still undefeated." Now the swaggering Weis had his wish. He also had the South Bend campus primed when the Trojans arrived for a late Friday afternoon walk-through.

TIM TESSALONE: Usually at a walk-through, nobody was around. You pull in and it's kind of quiet and your team gets off the bus, and Pete would then do these really loosey-goosey walk-throughs. This time our bus pulled in, and I'll never forget it. We had heard that Notre Dame was doing their Friday night rally, but they were doing it in the stadium this time. So as we are pulling up, everybody who is going to the rally after the walk-through ends is already outside waiting. And there's thousands of people out there because Joe Montana and these others ex–Notre Dame stars were going to speak.

SHELLEY SMITH: The Notre Dame fans lined the place where the bus would come in. They had anti-USC signs, and they were getting ready to heckle the players. Pete stops the bus about 100 feet before where they would usually pull up to because he *wants* to walk through the gauntlet.

LenDale had started this tradition of rocking the bus from side to side, so now the USC bus is literally rocking. Then they all kind of strutted through this gauntlet—not hurrying through—and just basically saying, "In your face, bring it on." Then we all went inside the stadium, and I was standing outside the USC locker room. They were screaming like crazy, they were so fired up. And this was Friday.

On Saturday afternoon, with 30 million viewers watching on NBC, Irish quarterback Brady Quinn led an 87-yard touchdown drive to put his team ahead, 31–28, with 2:04 left. USC had one more chance to preserve its 27-game winning streak and its quest for a third straight national title. But with 1:32 remaining, the Trojans faced a dismal fourth and nine from their own 26-yard line.

KEN FIELD: Again, our assignment was to follow USC until they lost. I said to Shelley Smith, "This could be it. This could be the end of our run." Then Leinart hit Dwayne Jarrett with a pass down the sideline. If the Notre Dame defensive back had turned for just a moment, the ball would've probably hit him in the arm. But it was a perfect pass and it wasn't played properly by the Notre Dame guy, and it kept the drive alive.

Jarrett's stunning 61-yard catch and run—on an *audible* called by Leinart—gave USC the ball on the Irish 13. Then a few plays later, with the clock ticking down, things got crazy again.

SHELLEY SMITH: It was first and goal near the 2-yard line. Leinart runs it himself near the sideline, and he fumbles. Everybody from Notre Dame rushes on the field. Notre Dame thinks they've won the game. USC is yelling that he fumbled *out of bounds* and there should still be time on the clock. There was a big argument, and they had to chase everybody off the field.

TIM TESSALONE: From where I was standing on the other end of the field, it looked like the ball flew over the goal line and then out of the side of the end zone. Which tells me: fumble, turnover, Notre Dame ball, game over.

But the ball went out of bounds at the one. They put a few seconds on the clock.

SHELLEY SMITH: USC had no time-outs left. They're down by three. They could spike it and kick the field goal and go into overtime, or they could score a touchdown and win the game right now. They went for the touchdown.

KEN FIELD: Leinart ran it again. Then the famous Bush Push happened, and Leinart scored the winning TD. I'll never forget how quiet the Notre Dame stadium got.

As Leinart bounced off the pile of linemen on his first surge, he was spun around with his back toward the line of scrimmage. As he spun back toward the goal line, Bush shoved him in the chest and into the end zone. Technically, pushing a runner forward is illegal. In reality, it's a penalty that's never called. After USC won, 34–31, Notre Dame fans complained about the Bush Push. USC fans exulted. America talked about an amazing football game.

SHELLEY SMITH: After the Notre Dame game, USC went viral. That's when they became the biggest celebrities in all of Los Angeles.

DARYL GROSS: I had seen things changing even before that season. Number one, the attendance changed. Pete's first game we played against San Jose State, we announced we had 46,000 there, but I don't think we did. By the time we got into 2003 and 2004, the attendance had grown up to 86,000 a game. That was a good indicator.

Then everyone wanted sideline passes, whether it was Arsenio Hall or it was Will Ferrell. The sideline became packed. It was a total zoo. By the time I left to become athletic director at Syracuse, you couldn't get a seat at the USC football banquet. That stock had hit its ceiling. The question I had when I left was, "How sustainable is this?"

BEN MALCOLMSON: In 2005 it became like a circus. The 2003 season came out of nowhere. And 2004 was like this childlike joy because it was still new and exciting. Then 2005 had all this media attention. It was Hollywood football. I remember being approached by *Us Weekly,* the tabloid, to report from games. They just wanted to know what celebrities were at the games. Leinart had buddied up with Nick Lachey, who I think was still married to Jessica Simpson. But then you also had the usual suspects: Will Ferrell, Snoop Dogg, the Fonz—all those guys were around.

LENDALE WHITE: We met everyone from Spike Lee, to Snoop, to Carmelo Anthony, to Shaq, to Puff Daddy. Who else? LeBron. He was our age, but he loved us. LeBron used to check us out. I think at that point in time, everyone who loved football knew who we were. Snoop would hang out with the team. He gave us motivational speeches. Pete knew how to get his team relaxed. He'd say, "Look, Snoop's coming to practice. He's gonna run around with you guys today. Everyone have fun. Just take it easy." One day the guys from *Jackass* showed up at practice, and they were filming. It was ridiculous, man. Hollywood is exactly what people dream of and think it is, especially when you're living it and you're somebody at the time.

PETROS PAPADAKIS: They went to those BCS bowl games, and they beat the crap out of Iowa and Oklahoma. Then, in 2005, they're trying to win three straight national championships. That's when they really found out what the city of Los Angeles becomes like when USC football has success. These guys weren't hanging out at the local bars near USC. They were hanging out at the Hollywood bars with Paris Hilton and Lindsay Lohan.

SCOTT WOLF: Leinart got mad at me because I wrote about him going to the club where Paris Hilton was. It was in the *New York Post,* too, but he blamed me. He had his head up his ass. He changed a lot when he got famous. I thought he was kind of a phony. He used to want security to walk him, like, 50 feet from the lobby at Heritage Hall to where they ate their meals after practice. It was ridiculous. He was a laid-back guy his freshman year, and he kind of turned into an arrogant jerk.

I think Bush changed, too, maybe because of that season. He was kind of a normal guy, and then he went through his whole egomaniac phase. But nothing they could do was wrong as a program. They just kept winning and winning. They were infallible.

SHELLEY SMITH: There were tons of people on the sidelines just for practice. But I don't think the players paid much attention to it. They were such a loose group, and every day was so much fun. Pete had the music blaring, and the practice was so fast-paced. Pete would be bopping around throwing the football. It was fun for the team and fun for the fans, and it was the place to be. I mean, these guys were bigger than any of the Hollywood stars who showed up to see them. It was the craziest atmosphere I've ever seen in college football.

In addition to that season's Hollywood story line, there was the Reggie Bush-LenDale White narrative. The more powerful White had led USC in rushing in 2003 and 2004. The more breathtaking Bush had finished fifth in the 2004 Heisman Trophy voting. Now, in 2005, Bush was being hailed as one of the Heisman favorites, but in the month of October, he seemed frustrated by his team's inability to get the ball to him in open space. Meanwhile, White was bulling his way to 24 rushing touchdowns, the single-season record at Tailback U. Of course, they both wanted the ball.

KEN FIELDS: I consider Reggie Bush the second most exciting player I've ever seen play in person. I'd put him right behind Michael Jordan just in terms of being a thrilling athlete to watch. But yes, there was some locker room strife early that season.

I think LenDale thought he might get shoved to the side because Reggie was the flashier running back.

SHELLEY SMITH: LenDale was a very sensitive guy, and Reggie getting all that attention bothered him. We ended up doing a story on LenDale. We went to Colorado, and he was really excited that we finally did a story on him about his family. Chauncey Billups is his cousin. Chauncey was always trying to counsel him, telling him, "Don't worry about it, you'll get the ball, you'll be fine." But yeah, he was a little disgruntled that season.

BRANDON HANCOCK: I thought they did a great job of sharing the football. Obviously, everybody wants the ball more. But I think they both understood that if they were unselfish, it would benefit them too. LenDale would pound up the middle and deflate a defense. Reggie would get on the edge and slash and dash. They were Thunder and Lightning.

The only tension I saw was in training camp. LenDale took Reggie's hat and hid it from him. They almost went to blows. Reggie was like, "Yo, dude, where's my hat?" LenDale was like, "I don't know what you're talking about, man." But everyone kind of knew he was in on it. That night they had to be separated because it looked like they were going to start throwing punches at each other's faces.

CHRIS HUSTON: LenDale was one of the guys who understood that he didn't need to always practice. The Carroll practices were like death matches. Human cockfights. They would have all these incredible athletes pounding each other during the week. And Mike Williams and LenDale White quickly realized that if you want to protect your body, you don't have to go through some of these practices. So LenDale might actually have a minor injury, and he would stay out of practice for a few days. Lane Kiffin hated that. So LenDale would get into the doghouse with the coaching staff. That's why he lost his starting job, officially, in 2005. And if you look at some of those games, you'll see that he's given short shrift as far as his carries—until they really needed him. Then they'd bring him in again because whatever they were doing wasn't working.

PETROS PAPADAKIS: There's only one football, and there were a lot of stars. And Pete Carroll at this point was riding this wave of superstardom that Leinart and Bush had. They were bigger than Kobe Bryant in this town. Carroll would run them past the autograph seekers like it was a presidential speech or something. They were trying to put on a show for the recruits. That's all it was really about: winning recruits. And it worked.

But LenDale White was really the unsung hero, and he didn't like it. I remember him walking off the field after the Hawaii game. I was the media, and he was telling me, "This is BS." He was unloading about the featuring of Reggie Bush and how he didn't get the ball until the end of that game. It was only the first game, but I think he saw the writing on the wall. He knew that Kiffin was trying to win Bush the Heisman, which he did. They only turned to LenDale when they were in big trouble that season.

LenDale has always been a little bit of a loose cannon. He brought a lot of the conflict upon himself, but I didn't blame him. He was really special. He's one of the greatest college backs I've ever seen. But there was nobody in his corner in this giant promotional machine that USC had become. LenDale White was kind of the odd man out in the celebration.

I asked White if his relationship with Pete Carroll changed over time.

LENDALE WHITE: Yeah, it definitely changed. When I first got there, Pete was like a father figure. I fell in love with the guy because of who he was. The thing is, I got to see Pete before he won a national championship. Then you win another national championship, and you play for a third national championship, and things change. You see a difference in people. And everybody saw how Pete was changing. It wasn't just me, this one person.

Pete probably felt the same way about me. I think we all were changing just because of being in Hollywood and then winning all those games. Matt Leinart is becoming the most famous bachelor in the world. Todd McNair is getting more love because he is coaching Reggie. There were a lot of things changing at the time.

I asked White to describe his relationship with Bush.

LENDALE WHITE: At that time, me and Reggie had this love-love-kind-of-hate relationship. It was only a kind of hate because we both thought we should be playing more than what we were. Nobody would ever say that, and he would probably never say that, but I'm gonna be realistic. I thought I should be getting the ball 30 times a game. I wanted to win a Heisman, too. So that's probably the only thing that that ever fueled us, but the fire *was* there because of the competition. I knew how great he was, and I wanted to outdo him, and I'm sure he wanted to outdo me. We were close, though, regardless. We were always roommates on the road. Reggie was my guy. He still is my guy.

After the Fresno State game on November 19, Reggie Bush was pretty much everyone's guy. Before then his Heisman hopes were still alive, but they had dimmed after a month in which his numbers were solid but not spectacular. Then Bush produced what the *New York Times* called "the signature performance of 2005."

The top-ranked and 10–0 Trojans and the 16th-ranked and 8–1 Bulldogs met at the Coliseum. Led by its coach Pat Hill, Fresno State lived by the mantra "Anyone, Anytime, Anywhere." Now the dangerous team from the Mountain West Conference was trying to keep USC from extending its 32-game winning streak.

The Trojans trailed at halftime, 21–13, and then erupted for 28 points in the third quarter for a 41–28 lead. Fresno State kept grinding and pulled ahead, 42–41. White scored the winning touchdown with 6:12 left in the fourth quarter, and USC persevered, 50–42. It was Bush who mesmerized, though, with an array of dazzling moves and 513 all-purpose yards—the second highest total in NCAA history. The night game ended after two a.m. on the East Coast, but Bush's fabulous highlights aired again and again on ESPN and Fox.

If the Fresno State game clinched his Heisman, his performance the next week in the regular-season finale guaranteed that Bush would win the award by a landslide. As USC improved to 12–0 with a 66–19 laugher over UCLA, he ran for 260 yards and two touchdowns.

The ceremony was held on December 10 in New York. With 1,658 rushing yards, an absurd average of 8.9 yards per carry, and 218 all-purpose yards per game, Bush won easily over Texas quarterback Vince Young and Leinart. When Bush's name was called, Bush and Leinart hugged and Young shook Bush's hand. But Young's disappointment was transparent. "Right now, I feel like I let my guys down," he said afterward. "Right now, I feel like I let my family down."

The Trojans saw Young again in exactly 25 days when they

took on Texas in the Rose Bowl. USC came in 12–0 with a 34-game winning streak and the No. 1 ranking in the BCS standings. The Longhorns came in 12–0 with a 19-game winning streak and the No. 2 ranking. Texas hadn't won a national title since 1970. USC had an unprecedented third straight national AP championship on the line.

This year the usual hype would not suffice. USC versus Texas was billed as one of those Games of the Century.

16

THE UNFORGETTABLE GAME:
JANUARY 2006

USC had Reggie Bush and Matt Leinart, the back-to-back Heisman winners, and an array of offensive stars, including LenDale White, Dwayne Jarrett, and Steve Smith. But Vince Young, the Heisman finalist, was the undeniable star of the Texas Longhorns. The 6-foot-5, 235-pound dual threat passed for 2,769 yards and 26 touchdowns that season. He also led his team in rushing with 850 yards and nine touchdowns.

Although Young, Bush, and Leinart stood out, the collective offensive numbers also were hard to ignore. USC led the nation with 580 yards of total offense per game, and Texas led the nation in scoring with 51 points per game. In the run-up to the Rose Bowl, Carroll likened the teams' offensive production to "video games. There are so many explosive players on both sides, offenses that are wide open; that is rare." Said Texas coach Mack Brown, "This is a great game for college football. It's a game that every college football fan will watch."

The opponents not only held the top two spots in the BCS polls, they also had the country's two longest winning streaks: USC at 34 and Texas at 19. There was also the endless talk of a possible three-peat, which the Trojans did their best to try to deflect. "We can't worry about the possible history that's going to play in this game," Bush told reporters. "We've got to focus on this team and this team alone."

The previous year at the Orange Bowl, USC had destroyed Oklahoma, 55–19, after coming into the game favored by 1.5 points. This year the Trojans were favored by a comparatively whopping seven points, which translated in Austin into "Nobody respects us." Mack Brown did an expert job of selling that to his players, who already felt aggrieved that Bush had just crushed Young in the Heisman Trophy voting.

SCOTT WOLF: USC had some close calls. The Fresno State game. ASU was ahead of them in the second half before they ran out of gas. The Notre Dame game, obviously. USC was mortal. But at least in LA, I think everyone expected them to beat Texas.

KEN FIELD: The game was going to be on ABC/ESPN. And leading up to the game, ESPN did a lot of stories. There was one series asking how USC compared to all the great college teams of the past: Oklahoma, Nebraska, etc. I remember thinking, *Wow. They're playing Texas, which is also undefeated and has also had a pretty remarkable season. Maybe we're jumping the gun.*

JOHN DAVID BOOTY: Texas was coming off a Rose Bowl win the year before. They were used to that stadium and the whole hoopla leading to that game, which was a little different from some of the other teams we played in the past. We had several injuries on defense, so we had some guys out there who typically would not be on the field. So knowing Vince Young and his running capabilities, I think that was probably a pretty big concern of our coaching staff.

On January 4, 2006, in front of a sold-out crowd of 93,986 at the Rose Bowl and another 35.6 million who watched on ABC,

LenDale White scored on a four-yard run to give USC a 7–0 lead in the first quarter. Still ahead 7–0 in the second quarter, the Trojans seemed poised to go up 14–0 or at least 10–0 when Bush broke loose for 37 yards on a perfectly executed screen pass. But as he was about to be tackled near the Texas 15-yard line, he attempted a lateral to walk-on receiver Brad Walker, who was not ready for it. Texas recovered the fumble and the game's momentum, scoring on its next three possessions to lead 16–10 at halftime. The *New York Times* later called it "the defining play of the first half," one that "would have been considered a major mental mistake in Pop Warner."

SCOTT WOLF: Kiffin still says to this day, "I never expected Bush to lateral to a walk-on."

DARYL GROSS: I went to the game. Here's what I saw: There was a little bit of hubris from USC in terms of, *We're really good, and we're just gonna beat the hell out of Texas.* And when Reggie was running down the field and decided to pitch it to another guy running down the field, that's where I thought the hubris was. Instead of, *Let's just get the yards, let's be fundamental, let's play USC football.*

BRANDON HANCOCK: He had never done that, even in practice. You could get your ass kicked doing that in practice. So here we are on the national, stage and he uncharacteristically pitches the ball to a guy who's a backup blocking receiver. It was a huge momentum change. And that took Reggie out of the game mentally for a couple of quarters.

LENDALE WHITE: At that time, I was pissed. It was like, *What's he doing?* But looking back on it, I can never blame a guy for trying to make a play. I also take nothing away from Brad Walker. But I want people to understand this: In urban areas, when you grow up playing football, where Reggie and I grew up, you do stuff like that. And I guarantee that if that had been Dwayne Jarrett or Steve Smith, that was a lateral they would have seen coming. And they would have caught it. Man, Reggie did that in high school. Worked perfectly. We've seen Randy Moss do that same shit in a game. Again, Brad Walker was a walk-on. This young man ain't never been on that stage. Me, Reggie, Dwayne Jarrett, Steve Smith—we were all ready for that stage, but Brad Walker, as good as he was, probably just wasn't ready to make that play.

After Bush's ill-advised lateral, Carroll made his own second-quarter mistake with USC ahead, 7–3. Texas scored an 11-yard touchdown after Vince Young pitched the ball to running back Selvin Young, but Vince Young's knee was down before he made the pitch. The play would have been overturned if the officials had reviewed it, but Carroll did not call time-out, Texas quickly kicked the extra point, and the bogus touchdown stood. The Longhorns led, 9–7, and then extended that to 16–10 at halftime.

White recalls the locker room scene as "kind of strange and quiet" for the first time all season. Still, the previously sloppy Trojans came out playing precisely in the second half. With White rushing for his second and third touchdowns, USC led, 24–23, after three quarters. Then with 6:42 left in the fourth quarter, Leinart connected with Jarrett on a 22-yard touchdown pass that pushed USC's lead to 38–26.

KEN FIELD: They were up by 12 with less than seven minutes. If they stop Vince Young on the next possession and they score again, they win by 19. Think about that. The game was actually close to being a USC blowout.

With about seven minutes to go and USC winning by 12, I was thinking to myself, *They've done it. Third straight national championship. Undefeated season, 35 straight wins. What a historic moment.* That's when Vince Young started going crazy. He picked them apart in those final two drives of the fourth quarter, and USC just didn't have an answer for him. Was it Pete's fault? I don't really know. But Vince Young killed them.

With Texas hustling into its no-huddle offense, Young led the Longhorns on a 69-yard drive that he capped off himself with a 17-yard scramble for a touchdown. USC still led, 38–33, with 4:02 remaining. The Trojans had a chance to put the game away with two first downs, but after one first down, the crucial drive stalled. USC faced a fourth and two at the Texas 45-yard line with 2:19 left. Carroll faced a tough choice: punt the ball out of midfield and put the onus on his defense to stop Young or go for the first down that probably would ice the game for USC.

When Carroll elected to go for the first down, White ran up the middle without a lead blocker and the blitzing Longhorns stopped him a few inches short. Meanwhile, Bush, the Heisman Trophy winner, stood on the sideline.

JOHN DAVID BOOTY: We had the utmost confidence in our coaching staff, and they had it in us. So when that decision was made, I don't think at the time anybody was really questioning it.

DARYL GROSS: What makes Pete so good and makes him so strong are the same things that can get you beat sometimes. Live and die by the sword. So you take that risk on fourth down, and you don't get it. It's like the pass that was called in the Super Bowl. It's a calculated risk. Both of them were *calculated* risks. Very scientific. And it doesn't always work out. But when you're playing at that level and you're playing for those stakes, you have to take those kinds of risks to even get yourself into those situations.

KEN FIELD: Carroll got some grief after the game for it. Part of it was, *If you don't usually have Reggie and LenDale in at the same* *time, why not have Reggie in at least as a decoy?* Pete's argument was, "That's not the way we did it. It's not what we did during the season."

JUSTICE WINSTON: That same play had worked earlier during that game in short-yardage situations. But I think Reggie felt slighted when he wasn't on the field. He had feelings about not being on the field. Reggie Bush is such a good player, and so is LenDale White. I would have probably had both of them on the field. But I wasn't a coordinator. I was a tackle.

Norm Chow was one season removed from being the offensive coordinator at USC and one season into his tenure with the Tennessee Titans. I asked him for his thoughts on the famous fourth-and-two play.

NORM CHOW: Well, I think the obvious thing is Reggie being on the sideline. I think, obviously, you keep them both on the field, and you motion one guy out or you do something. I don't necessarily think the play call itself was all that bad. But I think Reggie should have been out there somewhere. You gotta defend Reggie, right?

SHELLEY SMITH: I don't know who made that call, but we were all like, *Where's Reggie? Why are you gonna run the same play to LenDale?* Even though LenDale had been successful running the ball, Texas absolutely knew what they were gonna do. And even talking to Matt Leinart afterward, he said he saw the linebacker's eyes and he knew they weren't gonna make it. So everybody wondered why Reggie wasn't in the game. Why wasn't your most electric player in the game when you needed him most on a play that could have won the national championship?

LENDALE WHITE: People were saying that Reggie should have been on the field with me to take one of their players out of the box. If Reggie goes in motion, somebody's gonna run with him. And we had two formations, one called "horse" and one called "pony," that we ran all year where me and Reggie were both in the game at the same time. But that was how I was thinking *after* the game. I definitely thought Reggie should have been on the field.

But as a football player, at the time? We were killing their ass all day on the same play. It's the play I just scored on in the third quarter on a fourth and one. So I was okay with the call. And I guess Pete and Lane had confidence in that play. And I had confidence that I would get it. But in the back of your mind, before you run it, you're thinking: *We're putting in our jumbo personnel, and we're about to run this play that we've been running all night. Should we go quick count? Should we go hard count to try getting them to jump offside?*

Some people tried calling out our tackle Justice Winston, and it's not Winston's fault that he whiffed it, because, again, they knew that play was coming and they shot the gap. I also feel like maybe I took the ball to the left too much, and I could've just run behind Winston and punched forward for that yard. I remember praying, *Please, somehow, some way, let me get this first down.* But I didn't get it. And then I knew it was over. Vince Young's over there dancing, and it's just like, *Oh, my God, we can't give this guy the ball back. We can't.*

Young took over still trailing, 38–33, on his own 44-yard line with 2:09 left. After he moved the Longhorns 48 yards in nine plays, it all came down to one enormous moment. Facing a fourth and five at the USC eight-yard line with 26 seconds remaining, Young took a snap from the shotgun formation, dropped back to survey his receivers, bounced to the outside, and ran down the right sideline untouched and into the end zone for a 39–38 lead. His successful two-point conversion on a run up the middle made it 41–38, Texas.

The Trojans still had 19 seconds left but lost, 41–38, when they couldn't move the ball into field goal range. But first they put themselves at a disadvantage by calling their last time-out before that final possession.

SCOTT WOLF: After Vince Young scored the go-ahead touchdown, Carroll was talking to the offense about what they would do when USC got the ball back. In the meantime, Texas is trying to decide if they're going for one or two on the extra point. They were going back and forth, and finally they decided to go for two. USC couldn't find Carroll, so Jethro Franklin, the defensive line coach, called a time-out. Texas goes for two and gets it, and they're up three. USC gets the ball back, and they end up getting all the way past midfield. They could have run one more play and tried to set up a field goal. But they didn't have the time-out left to do that.

KEN FIELD: Vince Young started going crazy, so afterward it was mostly USC's defensive decisions that were questioned. But ultimately I don't know if that defense was good enough to contain him. Young got outside again on the winning play of the game, and he walked into the end zone.

SHELLEY SMITH: Pete admitted on that last play that Frostee Rucker was in the wrong place. He was supposed to keep Vince Young off the edge. Pete didn't want to blame it all on Frostee, but he basically blamed it on Frostee. They definitely had no answer for Young, and they never adjusted to that, and that's really what beat them.

LENDALE WHITE: Vince Young is the only guy in USC history that we've never been able to stop. Usually if a guy runs all over us in the first half, the second half we adjust and we shut him down. Our coaching staff was great at making adjustments. But when we came out the second half, Vince Young was still dancing.

BRANDON HANCOCK: There was definitely some mismanagement in that game. Defensively, we didn't make a single adjustment to stop Vince Young. He got around the corner every fucking play. It didn't make any sense with the defensive talent we had. Do *something*. Put a defensive end out there and tell him to *just* contain. Bring a free hitter down from safety and tell him to seal the edge. We're all in it together, the players and coaches. But it was not our finest hour coaching and not our finest hour defensively. We did hang up 38 points on that Texas defense.

JUSTICE WINSTON: It's not a science. It's football. You can't always control things. Overall, I think Pete Carroll is a very good in-game coach. He doesn't make his decisions based on the fear of losing. Some coaches do coach through fear. They don't win as many games as Pete Carroll wins.

KEN FIELD: Leinart kept saying while they were still on the field, "We're the better team. We're the better team." He sounded like a sore loser, and he later regretted that. But I kind of understood, in the moment, on the field, right after the game. He just couldn't accept the fact that they lost.

BEN MALCOLMSON: When you walked in the locker room, you felt this weight. You felt the heaviness of their grief. *They* felt the weight of trying to win three straight championships. Whatever your connection to the team was, it was hard in that locker room. You saw people crying, people not moving. It was a really dramatic moment.

JOHN DAVID BOOTY: It felt like all the life was sucked out of us. You put so much effort into every season. And to have the expectation of possibly winning a third championship, it was a tough pill to swallow. It was also Matt's last game and the last game for the entire senior class.

But at the same time, we felt over the last few years we had accomplished so much. It wasn't like that was our one time there and we didn't win it. We'd already won two straight championships before that. We'd won 34 games in a row. So yeah, it was a sad moment. But it was a proud one, too, especially for the senior class that was leaving.

In Leinart's final game, he completed 29 of 40 passes for 365 yards and one touchdown. Bush had 82 yards rushing and 95 yards in receptions. White rushed for 124 yards and three touchdowns and would have been named MVP if not for Young's masterpiece. He completed 30 of 40 passes for 267 yards, ran 19 times for 200 yards and three touchdowns, broke what seemed like 50 USC tackles, and won Rose Bowl MVP for the second straight year. Carroll said after the game that he had never coached against such a dominant player.

But Carroll and his Trojans had been ridiculously dominant, too. It was January 4, 2006. The last time they had lost was September 27, 2003, in the triple-overtime defeat at Cal.

LENDALE WHITE: I knew Texas was solid going into that game. I just felt that my team was better, and I knew that we would win. Nobody made me think otherwise until Vince Young scored that last touchdown.

Yeah, people were crying. Crying and sad. I think everybody was crying because we knew that it was over. It was over in the sense that Matt is gone. We know Reggie's outta there. And so at that point in time, when I walked into that locker room, my whole USC career flashed in front of me. I walked in and saw Pete Carroll, and he was one of the greatest coaches I ever could imagine playing for. I saw Lane Kiffin, this little pretty boy who turned into an amazing offensive coordinator. And then it starts sinking in that my guy Reggie is really leaving me. Yeah, I want the ball all the damn time, but I still want Reggie on the team. I don't want him to leave. Hell, no. There's no more Thunder and Lightning. It will just be Thunder. I was thinking all those things, and then I ended up leaving USC, too. Hindsight is twenty-twenty. They tell you that all the time. But at some point you realize you probably did make a mistake by leaving.

17

DYNASTY, INTERRUPTED:

2006–2008

One year earlier, after winning the Heisman Trophy as a junior, Leinart returned to play for USC his senior season. Bush now faced the same decision—remain in school or turn pro after winning the Heisman—and most predicted that he would leave for the NFL.

White's immediate future was harder to forecast. Despite splitting carries with Bush the last three seasons, he scored a USC-record 57 touchdowns while gaining 3,159 yards. White's Rose Bowl rushing performance (124 yards and three touchdowns) had established him as an early Heisman contender if he stayed in college. The guessing game ended on January 10, 2007, when he said he would enter that April's NFL draft.

LENDALE WHITE: I was struggling with that decision. I was struggling with it for sure. Then I had a conversation with somebody on our coaching staff. This is two, three days after the Rose Bowl. I'm not gonna name no names, but he basically said, "Either you stay or you don't. Either way, we're gonna keep marching on."

I didn't need to hear that at that time. Regardless of what anybody says, some of our egos need to be stroked a little bit. When they wanted Matt to come back, it wasn't, "Are you coming or are you going?" It was, "Matt, come back, make sure you come back." Then they put a big-ass party on for Matt. They knew Reggie was leaving, but they still tried to get him to come back. And when I was thinking about what I should do, I was told, "Do whatever you think you need to do, but we will march on."

I asked White who the USC coach was.

LENDALE WHITE: Again, I'm not gonna name names. I've put myself out there in the past with naming names, and it never comes back good. But if people are smart, they're smart and they'll figure it out. I'll just say that I knew the players wanted me back, but some people in the organization didn't want me. And that plays with your head a little bit. So it was like, *You already made the decision for me.*

One day after White's announcement, Bush said he also would skip his senior season. White and Bush leaving one year early was a bad development for USC fans, but the next major story would be exponentially worse. On April 23, one week before the NFL draft, Yahoo Sports reported that Bush's family had lived rent-free in a home near San Diego owned by Michael Michaels. Michaels and his partner, Lloyd Lake, ran a fledgling marketing firm that wanted to represent Bush when he turned pro. As more allegations surfaced, Yahoo reported that Bush and his family received nearly $300,000 in cash and goods from marketing agents during his career at USC.

In their quest to represent Bush when he joined the NFL, Lake and Michaels made an offer to Bush to *own* part of their firm. But first they had to sign him. Their stiffest competition was the controversial Mike Ornstein, a former NFL marketing executive who had pleaded guilty to defrauding the league before reemerging years later with his own sports marketing company in Southern California. Bush had gone to work for Ornstein as a summer intern before the 2005 season, reportedly with permission from USC. When Bush later signed a marketing deal with Ornstein—who also was alleged to have given Bush and his family improper gifts—Lake and Michaels felt spurned and blew the whistle to Yahoo.

It is hardly a secret that sports agents and marketers and their middlemen can figure out how to ingratiate themselves with college athletes. But did the particular culture of the Carroll years increase the potential for NCAA violations?

CHRIS HUSTON: I don't think there was any more messing around with agents than at other schools. But by 2003 the program was getting big, and just like any big program, you're going to have some goofballs doing stuff. But at USC the practices were open. Anybody could go—the agents, the media. We had reporters roaming around, ambushing players after they had dinner on campus. So USC could have done more to protect the program. But it was all going so good, why mess with it?

But the real hubris of Carroll was when he allowed Bush to intern for that agent, Mike Ornstein. To let your most high-profile football player go intern for a guy who has been a convicted felon? Bush didn't need to intern anywhere. I mean, is he really going there to be an intern or is he going there to make connections? If that doesn't happen, a lot of the stuff that happened at USC doesn't happen.

By then it was also part of Carroll's hubris that he thought he could talk his way out of every situation. And Mike Garrett wasn't giving him much oversight. It was basically: *Go do your thing; we're winning.*

In April 2006, after Yahoo's first blockbuster story, the NCAA began its investigation of the USC football program. The probe dragged on for four years with the chronic threat of heavy

sanctions if the NCAA determined that USC coaches or administrators either knew or should have known about the improper benefits allegedly received by Bush and his family. The investigation
cast an edgy four-year pall over the program even as USC mostly
continued its winning ways.

The 2006 Trojans also had some on-the-field issues. They somehow had to replace their trio of stars—Bush, Leinart, and White—
and eight other players drafted by the NFL from the powerful 2005
team. The starting quarterback job finally belonged to John David
Booty, the junior who had arrived in 2003 as the nation's top recruit at his position. As a heralded freshman, Booty had competed
with the unproven sophomore Leinart before Booty hurt his back
in the preseason. In 2004, Leinart won the Hesiman and Booty
redshirted after hurting his elbow. In 2005, when Leinart decided
to stay for one more year, Booty threw just 42 passes during mop-
up duty.

In late August 2006, as Booty prepared for his first career start,
USC entered the season ranked No. 6. I asked him if the painful
loss to Texas ever came up that week.

JOHN DAVID BOOTY: No. I don't recall it *ever* being referenced.
That's Pete Carroll, though. We're moving full steam ahead. It was a
whole new group, whole new season, all new opponents. We were
not going backward to discuss the Texas game.

SCOTT WOLF: After they lost the BCS title game to Texas, school
was out of session the next day because it was early January. But
Carroll was in his office later that night. It was weird to me that he
didn't even take one day to relax at home. He was already back in
Heritage Hall, working there late at night, looking ahead.

By late October 2006, the 6–0 Trojans were ranked No. 3, but to
some the ranking seemed bloated. USC had lost starting fullback
Brandon Hancock to a serious injury, Bush and White were gone,

and the running game had suffered. In their last three victories, all over unranked Pac-10 teams, the Trojans had won each time by seven points or less. Then Oregon State stunned sixth-ranked USC, 33–31, in Corvallis. The Beavers came in unranked, but that was just part of it. It was USC's first conference loss since the one at Cal in September 2003, which had been 27 Pac-10 games ago.

After dropping from No. 3 to No. 9, the Trojans won four in a row, including an impressive 44–24 victory over sixth-ranked Notre Dame on November 25 at the Coliseum. Now back up to 10–1 and No. 2, USC would play in its third straight BCS championship game if it handled 6–5 and unranked UCLA in the regular-season finale. Instead the Trojans lost a 13–9 shocker, their first defeat to the Bruins in eight years.

GARRY PASKWIETZ: I think the biggest thing was the lack of offensive output for the Trojans, which was squarely on the shoulders of Lane Kiffin. It wasn't even a very good defense for the Bruins. They just put together the plan that worked for them, and USC never made the right adjustments.

After scoring nine points in the first half—on a touchdown by the offense and a safety by the defense—the Trojans couldn't score, and the crowd in Pasadena sniffed an upset. Booty threw an interception on the last USC drive when a UCLA linebacker tipped a pass and then caught it himself. In the *Los Angeles Times* the next morning, columnist Bill Plaschke took him apart.

"The rush rattled him, the pressure rocked him and, in the end, the game was bigger than he was," Plaschke wrote. He also put a vote in for Mark Sanchez, the promising freshman backup quarterback. "Booty is a great guy, a stand-up guy," wrote Plaschke. "But for the Trojans to take this one-game leap back to the national championship game next season, he may not be the right guy. Mark Sanchez, anyone?"

One month later at the Rose Bowl, on the same field where he struggled against UCLA, Booty led the 10–2 and eighth-ranked Trojans to a 32–18 upset over 11–1 and third-ranked Michigan. The score was 3–3 at halftime as USC attempted to establish the run. Then Kiffin called for Booty to throw on 27 of the next 29 plays. Four of those passes went for touchdowns, two of them to Dwayne Jarrett, who also had 11 receptions for 205 yards. For the game, Booty completed 27 of 45 for 391 yards.

It wasn't the BCS national title game the Trojans expected to play in before their stunning loss to UCLA. Still, for the embattled Kiffin and Booty, there was some redemption in beating a solid Michigan team by two touchdowns in the Rose Bowl.

"I'm big enough to take the heat," Kiffin said afterward. "I still prepared for Michigan the same way. Still watched film."

Booty said, "I don't listen or mind what anybody says. I don't pay attention."

I asked him if that was really true.

JOHN DAVID BOOTY: I remember hearing things that season, but I never read it. I've met Bill Plaschke. I've talked to him many times. That's what those guys do, and that's how they make their money. I have no problem with it.

In his first year as a starter, Booty had passed for 3,347 yards and 29 touchdowns. As the next season approached in 2007, the senior quarterback was one of the primary reasons both *Sports Illustrated* and the AP media poll ranked the Trojans No. 1. There was also preseason talk of Booty perhaps winning USC's seventh Heisman Trophy.

Booty's offensive coordinator was gone, though. Kiffin had been hired away by Raiders owner Al Davis, who had long-standing USC ties after coaching the linemen there in the late 1950s. As an owner he had drafted Marcus Allen and Todd Marinovich. Now Davis made the 31-year-old Kiffin the NFL's youngest head coach since 1946. But that was only after the position was turned down by the USC quarterbacks coach, Steve Sarskisian. He was 33.

Yogi Roth was even younger. The 26-year-old had spent the last two years as a USC video assistant and was now in his second year as an assistant with the quarterbacks. He became close with Carroll, and they later coauthored the motivational book *Win Forever.* Roth is now a college football analyst for the Pac-12 Network.

YOGI ROTH: That was an interesting time. Anybody that was leaving USC was getting catapulted to other jobs, from Ed Orgeron to Nick Holt. Then here comes Al Davis. And Steve Sarkisian goes up there to interview for the head-coaching job at 33. Lane goes up there, too, and interviews to be Sark's offensive coordinator. Who knows if Lane would have taken it? But he goes up there to see what it's about, and everyone's kind of excited to be around Al Davis.

Suddenly Sark gets the job offer. He goes and talks to Pete, and he decides he doesn't want to leave. Sark came into his office, and it was already scrolling at the bottom of ESPN: "Steve Sarkisian turns down the head job with the Oakland Raiders to remain at USC." Sark looked at me in his office and he said, "I'll bet they go after Lane." And within 48 hours of Sark turning it down, Lane Kiffin was a head coach in the National Football League. It was an amazing time to be around the USC program and to see the power of what Pete had created.

As Kiffin struggled in the NFL—finishing 4–12 with a shaky roster while clashing immediately with the volatile Davis—Sarkisian moved up to offensive coordinator at USC. In addition to Booty, the 2007 offense featured what *Sports Illustrated* called the "mob at tailback," including Chauncey Washington, Allen Bradford, C. J. Gable, and freshman Joe McKnight, the supposed second coming of Reggie Bush. On defense, Brian Cushing, Rey

Maualuga, and Keith Rivers were perhaps the best linebacker unit in the country.

The Trojans were 4–0 when they hosted Stanford and its new coach Jim Harbaugh, who had irked Carroll back in March by telling a reporter that Carroll would leave USC after that season. Harbaugh made that brazen statement three months after arriving in Palo Alto from the University of San Diego, where receivers coach John Morton had been a Harbaugh assistant. With Morton now in his first year on the USC coaching staff, the media asked Harbaugh if Morton was his source on Carroll's alleged departure.

He said Morton was not. But Harbaugh being Harbaugh, he also did not recant. "I've heard it from multiple people secondhand, from people that have talked to people on the SC staff," he said.

Harbaugh's apparent attempt to undermine Carroll's recruiting brought this brusque denial from Carroll: "If he's going to make statements like that, he ought to get his information right. And if he has any questions about it, he should call me."

And just that quickly, the Pac-10 became even more interesting.

When they met on the field on October 6 in Los Angeles, the 4–0 Trojans had dropped to No. 2 after a sloppy 27–24 victory over unranked Washington. But the 1–3 Cardinal had just lost, 41–3, to Arizona State. Plus, it had gone 1–11 in 2006. Plus, it was starting a backup quarterback who had thrown three collegiate passes. Plus, USC had won 35 straight games at the Coliseum.

Harbaugh pulled a Lou Holtz after the oddsmakers favored USC by 41 points. He said with a straight face, "There is no question in my mind that USC is the best team in the country and may be the best team in the history of college football."

Stanford won, 24–23, beginning its sudden rise as a West Coast power, loosening USC's choke hold on the Pac-10, and stoking a quarrel between Carroll and Harbaugh that they later carried with them into the NFL in Seattle and San Francisco.

Marc Tyler was a freshman tailback from Oaks Christian, a

powerful private high school program in Westlake, California. The son of UCLA and NFL star Wendell Tyler, he had 8,000 all-purpose yards and 123 touchdowns during his prolific high school career. Then Tyler broke his tibia and fibula in a playoff game his senior year. His USC career began in 2007 with Tyler redshirting while rehabilitating his severe injury.

MARC TYLER: Stanford wasn't good yet, and they had a backup quarterback playing that day. We thought it was an automatic win. I remember the game-winning play when their guy caught the pass in the back of the end zone. You could just feel the air taken out of the Coliseum.

Carroll probably thought Harbaugh was arrogant. Harbaugh probably thought the same thing about Carroll. Carroll never said anything to us, but you could tell when we played Stanford, there was some extra feeling that week. But I think they also had a great amount of respect for each other.

Respect, and perhaps some other feelings, too. That season a writer for *Los Angeles* magazine hung out with Carroll for a lengthy profile and jokingly complained that Carroll told him all the good stuff off the record. In one off-the-record comment, Carroll called another coach both an "asshole" and a "fucking asshole." There were some Angelenos who swore Carroll was referring to the new provocateur in the Pac-10.

Sophomore quarterback Mitch Mustain sat out that season under NCAA transfer rules. In 2005, *USA Today, Parade* magazine, and Gatorade had all selected him as the country's best high school player. As a true freshman at Arkansas in 2006, he went 8–0 in the games he started. But his head coach, Houston Nutt, clashed with his offensive coordinator, Guz Malzahn, who had coached Mustain in high school. When Malzahn left Arkansas after the 2006 season, Mustain sorted through his suitors and chose USC.

MITCH MUSTAIN: When I left Arkansas, Stanford was calling my house. Every time I was gone for some reason, so my mom was picking up. They called three or four times, and then my mom would tell me, "Stanford's calling. Do you wanna talk to them?" I said, "No, I don't wanna talk to them."

Harbaugh had just arrived there, and Stanford was still at the bottom at that point. Then in 2007 we were supposed to kill them, and they beat us with a backup quarterback. That was the turning point for Jim Harbaugh's Stanford teams.

Pete Carroll seemed to have some personal grudges, and he wasn't afraid to take it to the other guy a little bit. He seemed to hate Stanford, and nobody really hates Stanford, I guess, except Cal. But I honestly think that both Carroll and Harbaugh became different people during games. Carroll was very laid back in the meeting rooms. He was sharp and focused, but he was chill. The competitor in him came out during games. Same as a player, you know? They put on a helmet and some eye black, and they turn into a raging machine. Harbaugh's that way, too. I've seen interviews with him where he seems very calm. You get him on the field, it's like he wants to fight somebody.

USC's 24–23 loss to 41-point underdog Stanford was one of college football's biggest upsets ever. Because it came after the two major upsets the previous season—against unranked Oregon State and unranked UCLA—Carroll's critics murmured that he might be losing his touch. But most of the shade got thrown at Booty, who had four interceptions in the second half.

JOHN DAVID BOOTY: I broke my right hand against Stanford in the first quarter. I threw a crossing route to Patrick Turner and got hit as I came down on a defender's helmet. I didn't have the control, the accuracy that I normally would. At the time, I felt I still gave us the best chance to win and I could do the things I needed to do.

Then it turned out my finger was completely smashed. There was a lot of bruising, and the doctor thought he saw some fractures inside the inner part of my hand.

GARRY PASKWIETZ: The decision by Carroll to stick with Booty, who had an injured throwing hand, instead of going to a more than capable backup in Sanchez was questionable. The Cardinal was also using a reserve QB who had barely played. It was the first glimpse that Harbaugh was going to be a serious adversary to Carroll.

Sanchez started his first college game the next week against unranked Arizona. USC came in as a 21-point favorite and trailed, 13–10, before rallying in the fourth quarter to win, 20–13. Sanchez passed for only 130 yards with two interceptions but made some big plays down the stretch. Bill Plaschke wrote in the *Los Angeles Times:* "Sanchez will be fun to watch, he is clearly the quarterback future of this program, and he should remain the starter even when John David Booty returns from his injury."

I asked Booty if it felt as if he was in the middle of a quarterback controversy.

JOHN DAVID BOOTY: No. I don't think there ever really was one. I'd been the only one that ever started. Mark played really well the next week against Notre Dame. Notre Dame was absolutely awful at that point. I'm not taking anything away from Mark. He played outstanding. We play Oregon the next week, a much better team, and we get beat.

You know how it goes, man. I had some passes that I sailed against Stanford, and I'd say 100 percent because of my hand. But there was kind of a knee-jerk reaction because we were such favorites. Obviously, the quarterback is the first one everybody turns on, and it goes with the territory. But I don't think there was a doubt among the players that it was still my team. And the second I was healthy and ready to go, I was right back in and getting all the reps with the first team. Nothing had changed.

In the loss to Oregon in late October, the Trojans had come in ranked No. 9 against the fifth-ranked Ducks, the first time USC had been the underdog since Leinart's first career start 58 games ago in the 2003 opener at Auburn. After Oregon won, 24–17, in Eugene, the *New York Times*'s Pete Thamel wrote, "The game may signify the end of an era of dominance in the Pacific-10 Conference for the Trojans."

Booty returned the next week, and 6–2 USC won its last four regular-season games, sending it to its third straight Rose Bowl and sixth consecutive BCS bowl game. On January 1, 2008, the 10–2 Trojans came in ranked No. 6 against 9–3 and 13th-ranked Illinois. Playing a team with three losses in a game with no bearing on the national title after being ranked No. 1 in most preseason polls could have been depressing, but USC looked frisky in a 49–17 rout.

Booty's three touchdown passes against Illinois and his four in the victory against Michigan the year before gave him a Rose Bowl–record seven. As he walked off the field, he was 20–3 as a starter and 9–0 against teams that were ranked. His 55 career touchdown passes in two years as a starter were the fourth highest ever at USC.

Bill Plaschke wrote a nice column in the *Los Angeles Times,* giving the underrated Booty his due. "I even called for Mark Sanchez to replace him this season after he suffered a broken finger against Stanford," wrote Plaschke. "A brilliant opinion. After Booty's return from that injury, the Trojans went 5–0 and outscored opponents, 165–68."

I asked Booty if the Rose Bowl felt bittersweet: playing well again in a postseason victory but knowing he'd no longer wear the cardinal and gold.

JOHN DAVID BOOTY: Yeah. I hated it. I had such a great time at USC and wish it could have lasted 20 years. But I'd seen all the guys come and go before me, and you kind of prepare yourself for it a little bit. What was more frustrating for me is the fact that we didn't win a national championship. I felt like I'd let the university down and my teammates down by not winning the big one, even though the Rose Bowl was our goal every year and we'd won it back to back. Still, to not even have a chance to play in that big game, that was more bittersweet for me than, hey, this is my last game at USC.

In 2008, with Sanchez at quarterback, a still-deep rotation at tailback, and perhaps the fastest defense of the Carroll era, the Trojans entered the season ranked No. 3. They moved up to No. 1 after crushing Virginia, 52–7, and fifth-ranked Ohio State, 35–3. Then they flew up to unranked Oregon State for a Thursday night game on ESPN. By then Carroll's Pac-10 record was 49–9 in the previous seven seasons, but one of those rare losses had been two years before in Corvallis against another unranked Oregon State team.

It happened again at a raucous Reser Stadium. USC arrived as 25-point favorites and left as 27–21 losers. The Trojans even trailed, 21–0, at halftime, thanks partly to two costly personal fouls called against junior nose tackle Averell Spicer. If you look up his name on the official site of USC Trojan athletics, you will read: "Spicer started the first 3 games (Virginia, Ohio State and Oregon State) of 2008 at nose tackle, then served as a backup there the rest of his junior season." It's a polite way of saying Spicer got benched.

The Oregon State upset dropped the Trojans to No. 9 and perhaps derailed their quest to win their first national title since 2004. Yes, it was only late September, but the Pac-10 was having a weak regular season, and it would be difficult for the Trojans to make up ground playing against schools the BCS computers did not respect.

MITCH MUSTAIN: That Oregon State game really broke our backs a few months later. And I think it's maybe the maddest I've ever seen Pete Carroll at a player. His rage at Averell Spicer was remarkable because Pete Carroll is the most engaging guy. He's so light on his feet and charismatic. But he can also be one of the most terrifying people when he's mad. I thought he was gonna run Averell Spicer out of there.

I remember Carroll once getting after Chris Galippo in a scrimmage. Galippo got an interception and did a front flip into the end zone, and Carroll—please excuse my language—"motherfucked" him from one end of the meeting room to the other the next day. You could hear a pin drop. The guy is full of passion. The guy is engaged. And sometimes that goes both ways. He can get you fired up when he's in a good mood, but the guy can flip the switch and just be breathing fire.

The Trojans showed some gusto of their own by shaking off the Oregon State loss and winning their last nine regular-season games. That included a redemptive 45–23 win over Stanford, with Carroll and Harbaugh mostly playing nice with each other. That would change in 2009 with their famous "what's your deal?" postgame exchange.

After pounding the Cardinal in November 2008, USC dismantled Notre Dame, 38–3, making Carroll 7–1 against the Irish and 4–0 against Charlie Weis. The last time Notre Dame had been even competitive in the rivalry was when USC had won, 34–31, in 2005. Two weeks after that loss and only seven games into Weis's tenure, he received a fat new ten-year contract. Weis later became a financial cautionary tale when he went 16–21 in his last three seasons and Notre Dame fired him in 2009. Between then and 2015, the Irish paid Weis an estimated $19 million in buyout money.

In 2008, USC again fell short of the BCS national title game and all because of the loss at Oregon State. Instead the 11–1 and fifth-ranked Trojans went to their fourth straight Rose Bowl, where they embarrassed 11–1 and sixth-ranked Penn State by storming to a 31–7 halftime lead. It was 38–14 early in the fourth quarter before Joe Paterno's team showed any fight in a 38–24 defeat. The Trojans stayed on point with the media afterward—yes, we were happy to play in the Rose Bowl—but the 2008 season still would be remembered as a near miss.

BEN MALCOLMSON: We had such high expectations. Sanchez was coming in as the starter and he had a lot of promise, and we had a lot of other players coming back. Then we lost on Thursday night at Oregon State. We never lost again after that. We were 12–1, won the Rose Bowl, finished number two in the country in the AP. That was such an admirable feat, but at the time it felt crummy because we lost game three in the regular season.

At the Rose Bowl, Sanchez passed for four touchdowns and a career-high 413 yards. Then he climbed the USC band's famous ladder as the chanting fans implored him to return for "ONE MORE YEAR!" Unbeknownst to the crowd and his own head coach, Sanchez had just played his last college game.

Carroll was 5–2 in the postseason, including three straight Rose Bowl wins after the epic Rose Bowl loss to Texas. He had won two national championships and seven straight Pac-10 titles while posting an overall 88–15 (85.4 percent) record in his eight seasons. As the Trojans celebrated in the Rose Bowl postgame locker room, it's unlikely anyone knew that Carroll's ninth season would be such a pivotal one.

18

CARROLL'S FAREWELL SEASON:

2009

In January 2009, shortly after the 38–24 Rose Bowl victory, Steve Sarkisian said his good-byes at USC. In December, the 34-year-old offensive coordinator had accepted the head-coaching job at Washington, where the Huskies were coming off an 0–12 season. He had worked at USC since 2001 except for a few brief stints at San Diego State and with the Oakland Raiders. Sarkisian was never a head coach, though. If he hoped to return someday and replace his mentor Pete Carroll, the Washington job could be an important stepping-stone.

Mark Sanchez departed next. On January 14, the junior quarterback said he would skip his senior season to enter the NFL draft. It was not an obvious move since he had started in college for only one full year and a total of 16 games. Furthermore, with his gambler's mentality, Sanchez had been inconsistent before throwing for 413 yards and four touchdowns at the Rose Bowl. Still, he and Georgia's Matthew Stafford were projected as the draft's two leading quarterback prospects.

Sanchez spoke first during a news conference in a meeting

room at Heritage Hall. "It is with a heavy heart that I say good-bye to this university," he said, fighting back tears. "But I can't tell you how excited I am for this dream to come true."

When Carroll began to weigh in, it could not have been more awkward.

"The facts are so strong against this decision," said Carroll, who did not sit next to Sanchez. "After analyzing all the information, the truth is there, he should have stayed another year. He lost out on a chance to fully prepare himself. The facts are there's a 62 percent failure rate for underclassmen quarterbacks."

Carroll also said he talked about Sanchez with several NFL teams and "they all think he should stay in school. But that doesn't mean they're not going to pick him. They just know he would be a better product for the league if he took another year to prepare for it."

Carroll impatiently took a handful of questions from the media. Then, as Sanchez prepared to take questions, Carroll acknowledged him halfheartedly before leaving the room.

GARRY PASKWIETZ: I think Pete had a feeling his time at USC might be coming to an end sometime soon, and he badly wanted to leave on a high note after a few years where things had slid a little. If Sanchez stays, that team legitimately has a chance to compete for a national title. But the outlook is a little different if he is gone, and Pete knew it.

PETROS PAPADAKIS: Matt Barkley was going to be a true freshman that season. I think Pete was so angry when Sanchez left because he made a deal with Barkley when he recruited him that Barkley would be the guy after Sanchez graduated. So Pete lost his mind at the press conference because he knew that he'd have to start Barkley no matter what. That's how you got Matt Barkley starting at USC as a true freshman.

Carroll and Sanchez said later they were still on good terms. At the time, however, Carroll took a beating from the Los Angeles media. Michael Lev wrote in the *Orange County Register*: "Carroll openly criticized Sanchez" at the news conference and "didn't hide his disdain for Sanchez's decision." Bill Plaschke wrote in the *Los Angeles Times* that Carroll "publicly treated him like a traitor."

As for the suddenly scrambled quarterback situation, the top candidates were Barkley, the true freshman who had starred at Mater Dei, the same high school that produced Leinart; Aaron Corp, a mobile redshirt freshman who had been the No. 3 man in 2008; and Mitch Mustain, who had thrown just 16 passes as Sanchez's backup.

MITCH MUSTAIN: Steve Sarkisian left. Then Mark Sanchez. So that was a freaking whirlwind. And I still hear people talk about how pissed off Carroll was when Mark left. For a guy that was very diplomatic, Carroll kind of showed his stripes a little bit.

We were all in the building that day. It was like ice in the building. Everybody's going, *Holy crap. What is going on here?* And Mark wears his emotions on his sleeve. You can see everything on his face, and you could tell he was incredibly uncomfortable. He kind of looked like a beat kid, you know? Like he just let his dad down.

By the eventful 2009 season, there was also increasing tension between Pete Carroll and athletic director Mike Garrett.

CHRIS HUSTON: The relationship had been fine because Garrett was hands-off when Carroll had all that success. Then the relationship started to fray. I don't think it was this terrible situation. But because of the NCAA investigation, Garrett may have had to become more hands-on. I think Garrett was meddling a bit more, and Carroll may have chafed a bit under that.

SHELLEY SMITH: Garrett started trying to take credit by saying he had hired Pete when nobody wanted Pete. Garrett would also come in the locker room, and I think it really irritated Pete. Then when Garrett started coming in the locker room and he wanted to address the team, Pete was like, *What are you doing?* Then it became adversarial at a point because Garrett was starting to say, *Why don't you run this and that?* He was suggesting plays. I don't think Pete felt any pressure from that, but he felt like Garrett was invading his space. You could tell that was happening more as time went on.

SCOTT WOLF: One time Garrett chewed out a defensive player named Lawrence Jackson so bad that Carroll told him to apologize to Jackson afterward. Garrett refused.

MITCH MUSTAIN: Oh, jeez. Pete Carroll and Mike Garrett is like throwing a book of matches on a crate of TNT. I think it was one of the most volatile relationships you'll ever see in a professional setting.

Mike Garrett's one of those guys who does not hold back anything. If he thinks it, he says it. I've heard him say stuff to players that you just think, *Oh, my God, if somebody heard that, the NCAA would be in here, the media would be in here. He would just get roasted.* But Mike Garrett was just one of those guys: You either love him or hate him. He was always extremely good to me. I don't know why.

So I've seen both sides of that relationship. I remember the yelling matches between them. Carroll would be late for our team meeting, and you could literally hear them yelling at each other in Garrett's office or in Carroll's office. I don't know the content of it. I think they just disagreed on everything by then.

GARRY PASKWIETZ: It was a very good mutual relationship at the beginning. Mike Garrett needed a winner, and Pete Carroll needed a chance. But as Pete got more and more success, he began to wield more and more power within the athletic department, and that was tough for Mike because he liked being in control. Mike knew that if he did anything that was perceived as pushing Pete back to the NFL, USC fans would hold that against him, and he was probably right.

PETROS PAPADAKIS: Carroll had taken control of everything in the program, and Garrett had lost his power. Carroll was such a big star that Garrett became very ancillary. Carroll was just so much more charismatic that Garrett, who really didn't like publicly speaking.

But Pete didn't endear himself as much as you might think to the alumni base and the big donors. Pete was cultivating his relationships with restaurateurs and Hollywood actors. He was going outside USC, into the Los Angeles community, and cultivating relationships with people like the Leiwekes, which ended up helping him get that NFL job in Seattle.

With Garrett's history of being especially tough on USC running backs, I asked tailback Marc Tyler about Garrett and also the Garrett-Carroll relationship.

MARC TYLER: Mike Garrett *loved* Joe McKnight. Joe could never get in trouble for anything. But Garrett used to cuss at a lot of other guys. He would call the guys who got in trouble up to his office. He called a few of the black guys the N word: *I should stop recruiting you N words.*

He used that word with me. I spoke to my mother and father about it. My mom's sister's husband actually played at USC, and he didn't like Garrett. So my family didn't like him too much going into it. But my dad took it in stride. He said, "Just handle your business and stay out of his way. Don't let him affect you."

If you missed a class at USC, you could get a point. I think I had over ten points, so he wanted to talk to me. So that part was my fault. But the way he talked to you wasn't the right way you should talk to a student athlete.

I never saw any conflict between Mike Garrett and Coach Carroll. But I could see how it could happen. I could see Garrett wanting to be in the limelight of everything and Coach Carroll not liking that. I could see Garrett doing a Jerry Jones type of thing.

By the summer of 2009, the threat of NCAA sanctions only added to the pressure inside Heritage Hall. The Reggie Bush investigation had stretched into its third full year. Furthermore, the NCAA had started investigating the USC basketball program and its former star guard O. J. Mayo. In 2008, one of Mayo's ex-confidants told ESPN's *Outside the Lines* that an NBA agent had funneled cash and gifts to Mayo at USC through his adviser Rodney Guillory. That name was all too familiar to USC insiders. Back in 2000, Guillory had helped get the basketball program in trouble when the NCAA suspended a player for allegedly accepting free airplane tickets provided by Guillory. When Guillory showed up on campus several years later—this time saying Mayo wanted to play there—USC went forward with his recruitment. That risky business backfired when the NCAA launched its Mayo probe in 2008. In 2009, the NCAA combined the Bush and Mayo cases into one investigation of the athletic department.

On the football field, the 2009 Trojans attempted to maintain the towering standards of the eight-year Carroll era, which included the last seven seasons of 11 wins or more.

BEN MALCOLMSON: Sanchez leaving early caught people off guard. Barkley obviously had a lot of talent, but playing an 18-year-old quarterback on a major college football team is pretty hard. I also think the Pac-10 had caught up to USC in a sense. Teams had figured out ways to strike USC's weaknesses.

MARC TYLER: You could feel the environment was different than in the past. A lot of guys were playing for themselves. They were looking forward to leaving after the season and going to the NFL, so they didn't want to get hurt. We didn't have the same swag or the same mind-set.

At a certain point, the coaches checked out, too. It seemed like they knew they didn't have the talent they previously had. It seemed like they were looking ahead to getting a new class and building back up again. Or maybe Coach Carroll knew that he was leaving. Maybe he was looking elsewhere.

MITCH MUSTAIN: I think Carroll and his coaches were burned out. It showed in his demeanor. It showed in the guys he recruited leading up to that season. If you look at those last two recruiting classes, there were guys who had no business being at USC. They were getting busted for drugs; they were light drug infractions, but it was affecting the program. By 2009, we had a lot of cowboys on the team.

It didn't help USC when its junior center and best offensive lineman, Kristofer O'Dowd, dislocated his kneecap in fall camp and never fully recovered until the next season. As a sophomore in 2008, O'Dowd made first-team All-Pac-10. Before his injury in 2009, he was on *Playboy*'s preseason All-American team.

KRISTOFER O'DOWD: I felt like our team in 2009 had a sense of complacency. Not to point fingers at a certain group of players or coaching staff. It just felt a little lost.

The season began with the Trojans ranked No. 4, a nod to the program's prolonged success and the previous 12–1 season and Rose Bowl win over Penn State. Still, with Sanchez gone, Barkley was the first true freshman to start at quarterback in USC history.

After two victories—56–3 at home against San Jose State and 18–15 at eighth-ranked Ohio State—third-ranked USC went north to play Steve Sarkisian's 1–1 Huskies. As mentor and protégé met for the first time, Washington had lost its last ten conference games and hadn't beaten the Trojans since Carroll's first season in 2001. But for the fourth straight year an unranked Pac-10 team upset a highly ranked USC team.

MITCH MUSTAIN: Barkley had injured his shoulder the week before. They made Aaron Corp the starter, and he just fell apart. I didn't play at all. They talked about putting Matt back in, so that was kind of a weird contentious moment with Carroll and I. I didn't really say much, but I certainly felt that I could've played better than Corp did at Washington.

By that time, I think Carroll had lost his edge. My main example would be that Washington game. On the Tuesday before, we had a bad practice. Carroll called us in, I think, on Wednesday. He was always Mr. Cool in the media. He was Mr. Cool in our meetings. Then all of a sudden you could tell he was rattled. He referenced Steve Sarkisian by name no fewer than probably ten times in this eight- to ten-minute talk. You could tell he was afraid of losing to Steve Sarkisian. Not to Washington. To Steve Sarkisian. That was a very demoralizing moment. That's when some players said, *What the hell is going on? Why is he so worried?*

Then we lost against a terrible football team. They were terrible, and we were like ghosts on their field. Looking back on it, that Washington game was the end of that season. And maybe the end of the run at USC.

The Trojans arrived in Seattle favored by 17 points. But after blowing an early 10–0 lead, committing eight penalties, and going 0 for 10 on third down, they lost, 16–13, to the scrappier Huskies on a short field goal with three seconds left. "It's unbelievable,"

Sarkisian said. "It's a great moment for our program and hopefully sends a message of where we're headed."

Back in Los Angeles that Monday, the headline in the *Daily Trojan* read CARROLL IS RESPONSIBLE FOR THE LATEST LETDOWN. When the school paper calls out the powerful football coach, the climate on campus has changed.

The Trojans dropped nine spots to No. 12. Then they easily defeated Washington State and Cal before beating Notre Dame, 34–27, in South Bend. Still, the seven-point victory felt somewhat hollow. The 25th-ranked Irish were mediocre—they would finish 6–6, and Charlie Weis would be fired—and it was the first close score since the 34–31 game in 2005. Since then USC had owned Notre Dame, 38–3, 38–0, and 44–24.

On October 31, the Trojans were 6–1 and ranked No. 4 when they faced 6–1 and tenth-ranked Oregon on national television. Although it was cold and foggy in Eugene, Chip Kelly's offense looked fluid in a 47–20 Halloween blowout.

More alarms went off in USC nation. The 47 points was the most the Ducks had ever scored against the Trojans, and the 27-point deficit was the largest of the Carroll era. Before that his worst loss had been by 11 points to Notre Dame in his first season. That statistic shows how remarkably proficient Carroll was, but right now the focus was elsewhere. Carroll had made his name as a defensive expert, and the Ducks rolled up 613 total yards.

MITCH MUSTAIN: Their players were so quick and their tempo was so quick. They were so much better than us that night. And I think it was the first time our team realized it, to be honest.

KRISTOFER O'DOWD: I've never won in the state of Oregon. I don't know if it's the air, the water, the atmosphere, but things never really fell in place for USC when we went up there.

After a shaky 14–9 win at unranked Arizona State, USC met Stanford at the Coliseum after having split their last two encounters. The 7–3 Trojans were ranked No. 11. The Cardinal were 6–3 and ranked 25th but had just shocked Oregon, 51–42, the previous week.

Stanford won, 55–21, as running back Toby Gerhart shredded USC for 178 yards and three touchdowns. The controversy started midway through the fourth quarter when Harbaugh called for a two-point conversion with a 48–21 lead. Harbaugh reportedly told a surprised Gerhart on the sideline, "I want to put 50 on these motherfuckers."

The two-point conversion failed, but Stanford scored again a few minutes later for the 55–21 final. Carroll said to Harbaugh as they met for the postgame handshake, "What's your deal? You all right?" Harbaugh said, "Yeah, I'm good. What's your deal?"

Their testy exchange went viral, but the real story was Stanford's resounding win at the Coliseum. USC had *never* allowed 55 points in one game.

GARRY PASKWIETZ: What Harbaugh did with Toby Gerhart at the Coliseum in 2009 changed things. I didn't think you could do that to a Pete Carroll defense, and my guess is Pete didn't either. I'm also guessing a lot of conference coaches appreciated what Harbaugh did after the way Carroll had run roughshod over the conference in previous years.

PETROS PAPADAKIS: I'd never seen USC absolutely pounded to death physically on its own football field, especially during the Pete Carroll era. You just didn't see it, you know? But Stanford must have run Power a hundred times, Toby Gerhart just right up their ass, and it was ugly. And Harbaugh was trying to prove a point obviously. He probably went for two on that conversion because he couldn't go for three.

From then on Harbaugh and Carroll hated each other, and their programs were also headed in different directions. That game was the end for Pete. Some people even said that Harbaugh ran him out of the Pac-10. Even today, Stanford's never as physically gifted as USC, but they have a game plan they stick with, every guy knows his role, and they go out and execute it. Meanwhile, if USC's not playing on the same page, they can be beaten by Stanford. Jim Harbaugh started all that in this very exciting rivalry with Pete Carroll. That's over now, kind of sadly.

On November 14, the 55–21 defeat to Stanford dropped USC to 7–3 overall and a hard-to-believe 4–3 in the Pac-10. I asked O'Dowd if he had any inkling then that Carroll was on his way out.

KRISTOFER O'DOWD: Yeah. There, of course, is talk, and you get inside information. I'd say that late October would be a defining time where I personally felt that he might leave. It was just a really strange season overall because it felt like the transition to the end of a dynasty. Then, of course, you know that the sanctions might come down and also that Coach Carroll has been getting all these offers year after year to coach these NFL teams and get a ridiculous salary. So I think it's safe to say that a lot of us believed this would be his last year.

GARRY PASKWIETZ: Things had gotten a little loose at that point under Pete, with assistant coaches that weren't at the same level as where they were earlier in his tenure, and some players like Joe McKnight who wanted to be a Trojan star more than they wanted to put in the work needed to get there.

So it felt like there was a little more of a possibility this time. One of the things that Pete had always talked about when the team was at its peak was, "How long can we keep this fire burning?" And by that time the fire had dimmed a bit. He was either going to have to dig in his heels at SC or choose that time to make a move back to the NFL.

On November 28 at the Coliseum, in Carroll's final game against UCLA, the Trojans won, 28–7, with most of the excitement coming in the last 54 seconds. USC had the ball at midfield with a 21–7 lead. In contrast to Harbaugh, Carroll instructed Barkley to take a knee twice and let the clock run out. After Barkley knelt the first time, though, Bruins coach Rick Neuheisel called a time-out, probably to irritate Carroll. On the next play Barkley threw deep to Damian Williams for a 48-yard "screw you too" touchdown pass that nearly resulted in a postgame brawl.

The 20th-ranked Trojans ended the regular season in Los Angeles with a 20–17 defeat to unranked Arizona. USC had now lost three of its last five games, including two at the Coliseum, where it had lost only twice in the previous seven years. At 8–4 overall and 5–4 in the Pac-10, there would be no eighth straight BCS bowl game or fifth consecutive Rose Bowl. Instead the Trojans would play in the Emerald Bowl, their first lower-tier postseason berth since the Las Vegas Bowl in 2001.

Two weeks before the December 26 game in San Francisco, Garrett appeared on the popular *Petros and Money* radio show hosted by Papadakis and Matt Smith. "I was very dismayed by our whole season," said Garrett. "I don't think we had one good game. I think we sloppily won some and sloppily lost four, and it was not a picture-perfect kind of season."

Garrett's comments reverberated across Los Angeles. He honestly didn't think eight-win USC played one good game? Or was he kicking Carroll when he was down? "Mike can say whatever he wants," Carroll responded. "He's the athletic director. He calls it like he sees it, which he pretty much is always going to do."

Although it felt like much longer, it had been only three months since USC had entered the 2009 season ranked No. 4. Now the 8–4 and unranked Trojans defeated 8–4 and unranked Boston College, 24–13, in the largely ignored Emerald Bowl. Barkley ended his true freshman season by passing for two touchdowns and running for a third. After USC improved to 9–4, junior linebacker Chris Galippo told reporters, "There's nothing like winning the last game of the year. It's going to be a long, fun off-season."

He was right about the long part.

Sixteen days later, on January 11, 2010, Carroll announced his resignation at USC to become head coach of the Seattle Seahawks. The Seahawks made room for Carroll by firing Jim Mora after one season. Though his team went 5–11, Mora said he was "extremely shocked" when Seattle dismissed him a few days before hiring Carroll. One year later, Mora became head coach at UCLA.

The Seahawks were owned by Paul Allen, the billionaire co-founder of Microsoft, and operated by CEO Tod Leiweke, the younger brother of Tim Leiweke, the president and CEO of the powerful Anschutz Entertainment Group (AEG) headquartered in Los Angeles. Seattle reportedly gave Carroll a five-year deal worth $7 million per season, about $2 million more than USC had paid him.

"It wasn't about money, it wasn't about tangible issues. It was about the challenge," Carroll said at his farewell news conference in Heritage Hall. "I thought I'd be here forever. The emotional part is ongoing. It should hurt. My body is in shock. I haven't slept in days."

The recipients of the news also experienced a wide range of emotions. One of them was Malcolmson, the former reporter for the *Daily Trojan* who worked at USC after his graduation as a personal assistant to Carroll.

BEN MALCOLMSON: It was definitely a gut punch. I thought he would be the John Wooden of college football and stay at USC forever. You don't think anything that good is going to change. It was hard to take at first.

MARC TYLER: I was definitely mad because when players transfer, coaches get mad, or when players want to leave early for the NFL, coaches get mad. So for him to leave, we were kind of upset because he recruited us. At the same time, for me, it was a new opportunity to have a new coach and a new staff and get a fresh look again when I was finally healthy. So I was kind of in between.

KRISTOFER O'DOWD: To be honest, I felt a little bit abandoned. When you have a leader and a father figure and he just kind of jumps ship, it was really hard to bear.

He called us into a team meeting. He laid out the situation and why he was taking this opportunity. I couldn't even look at him because of how I felt. I was a part of the Trojan community, and I believed in being a Trojan—everything that he had taught me. And then the mentor himself leaves.

At the meeting, he invited all the players to come up and say good-bye and any last things. A lot of players went up to his office to congratulate him, but I didn't do that. I didn't say good-bye and wish him luck. I just had no inclination to go up there.

MITCH MUSTAIN: They brought us into a team meeting. I forget who briefed us first, but they briefed us. Then Carroll came in, and it was a pretty cold reception. We were all in shock. I remember some guys being angry and feeling betrayed. I personally had a sense of relief, followed by a mild sense of fear for the program: *Who the hell are we gonna bring in?* At that point I hadn't even considered Lane Kiffin. I was thinking, *Maybe they're bringing Sark back.*

Carroll had not become a hot NFL commodity overnight. When he announced his exit after a glorious nine-year run at USC, he knew there would be questions about the timing. Carroll emphasized that his decision had nothing to do with the possible NCAA sanctions hanging over the program. "Not in any way," he said.

"Because I know where we stand. It's just a process we have to go through. We know we've fought hard to do right."

Five months after Carroll left USC, the NCAA crippled the football program with severe penalties primarily related to the improper benefits given to Reggie Bush and his family by marketing agents. "I am absolutely shocked and disappointed at the findings of the NCAA," Carroll said on a video posted on YouTube. "I never ever thought it would come to this."

Still, the monumental news raised the question, again, even more resoundingly: Did Carroll know USC would be sanctioned before he left for Seattle?

BEN MALCOLMSON: No. To have control of an NFL team like that and to have the total backing of the owner, you couldn't ask for a better situation. He's the ultimate competitor, and when you give someone like that a chance to prove himself at another level, you can't turn that down. It was just too good an offer not to take.

YOGI ROTH: He'd been in the NFL at every level. That's how he grew up as a coach for the most part. I just don't think he believed he could ever go back and do it the way he wanted to. Until he got the call from Tod Leiweke, he didn't expect it to happen. But when it did, it was everything he knew he needed to succeed at the highest level. I think SC fans respect that now. I think they understand that what he did for that program and for that university was really unique.

TIM TESSALONE: Going into Pete's last season at SC, we were coming off a 12–1 year and a Rose Bowl win over Joe Paterno. And I think Pete was already being courted by some NFL teams. So that discussion was starting to happen before Seattle.

I remember we were in a car in Miami once talking about the NFL. He said he loved being at SC and he had already done the NFL.

But if the team was right and the control aspect was right, he would consider going back to the NFL. How can you fault him for doing that? It made a heck of a lot of sense for him to do that. Nothing lasts forever. I do understand the perception that people have. But I will never be convinced that was the case.

CHRIS HUSTON: I don't necessarily think he was beating the NCAA posse. That may have been part of it. But he'd always been interested in going back to prove he could win a Super Bowl. He had conquered the college world, and I think he was bored with it. He also went 9–4. I think he realized this was as good a time as any to leave because if you don't win ten or 11 the next year, people will say you've lost it.

SHELLEY SMITH: I honestly don't think he knew it was about to come down. I think they presented him with an amazing offer up in Seattle. Paul Allen is a great salesman. The facilities up there are unbelievable. The idea that he could get away from Mike Garrett, I think, was extremely attractive. There was also the money.

So my sense was that it was too good of an offer to refuse, coupled with the way Garrett was hovering. Plus, he took the whole strength-coaching staff with him; he took several of his assistant coaches. It was a way for them to get out of the whole college football recruiting world mess. Maybe that's wishful thinking because I really like Pete, but I just don't think he would cut and run. I don't think that's in him.

MARC TYLER: He had to know something about the sanctions. But I also feel he left because he didn't think he could be as successful as in the past. He saw the other teams in the Pac-10 catching up to him. They were gaining on us because they brought in better head coaches. Jim Harbaugh at Stanford. Chip Kelly at Oregon. Arizona had Mike Stoops.

But I do think he knew about the sanctions. I think the NCAA came down so hard on us because Mike Garrett was being so arrogant about it. Pete Carroll had to have known that it was going to be bad.

LENDALE WHITE: That man knew when I was having a party at my dorm room, before it happened. So we have to be realistic about the timing. It's one thing to get the sanctions and then be like, *I've decided to step down because it's the proper thing to do.* But to me, it's just so weird that a few months before this stuff gets handed down, you go to Seattle after you've been offered so many jobs. And you take half the staff with you, and it's like USC at Seattle. It was just weird, man.

KRISTOFER O'DOWD: Undoubtedly he left because of the sanctions. Undoubtedly. He had plenty of opportunities to leave the years prior, and he never did. And especially with a resource like Todd McNair in your coaching room giving you updates on the NCAA and what's going on? With Todd McNair being an integral part of that investigation and the NCAA being who they are? He definitely left because he had the sanctions coming down.

In the moment, like I said, I wasn't happy about it. I couldn't believe he was leaving. I couldn't believe he was turning his back on us, especially the seniors. But now that I look at it from just a logical standpoint—and knowing what we went through after the sanctions came down—I don't blame him for leaving. I would have done the same thing as a head coach.

MITCH MUSTAIN: I think Carroll knows a lot more than he ever let on. I've seen interviews since where they ask him, and I just don't buy it. And of course he's not gonna say it, and I don't expect him to say it, but I think 100 percent he knew they were coming. He's an extremely savvy person. I think Carroll's the kind of guy that has his own little intelligence network. And I say that in the best way possible. Why not? I think he had ways of knowing, of gathering stuff, even if it wasn't public knowledge.

But I *don't* think he left USC because he knew. And I don't blame him for leaving. I think he made the right move. Pete Carroll holds grudges. He does not forget. I think there was always a sense in his ego that no matter how well he did at USC, he would always be remembered for his failure with the Jets and the Patriots. I don't think he ever felt he would live that down. He could win ten college championships, and people would still be saying, "Yeah, but he can't coach in the NFL." I don't think he could live with himself if he didn't challenge that.

We were also on the decline at USC. We were done. He knew it. I don't think our players knew it as much, but he certainly did. Now he gets a chance to go to an ownership that gives 100 percent deference to him. What's not to jump at? I think Pete Carroll built himself for that moment. I think he stayed awake at night thinking about that moment, and it came knocking. So 2009 was a really pivotal season for the USC football program. That was the season we fell. Then Carroll leaves. Then there are sanctions.

PETROS PAPADAKIS: Carroll had created this big relationship with the president of AEG, Tim Leiweke, whose brother was running the Seahawks at the time. So I think it was probably, *Hey, bro, I can get you Pete Carroll.* Once the offer comes in, Pete's about Pete. Not that that's a terrible thing. But Pete's got no trouble leaving anybody in the dust.

I think he was always looking for a job in the NFL that was suitable to him. I think San Francisco was his dream job. He wanted a coastal team. He once had a secret meeting with Wayne Huizenga in Costa Rica or something weird like that to talk about the Miami job. He wants to be on the water so he can ride his beach cruiser, and he wants to have control. He looked into it with the Chargers; he looked into it with Miami.

He flirted with all those teams throughout his career at SC, but it finally came to fruition with Seattle. Of course it took a coup, and they had to catapult Jim Mora out of town. Mora was in Seattle only for a year. They didn't give him a chance to build anything. They basically said, "We got a better guy. You gotta go." And Mora, I don't think he's happy still. That was a pretty bad deal. It was kind of a midnight stabbing.

Carroll finally got what he wanted, and he left. I know the timing looked bad, but I don't think he left because he knew the sanctions were coming down. I think once the sanctions *came* down, he would have been fired just like Mike Garrett. I don't know of any coach in America that could've survived those sanctions. I mean, if anybody could, I guess it would've been Pete, but I still don't see it.

19

NCAA VERSUS USC:

2010

How do you replace Elvis once he leaves the building?

In his nine seasons at USC, Pete Carroll went 16–2 against Notre Dame and UCLA. He won seven Pac-10 titles and six out of seven BCS bowl games. He won national championships in 2003 and 2004 and nearly won a third straight in 2005. He went 91–19 overall, winning more consistently (.836) than anyone at USC since John McKay.

On January 12, 2010, the Trojans replaced Carroll with the controversial Lane Kiffin. Kiffin had worked under Carroll at USC from 2001 to 2006. Then he left for the NFL and went 5–15 as head coach of the Oakland Raiders before Al Davis fired him four games into the 2008 season. By 2009 Kiffin was head coach at the University of Tennessee, where he went 7–6 in his one season and was cited for six secondary NCAA violations. The NCAA later determined that he and his team had committed a total of 12 secondary violations, all of them connected to recruiting.

The hiring decision by USC athletic director Mike Garrett struck some people as bold and others as shocking. Kiffin was 34.

His combined NFL and college head-coaching record was 12–21. He already had been rebuked by the NCAA and now would take over a USC program under a major NCAA investigation.

TIM TESSALONE: Lane had been here in the glory years of Pete and was a key factor in that. He's an incredible recruiter. People will say what they will about Lane. It's kind of amazing that he's the most hated coach in sports, I think. People have a perception of him that is jaded from previous stops. I think the media has done a great job of kind of perpetuating that. And some of it is self-inflicted, obviously. It's not important to Lane to be well liked. There's also his age. To have that kind of success and make that kind of money at his age sets people off. The reality of Lane—and I think I know him very well—is that he's a good guy. He's not this ogre who is so vilified.

GARRY PASKWIETZ: Mike Garrett had a good relationship with Lane's father, Monte Kiffin, from when Monte would time spend time at USC while Lane was an assistant. Pete Carroll considered Monte his coaching mentor. After Carroll left, Garrett and Monte talked about having Monte, Lane, and Ed Orgeron come to USC as a package deal. Garrett thought Lane had a bright offensive mind, the thought of Monte running the defense sounded good in theory, and the chance to bring the beloved Coach O back to USC was huge.

But Ben Malcolmson says the players had a different head coach in mind. After working at USC as Carroll's personal assistant, Malcolmson recently had said yes when offered the same position with the Seahawks.

BEN MALCOLMSON: I didn't move up to Seattle right away. It took me a couple weeks, so I stayed working at USC. It was just a really weird time. There was still the aftershock of losing Pete Carroll. And then there was no head coach for about the first 48 hours. The media was starting to point to Sark. Then a lot of the players rallied together and wanted to share who they wanted. They went up to the athletic director's office and told him, "We want Sark." So the players are pushing for Sark, and then Kiffin comes out of nowhere. That was out of left field, for sure.

KRISTOFER O'DOWD: I know that myself and other players were surprised that he ended up getting the position. I think a big part of it was Mike Garrett knowing he would be leaving USC soon and knowing that Pat Haden would replace him. I think Carroll and Garrett both knew the NCAA sanctions were coming. And after Carroll left, Garrett knew he would be leaving next. So I think hiring Kiffin was a ploy to set up Pat Haden with a head coach that he doesn't want.

That is just my opinion. But it makes perfect sense to me. I think there was some spite behind that hire. That was a Garrett hire when Garrett knew he wouldn't be here.

PETROS PAPADAKIS: It boggles my mind that they made that decision. But I think because Lane's dad was gonna come and Ed Orgeron was gonna come, that kind of softened the blow, and it sort of made people feel like: *Things aren't going to change. Here's Pete's disciples coming back.*

But obviously it wasn't the same. Kiffin and Sark were the two guys Pete chose to give credit to and control their careers, and to a certain degree he might still be doing that. But there was never any good reason to celebrate those guys other than that's what Pete told us. I'm sure they both can teach offense. But I don't think Kiffin or Sark ever proved themselves worthy of such a big job as USC head coach.

SHELLEY SMITH: When they hired Lane Kiffin, Garrett told him he had to hire Norm Chow along with Lane's dad and Ed Orgeron.

Norm wouldn't do it. He didn't want to work for Lane, and Lane didn't want to have him on staff either. But that was one of the conditions that Garrett set down.

Kiffin just really wanted to get back to USC. I think he hated it in Tennessee. His relationship with Matt Barkley was also big. Nobody would say that Barkley was consulted, but I wouldn't have been surprised. It was Kiffin who recruited him as a 13-year-old. And Barkley was standing right there when Kiffin walked in the door at USC. There was a lot of anger at Tennessee when Kiffin left so abruptly. There were death threats and almost riots outside their house in Knoxville. Then Kiffin and his wife and their three little kids walk in at USC, and Barkley is the first one to shake his hand. I think it was a huge relief to Kiffin just to get back around friendly people.

MARC TYLER: I kind of liked it when they hired him. As a player, you didn't want the whole way we did things to change: Competition Tuesday and No Turnovers Wednesday and all that stuff we did with Pete Carroll. Kiffin was there for all that.

But then Kiffin and Coach O were over the top. It was like they were trying too hard to be tough and disciplined and yell at people. It almost seemed kind of fake.

MITCH MUSTAIN: When Kiffin first came in, we were all contrasting him with Carroll. Carroll's this great motivator. And then you get Kiffin, who I think is a brilliant offensive football mind. But I don't think he's built to be a head coach. I remember thinking: *This guy is like Debbie Downer in every meeting.*

And you also had Coach Orgeron back. So you had this huge dynamic shift where we went from Pete Carroll being the life of the group and also the head coach. Now our head coach is kind of an Eeyore. And Coach Orgeron's cracking the whip. He's just beating people down and scaring people into this and that.

Then the real fun started. They ran the shit out of us that spring.

They ran us until we were about to die. But I will say this to his credit: In 2009 we had some Lone Rangers in the program, just troublemakers out to do their own thing. Kiffin came in and he said it explicitly: "There's some of you that don't belong here, and we're going to run you until you leave." And for however many weeks, he ran the crap out of us, and it worked. We lost at least three or four guys that should have been gone.

KRISTOFER O'DOWD: A lot of the rah-rah, a lot of the juice, came from Ed Orgeron. They would condition us four days a week that spring, and it was pretty brutal. They wanted to weed out some guys so they could make some more scholarship room.

If it wasn't fun for the players, it wasn't unusual, either. New college coaching staffs commonly trim the herd so they can give scholarships to other players they hope will be improvements. Furthermore, at USC, every football scholarship was about to become even more precious. Finally, after a four-year investigation, the NCAA sanctions struck.

On June 10, 2010, the NCAA determined that football's Reggie Bush and basketball's O. J. Mayo violated rules by accepting improper benefits. By then USC had imposed its own sanctions against the basketball program: the loss of two scholarships, a one-year postseason ban, and the forfeiture of the 21 wins from the season Mayo played there.

USC never sanctioned its football program, though. The university chose to fight those allegations. Then the NCAA chose to cripple the football program with some of the most severe penalties in college sports history.

The Trojans received a two-year bowl ban, the loss of 30 scholarships over three years, and 14 victories vacated from the 2004 and 2005 seasons. The NCAA spread the blame around but took special aim at running backs coach Todd McNair, alleging that he knew marketing agent Lloyd Lake and "knew or should have known" about the benefits lavished on Bush and his family. McNair soon lost his job at USC and then sued the NCAA for defamation.

The NCAA's 67-page report made no similar "he-knew-or-should-have-known" charge against Carroll. But it said he developed a program "in which student-athletes could feel entitled to special treatment." The report reprimanded Garrett for making a lackluster effort to investigate the allegations and placed the entire athletic department on four years of probation. The NCAA also cited the school's administration for "lack of institutional control."

GARRY PASKWIETZ: You knew sanctions were coming, but these penalties were arguably the stiffest since the SMU death penalty. Yes, there were some infractions, so some kind of penalty was warranted, but it was hard to imagine what actually got handed down.

I thought it was an overreach by the NCAA. I will always believe a big reason for it was the bad luck for USC to draw Paul Dee as the head of the Committee on Infractions for the USC case. In hindsight, it's pure irony for the guy who was AD at Miami during the Nevin Shapiro years to sit in judgment of any USC violations. But when you see the paperwork and internal NCAA e-mails that have come out in recent years, it is absolutely amazing to read what they did and how it violated their own procedures.

Paskwietz is referring to the now-public court documents from the defamation lawsuit filed by McNair. While trying to have the case dismissed, for years the NCAA fought to seal the documents, but that attempt was rejected in 2015 by a California appellate court. Some of the more inflammatory e-mails and memos were written by the NCAA's Rodney Uphoff, a member of the Committee on Infractions. By the NCAA's own rules, though, he was not allowed to vote on the USC case and was not supposed to influence other committee members. Still, Uphoff wrote to a group of his colleagues, "USC has responded to its problems by bringing in Lane Kiffin. They need a wake-up call that doing things the wrong way will have serious consequences." Uphoff also wrote in an e-mail to one colleague, "As you know I favor strict penalties in this case" and "this case cries out for something dramatic." In another e-mail written by the infractions committee liaison Shep Cooper, McNair is described as "a lying, morally bankrupt criminal" and a "hypocrite of the highest order."

The McNair case is still in the courts. But if you're wondering how the NCAA can operate in such an arguably hostile and biased manner, it is partly rooted in a famous Supreme Court ruling in 1988 during the NCAA's lengthy legal battle with UNLV basketball coach Jerry Tarkanian. The court essentially ruled that the NCAA was not a government entity and therefore not required to give due process to the athletes, coaches, and schools it investigates. Almost 30 years later, the NCAA can still mete out punishment *without* providing due process and *with* what its critics call impunity.

TIM TESSALONE: We felt the penalties far outweighed the crime, if you will. And if it had come down two years later, I don't think the penalties would have been the same. You just have to look around at other schools with comparable issues, or arguably more serious issues, that were not penalized as heavily. We happened to be at a point in history when people wanted to make a statement about penalties and infractions.

For the three years of scholarship restrictions, we were only allowed to sign 15 players per year instead of the 25 everyone else was allowed. We were also not allowed to have more than a total of 75 scholarship players on our roster while everyone else was allowed to have 85. That sounds manageable, but then you lose some guys through transfers and injuries that you can't really make up because you already signed your 15. So you can't just catch up overnight after losing that many scholarships. It takes several years. By 2014 the sanctions were over and we still had games when we suited up 50 recruited scholarship players.

These things were done to kill USC. But we still ended up winning eight, nine, ten games a year with those kinds of penalties. Looking back on it today, I think we got through it pretty well.

MARC TYLER: It was really hard at the time. Some guys wanted to transfer. And the NCAA said we could have without sitting out a year, so a lot of guys looked around and some guys actually left. I thought about leaving. I was talking to other schools. Then my dad told me, "Football doesn't last forever anyway. You should stay there and get your degree from USC."

But I still thought the sanctions were too harsh. They were terrible. The Reggie Bush stuff? I think a lot worse has happened around the country. I don't think the NCAA liked that a West Coast school was dominant for so long. I feel like if it were an SEC school, it definitely wouldn't have been that bad.

MITCH MUSTAIN: Part of the ruling was that juniors and seniors could leave without penalty. I obviously had that option as a senior. I remember Tennessee calling me, jeez, 20 times in a week and trying to pull me in there. At that point I'm in my last season and I'm thinking: *I don't want to go. I've really liked my time at USC, even with all of the weirdness going on here right now.*

KRISTOFER O'DOWD: The coaching staff tried making sure that we didn't leave when the sanctions got dropped. We were all getting these phone calls from other coaches. There was no way in hell I was leaving. I'm a Trojan for life.

I considered the sanctions extreme and outrageous. By then Pete

Carroll is gone. Mike Garrett is going to be gone in a few weeks. It's like, *Well, then who is left? There's these kids that have worked their ass off for three years. Let's nail THESE guys.*

You can ask any player what they think of the NCAA. Nobody respects them. Some college kid gets a free meal or sends a few dollars back to his family of six and someone reports him and he gets suspended for three games? Are you kidding me? Come on.

MITCH MUSTAIN: The NCAA is like a kangaroo court. There's no legal basis; there's no precedents. It's just kind of whatever they want to conjure up and go with. I felt it was extremely arbitrary. They're penalizing about 100 players, and not one of us played with Reggie Bush. We didn't participate, didn't take any money. But now we're gonna have all these players who can never go to a bowl game?

I was also thinking: *You've got a marketing agent that's not affiliated with the program. Reggie Bush's parents lived in his house that was 120 miles away. Is USC supposed to send somebody to check on all the parents' houses? And how do they do that?*

One of the popular notions was that Garrett's arrogant stance toward the NCAA—his prickly insistence that the football team had done no wrong and his tone-deaf hiring of Kiffin—was partly responsible for the severity of the sanctions. This idea was buttressed when the NCAA report came out and Garrett told a USC booster group, "As I read the decision by the NCAA, all I could get out of all this was . . . I read between the lines and there was nothing but a lot of envy, and they wish they were all Trojans."

PETROS PAPADAKIS: He went up to San Francisco and gave a speech to a private room and basically said, "Everybody's jealous of us." But that really wasn't that weird. That's what happens in those booster meetings. Then someone reported it, and I really think that thing was kind of blown out of proportion.

Nobody said Garrett was an innocent bystander in this. But with the Reggie Bush investigation, USC simply wasn't cooperative and Pete Carroll was the most uncooperative. They're the governing body, and obviously no, I don't think it was fair. But you can't have contempt for the court in a place that's not really a court of law. They'll go after you. They'll make it hard on you. And Pete made it hard on them the whole four years, so then they made it hard on USC, especially after Garrett hired Kiffin, which was also spitting in the face of the NCAA because they were dealing with a bunch of stuff with him from the Tennessee thing.

And sure, the NCAA is disreputable and a mess. But they're not a big organization. They don't want to send a bunch of people out here to investigate something and figure it out. They want you to fly to Indy, say you're sorry, self-impose something, and come to some kind of negotiable agreement, and USC didn't do any of that. They acted like the NCAA was a solicitor calling, and that pissed them off, so then USC got whacked. That's exactly why it happened. USC could have handled it in a much more diplomatic and pragmatic way. They chose not to because they were riding so high in the moment.

I asked LenDale White, whose teams lost 14 wins to the NCAA sanctions, for his reaction when he heard the news.

LENDALE WHITE: I thought it was a bunch of bullshit. I'd seen other programs get in trouble, and it was sanctions, but it wasn't *forever* sanctions where they take away your wins. I've seen a *bunch* of guys on one team get in trouble for taking stuff, and penalties weren't as harsh as we got for one guy. Whatever Reggie was doing, we had no idea, but we're all punished for this *forever.*

I also felt like the whole staff was responsible, mainly our head coach. Reggie did whatever he did, but it's easier to let him take the whole blame and you move on with your life. Then the NCAA pointed fingers at Todd McNair? Somebody needed to be a scapegoat. Pete got outta there so fast it was ridiculous, so who else was next? Who else on that staff was the closest to Reggie that you could possibly point some fingers at? To me it's unfortunate that a running backs coach would take more responsibility on a team than a man who's a head coach. If you're a head coach, you should know what your assistants are doing, and if not, you should be responsible for that.

As part of the sanctions, the NCAA ordered USC to permanently disassociate from Bush by removing all evidence of his time spent at the school. During that process USC returned its copy of his Heisman Trophy. Bush later returned his own copy voluntarily. He said in a statement, "I have made the difficult decision to forfeit my title as Heisman winner of 2005."

LENDALE WHITE: He didn't probably have to do it, but we gotta be real about the situation. When the world is calling you a cheater, you don't feel right about that. We all know damn well that Reggie won that trophy hands down. Whatever he was doing or whatever his parents were doing on the back end didn't have shit to do with what he was doing on the field. He was probably just sick of hearing all that stuff. I mean, you can only imagine when you're that age, the pressure. Man, he was what, 21 years old? He just got into the league. He didn't know what to do. It was mind-blowing. So he ended up giving it back.

On July 20, 2010, almost six weeks after the sanctions came down, USC ousted athletic director Mike Garrett. President Steven Sample, who had hired Garrett 17 years earlier and then frequently stood by him during his stormy tenure, had announced his own retirement in August. With Sample on his way out and Garrett's power base already eroded, his dismissal was expected once the NCAA handed down the harshest football sanctions since SMU received its two-year "death penalty" in 1987.

USC's president-elect, C. L. Max Nikias, replaced Garrett with

Pat Haden, the former star quarterback for John McKay, an influential alum and a longtime member of the school's board of trustees. Haden hired J. K. McKay, his former wide receiver and McKay's son, as a liaison between himself and the football program. Haden's hiring, for the moment, brought some degree of calm to beleaguered Heritage Hall.

Garrett, the school's first Heisman Trophy winner, left the athletic department with a mixed legacy. For all his public and private clashes with USC coaches and the NCAA, his hiring of Carroll had sparked the resurgence of the football program and generated millions for the university. Garrett also led several major fund-raising drives, including the one for the Galen Center, which opened in 2006 and finally gave USC its own basketball arena after several failed attempts. Perhaps most important to the hypercompetitive Garrett, the school's athletic teams won 23 national titles on his 17-year watch.

In September 2010, a new football season finally arrived with the Trojans ranked No. 14 and banned from postseason play for the first of two years. After starting 4–0 in the soft part of its schedule, USC ended up at 8–5 overall, 5–4 in the Pac-10, and unranked. Two of the defeats (to Sarkisian's Washington Huskies and Harbaugh's Stanford Cardinal) came by a total of only 3 points. There was also a bad loss (53–32) to top-ranked Oregon and an even uglier one (36–7) to unranked Oregon State.

Marc Tyler was finally healthy again after his badly broken leg his senior year of high school, but he had still entered spring camp as the No. 5 tailback on the depth chart. Tyler left camp as the starter and wound up rushing for 913 yards and nine touchdowns.

MARC TYLER: That was our first year with no bowl game, so I feel like some guys didn't stay mentally sharp. There was nothing for them to look forward to at the end of the season.

For me it felt good to get back out there, and I actually liked playing for Kiffin. I can see how other players didn't like him. He would walk by guys in the hallway and not say anything. He never did that to me, maybe because I was his starting running back. But he could be a little arrogant. He could rub people the wrong way.

In stark contrast to Tyler, a five-star recruit who had entered USC as the top-rated running back in the nation, Emon Saee was a junior college transfer who walked onto the team as a quarterback in 2010. A student of the game and a good student period, he later received a master's degree from USC's acclaimed Marshall School of Business.

EMON SAEE: When the news came out about the sanctions, I hadn't stepped foot on campus yet. When I actually came in, the atmosphere didn't seem down. It wasn't like, *Oh, shoot, we have the bowl ban, and we got 30 scholarships taken away.* Everyone seemed excited to get the season started.

But you could tell that Kiffin was under a lot of pressure. You go to the NFL, and you're not successful. You go to the University of Tennessee, you hype up how much you're gonna change the program, how you're gonna beat Florida and Urban Myer. Then suddenly you get this offer at USC, one of the most historic programs of all time. This is your opportunity to prove to everyone how great a coach you really are. That had to be in his mind, right? And that's lot of pressure.

I began to think Kiffin was in over his head when he wanted to take control of the play calling and not let Clay Helton, our quarterbacks coach, have more input. You can name a bunch of college head coaches from Kiffin, to Brian Kelly, to Chip Kelly who were offensive-minded guys and wanted to control that part of the game. Some of them were successful, such as Brian Kelly and Chip Kelly, and some of them were not, like Coach Kiffin. He should have relied more on Coach Helton. Kiffin's ego got in his own way that season.

Still, at 8–5, the 2010 Trojans would have qualified for a semi-decent bowl game. Under the sanctions, however, they sat out the postseason for the first time since Paul Hackett's final year in 2000.

A few weeks before that, in late November 2010, USC played Notre Dame at the Coliseum. After two years of backing up Sanchez and Barkley, Mustain finally made his first start in place of an injured Barkley. With 1:17 to play and the Trojans down, 20–16, the senior quarterback threw to Ronald Johnson at the Irish 15-yard line with no defenders in sight, but Johnson dropped the sure touchdown pass that would have won the game. Johnson, a senior receiver, looked mortified in front of the home crowd. When Mustain threw an interception moments later, it signaled the end of the eight-year winning streak against Notre Dame.

KRISTOFER O'DOWD: I'll never forget that game. It was in the Coliseum on Senior Day. I couldn't believe we lost to Notre Dame. And I felt that the way our younger guys reacted in the locker room after the game was really a testament to where that program was and where it was going. And it wasn't going in the right place. If we lost on Senior Day in '07, '08, or '09 and the young guys were cracking jokes and laughing in the locker room, I can guarantee you they would have been knocked out. I can also guarantee you that I almost knocked somebody out after that game.

I asked O'Dowd, the senior center who started for all four seasons, to sum up his particular era at USC.

KRISTOFER O'DOWD: Man, it was crazy. There was *so much* going on there. And I come from Tucson, Arizona. I don't know if you've ever been to Tucson, Arizona. But it sure as hell isn't Los Angeles.

20

CHAOS AND CONTROVERSY:

2011–2013

In 2011, the Pac-10 became the Pac-12 with the addition of Utah and Colorado. The conference was split in half, and USC resided in the Pac-12 South.

That season could have been dreary. The Trojans started out ranked 25th after finishing just 8–5 overall and 5–4 in the Pac-10 the previous season. In the second year of the sanctions, they were still ineligible for a bowl game as well as the newly created Pac-12 title game. But USC seemed inspired and businesslike while going 10–2 and 7–2, which was good for first place in the Pac-12 South.

Barkley had a terrific junior year, breaking school records with 39 touchdown passes and a 69.1 percent completion rate. His two dangerous receivers, Robert Woods and Marqise Lee, combined for 26 touchdown receptions. There was veteran leadership from the final Pete Carroll holdovers, and Lane Kiffin took a step forward in his second season in charge.

GARRY PASKWIETZ: Kiffin did a lot of things right. They avenged losses from the previous year to Oregon, Washington, and Notre

Dame. That meant Kiffin going head to head in battles with three pretty good offensive football coaches in Chip Kelly, Steve Sarkisian, and Brian Kelly.

One sign of Kiffin and his handling of the team involved Marc Tyler, who had been suspended from the team over the summer due to alcohol-related issues. Kiffin worked hard to bring Tyler back at a time when the popular senior was considering giving up the game, and that move resonated with his teammates.

After finally getting healthy in 2010 and rushing for 913 yards and nine touchdowns, Tyler's three alcohol-fueled incidents included an impromptu appearance on *TMZ* when the tabloid TV show filmed him outside a Hollywood nightclub. Asked why USC had so many running backs, Tyler said, "'Cause we're RBU [Running Back University]. That's how we get down. We all win our Heismans, we all gonna ball." That was only the prelude. When asked if USC or professional players were paid more, he said, "USC. They breaking bread." The video went viral and led to a one-game suspension for the 2011 season opener.

MARC TYLER: I was hoping they wouldn't air that because I wasn't a big celebrity or anything. But I figured that they might because I looked so dumb.

We were at a Matt Leinart charity bowling event. Then some of the guys went out, and I was leaving a club. One of my friends, who wasn't on the team, I guess wanted some attention. He called to the camera guy and said, "This is Marc Tyler, the USC running back." I was drinking and kidding around, and I said a whole bunch of dumb things. Kiffin could have kicked me off the team. But he stood up for me.

When I look back on it now, I had waited so long to start and be the man. And when it came, I didn't handle it. I got caught up in the scene. It's USC and Hollywood. People want to hang out with you and take you to clubs. I never got in trouble before, and then I'm in trouble three times. I wasn't taking football seriously enough.

Pat Haden suspended me for the first game, and he said I had to go to rehab. I didn't think I had a drinking problem. I went out on Thursdays like the rest of the kids. But I feel like it was a good learning experience to go into counseling and hear the people's stories that were in there. It helped me grow up.

In the second-to-last week of their satisfying season, the 8–2 and 18th-ranked Trojans upset 9–1 and fourth-ranked Oregon, 38–35, in Eugene. Then the tenth-ranked Trojans returned to the Coliseum to face the unranked Bruins. UCLA coach Rick Neuheisel would soon be fired but nonetheless told reporters that his program had "closed the gap" with USC. The Bruins also announced that rather than wear their traditional blue and gold, they would play that Saturday in all-white uniforms and helmets for the first time ever. The Adidas uniforms looked sharp and yet also absurd when Barkley threw for six touchdowns in a 50–0 demolition.

EMON SAEE: That entire season, we wanted to prove to the world: *Hey, this is USC We're coming back.* But beating UCLA 50–0 was the best feeling ever, hands down. Kiffin just let Matt Barkley keep throwing the ball. That's the thing about Kiffin: He likes to keep throwing the ball no matter what. He wants to pad the stats. But at the same time, when your quarterback is performing that well, you want to keep feeding him the ball and showcasing his skills. Also, this was the time when everybody was asking: *Is Barkley going to leave USC early or will he come back next season to try and win a national title?*

In 2011, the NCAA sanctions not only kept the Trojans from the postseason, but with their 10–2 record and final No. 6 ranking in the AP, the sanctions probably kept them from playing a BCS game.

In 2012, the two-season bowl ban ended, but the scholarship reductions were just beginning: only 15 new scholarship players per year instead of the regular 25 and only 75 total scholarship players on the roster instead of the 85 the other teams could have.

Still, the talented and apparently resurgent Trojans were ranked No. 1 in several preseason polls. Barkley, who chose to forgo the NFL, made the cover of the August 12 edition of *Sports Illustrated* next to a headline that read MATT BARKLEY IS BACK, AND HE DIDN'T STAY TO PLAY IN THE HOLIDAY BOWL.

Offensive tackle Zach Banner made several high school All-American lists before redshirting as a freshman in 2012. USC's biggest player at 6-foot-9 and 360 pounds, he later would be voted first-team All-Pac-12 as a junior in 2015. I asked Banner, in retrospect, if the 2012 Trojans were overrated when the season began.

ZACH BANNER: No. I think with the talent we had, we definitely should have been ranked No. 1. I just don't think we were put in the right places to succeed by the coaching staff.

EMON SAEE: We had Matt Barkley, the face of the USC program during the sanctions and a great college quarterback. We had two 1,000-yard receivers: Robert Woods and Marqise Lee. We had two 1,000-yard runners: Curtis McNeal and Silas Redd. We had a big strong offensive line. That's a lot of firepower. There was no way you would think you could ever lose a game, right?

GARRY PASKWIETZ: It was supposed to be the dream season. Entering the year No. 1—while on sanctions, not a small accomplishment—and with the No. 1 recruiting class as well. Matt Barkley was the Heisman favorite, and Trojans fans loved him for coming back his senior year to make a run at the national title. On top of that, Barkley and a group of his teammates went on a mission trip over the off-season to Haiti to build homes for victims of an earthquake.

But the preseason No. 1 ranking and all that came with it was too much for Lane Kiffin. To be honest, it would probably be too much for 99 percent of the coaches out there. But for Lane, at that point in his career, he just got wound too tight and choked the life out of the team.

In August, Kiffin triggered the first of several small controversies after he was told that Arizona coach Rich Rodriguez said he voted USC first in the USA Today Coaches Poll. Kiffin told reporters, "I would not vote USC No. 1. I can tell you that much." *USA Today* then disclosed that Kiffin had in fact voted his team No. 1. To outsiders it seemed a minor embarrassment, but Saee says it marked the beginning of Kiffin losing his own locker room.

EMON SAEE: We were like, *Hey, why are you lying?* Because he said the same thing to us. He said, "I didn't vote us number one. I don't think we *should* be number one." When we found out, we were saying, "What else could he be possibly lying to us about?" I mean, why would a head coach lie about that? Especially to his players that sweat and bleed and do all that stuff for him? And this was before the season even started.

SHELLEY SMITH: When they went 10–2, Kiffin was getting all the credit for calling offensive plays and Barkley was playing great. So now they're odds-on favorites to win it all, which is stupid because they're down scholarships and they were so thin. I think the pressure that came with those expectations got to Kiffin. He created a lot of drama that didn't need to be created.

For example, he stopped letting visiting teams do their walk-throughs at the Coliseum the day before a game. He did it for no reason. He said he didn't want them to tear up the grass. We were all like, *That makes no sense, and it just calls more attention to the program.*

Then an injured player comes back, a reporter mentions it to Kiffin, and he storms out of the daily news conference. And of course it was all caught on video. All he had to say was, "I don't talk about injuries," and move on. Instead it became the lead on *SportsCenter,* right?

USC won its first two games against Hawaii and Syracuse but lost a crucial player when senior center Khaled Holmes injured his ankle. He was a team captain and an All-American candidate who had protected Barkley since they were ninth-graders at Mater Dei High School. Holmes was still sidelined when the 2–0 and second-ranked Trojans traveled to Palo Alto to play 2–0 and 21st-ranked Stanford. Cardinal coach David Shaw, knowing that USC had an untested redshirt freshman playing center, ordered his defense to keep attacking the middle. When USC never adjusted in any meaningful way, Stanford sacked Barkley five times and hit him repeatedly in a 21–14 Stanford upset.

PETROS PAPADAKIS: Barkley got his head knocked off. Then Kiffin blamed the left tackle, Aundrey Walker. I don't think the guy played well. They didn't play well on the entire offensive line. The point is, you don't publicly call out your players after the game. You don't single out an offensive lineman and say that's the reason you lost because *you're* the one being criticized.

After losing to Stanford and dropping 11 spots to No. 13, the Trojans won four straight Pac-12 games. They were 6–1, ranked No. 10 and predicted to hammer unranked Arizona in Tucson. They lost, 39–36, after leading by 15 points deep into the third quarter.

The next Saturday at the Coliseum, second-ranked Oregon

rang up 62 points and 730 total yards, which were both the most allowed by USC since it began playing football in 1888. The 62–51 loss to the visiting Ducks shifted the media heat to Monte Kiffin, Lane's father and defensive coordinator. The Trojans then beat Arizona State but lost the rivalry games to UCLA and Notre Dame.

A star-studded team allegedly in the hunt for a national title had lost four of its last five games while dropping to 7–5. And both before and during the late-season skid, there were more distractions and signs of Kiffin's immaturity.

PETROS PAPADAKIS: In the middle of the Colorado game, they changed the numbers of the quarterback and a special teams guy. I guess they were trying to be deceptive or something. But for what? They beat Colorado, 50–6. It was a stat-padding game.

The week after they lost to Oregon, they got in trouble for deflating some of the balls in that game. They were the original ball deflators. They got fined by the Pac-12. Then they blamed this kid, this student manager, and they fired him from the program.

GARRY PASKWIETZ: I don't think the real story has come out on that one. The USC athletic department pinned it on a "rogue team manager" who they said acted alone and who quickly left the program and has not been heard from since.

SHELLEY SMITH: Barkley likes the ball a little bit underinflated. Nobody likes to talk about that incident, but everyone believes the ball boy took a hit for the team. I'm sure someone paid his way to leave. Some USC booster's probably paying his tuition at another school.

PETROS PAPADAKIS: I think he went to grad school somewhere for free. I'm not kidding. He might be in, like, fucking Brandeis or something.

SHELLEY SMITH: It was these constant things that caused the program tension. Also, Barkley wasn't happy and sort of saying it, and Kiffin was not on the same page with his players.

ZACH BANNER: He obviously wasn't a player's coach. I don't think he grasped the idea of playing as a team. He talked about it, but I think he was more focused on setting offensive records and things like that.

EMON SAEE: After every loss, he gave us literally the same speech. He said, "They came out and played better than us. We didn't execute."

When you keep on giving your team the same speech, especially after we lost 62–51 to Oregon, it was like, *Come on, man, is that really all you got in your back pocket as the head coach? Can't you tell us straight up what's going on and how we can get better?* Then you started hearing it from the media: *What a disappointment of a season. Should Barkley have left? Is Kiffin on the hot seat?*

PETROS PAPADAKIS: Kiffin never really had the respect of those players. He was a weak leader. I knew of one incident where Barkley told him to fuck off in front of the whole team. And in 2012, they just laid a gigantic egg. A lot of guys from that team are in the NFL now. But they didn't play together. And when things go bad at SC, they go pretty bad in a hurry, and Lane couldn't hold it together.

In the second-to-last game on November 17, the Trojans lost, 38–28, to the Bruins one year after crushing them, 50–0. By then UCLA had improved dramatically with a mobile freshman quarterback named Brett Hundley and first-year head coach Jim Mora, the man fired after one season by the Seahawks to make room for Carroll.

It was USC's first loss to UCLA since 2006, and making a dark day at the Rose Bowl darker, Bruins linebacker Anthony Barr blitzed with a few minutes left and came roaring through the line of scrimmage unblocked. Barr drilled Barkley in the back, knocked him flat, and injured his right shoulder. After the game with reporters, Barkley concealed his shoulder inside a sweatshirt, but he appeared to be wearing a sling. Meanwhile, his coach threw him right under the bus.

"You wouldn't think that we would lose this game with a senior quarterback versus a freshman," said Kiffin. "Usually you don't, just like a veteran versus a rookie."

The *Los Angeles Times*'s Bill Plaschke spoke with athletic director Pat Haden about Kiffin's status after the UCLA game. Although Mike Garrett had hired Kiffin in 2010, Haden had now become Kiffin's staunchest defender. Plachske quoted Haden saying Kiffin was still his coach "150 percent," a statement that got wide play in the mainstream media and on social media, too.

In the regular-season finale, redshirt freshman quarterback Max Wittek replaced the injured Barkley and played respectably in a 22–13 loss to top-ranked Notre Dame. At 7–6 overall and 5–4 in the Pac-12, the Trojans qualified for the postseason after their two-year ban from the NCAA ended. But in the run-up to the lower-tier Sun Bowl, USC absorbed another public relations hit when it alienated the host city. At one point the exasperated *El Paso Times* ran a headline on the front page: TROJAN TROUBLE.

EMON SAEE: After we lost to Notre Dame, we thought we might go to the Holiday Bowl in San Diego or maybe the Las Vegas Bowl. Then Kiffin comes and tells us, "I chose a bowl game for us." And we were like, *Okay, you chose it, but you didn't ask the captains or anybody?* He said, "I decided to go to the Sun Bowl."

So we go to El Paso, Texas. You're literally right across the street from Juarez, so there's not a lot going on there. But some of us thought the experience was cool because we got to go to the army base there. But then what messed up the trip was that we kept running late because Kiffin ran these overlong practices. One night we had this joint dinner with Georgia Tech and the bowl game people. So out of respect, get to this joint dinner on time, right? But Georgia Tech was leaving when we got there.

We also had a few guys that went on social media, and they were bad-mouthing the city of El Paso. That kind of put a target on our back, not just for Georgia Tech but also the people of El Paso. The only people rooting for us in that stadium were our own family members and some fans that came from Los Angeles. The residents of El Paso were rooting for Georgia Tech. I think they saw us as spoiled guys from Los Angeles who stepped onto their land and pretty much said, "This is crap." That's not appropriate.

ZACH BANNER: No one wanted to go to that bowl game. We were the number one team in America, and we wind up in El Paso, Texas, at the Sun Bowl against Georgia Tech. Seriously? You know what I mean? That's not why we came to USC, to play in games like that. It still wasn't the right way to handle it as a team, but the coaching and the leadership just wasn't there.

On December 31, 2012, unranked USC faced unranked Georgia Tech, the least successful team that had qualified for the postseason. What's more, the Yellow Jackets had not qualified the way the other teams had: They had required a waiver from the NCAA to participate in a bowl because they were 6–7.

With Barkley's shoulder still not fully healed, Wittek threw three interceptions in the windy conditions and the offense gained only 205 total yards against a team that had allowed 510 yards to Middle Tennessee State. The USC defense fared better in Monte Kiffin's last game before stepping down but still gave up 294 yards rushing.

When Georgia Tech won, 21–7, it was the fifth loss in six games for a team that had entered the season ranked No. 1. But the collapse was not just epic. It was historic. The Trojans became the first team in 48 years to start a season at No. 1 and end up being unranked.

Kiffin did not attempt to deflect the blame this time. "You look at yourself first," he said. "We can't be 7–6. Not at SC." But when asked if he was concerned about his coaching status, he said, "No."

EMON SAEE: At that point I think he *was* worried for his career. And I don't blame him. You have all those weapons, especially on offense. Then you lose to Notre Dame and UCLA, which is a big no-no to the boosters. You don't make the Rose Bowl or play for the national title when everyone says you will. Then you lose the Sun Bowl.

ZACH BANNER: When you lose to UCLA and Notre Dame and then you go to a lower-tier bowl, you're already feeling shitty if you're USC. So the mood wasn't great going into that game.

GARRY PASKWIETZ: Kiffin had told offensive coaches Clay Helton and Kennedy Polamalu that they would call the plays in the Sun Bowl, only to change his mind in the days leading up to the game. Kiffin wore a hoodie and sunglasses during the game, even during a halftime interview on camera. There were lots of rumors about whether he wore them to cover up a gash on his forehead.

One of the biggest memories of that game is how much Max Wittek struggled, and you never saw Kiffin go over to talk with him, give him support. Then things got heated in the SC locker room afterward, lots of emotion from players who were frustrated with the way the season ended and with Kiffin.

EMON SAEE: Some of the younger guys were calling out the seniors, saying you're the reason we lost the season, not just that game but the season. The media said there was an actual fight. I didn't see any punches thrown. Guys were calling each other out. Tempers flared. Everyone in that locker room was upset. I really think that season was the most disappointing ever in college football.

ZACH BANNER: Nothing happened. Some guys went face to face. There was no fistfight. Guys were pissed about losing. That was not how we wanted to end the season.

At that point, I didn't think Kiffin would be my coach for much longer. I expected him to be done. I think everyone did.

GARRY PASKWIETZ: As far as the fans were concerned, Kiffin should have been gone. Pat Haden made his case for why he was supporting Lane, and in hindsight that turned out to be a very questionable decision.

In 2012, the preseason No. 1 ranking had made the pollsters look naive when USC ended up 7–6. By 2013 that faith was gone, and the Trojans entered the season ranked 24th. Cody Kessler and Max Wittek competed to replace Barkley, who slid all the way to the fourth round before the Philadelphia Eagles drafted him. Barkley, in retrospect, should have left USC after his junior season, when his 39 touchdown passes and 69.1 percent completion rate both set school records. Returning for his senior year to play for a lousy team while injuring his right shoulder cost him millions.

As the 2013 season began, Kiffin couldn't decide between Kessler and Wittek as his starting quarterback. He also kept calling the plays even though Haden preferred that he delegate that role and focus more on being the head coach. After USC beat Hawaii in the first game, the tipping point for Kiffin came in the Pac-12 opener against Washington State. The Cougars came in unranked and had not beaten USC since 2002. Yet matched against a perennial conference lightweight—in the first game of the season at the Coliseum—the Trojans gained only 193 yards as Kiffin played Kessler one half and Wittek the other.

ZACH BANNER: We lost 10–7 to Washington State. I knew his job was in jeopardy after that game. Everyone knew it was a squad we shouldn't have lost to. The crowd was booing us. Not only that, they were chanting, "Fire Kiffin." Sooner or later, things were going to start happening.

On September 28, after beating Boston College and Utah State, USC returned to Pac-12 play with a 62–41 loss at *unranked* Arizona State. The Trojans were a middling 3–2. They were 0–2 in the conference for the first time in 12 years. They were 4–7 in their last 11 games. Despite the annual talent flowing into the program, Kiffin was 2–7 against ranked opponents and 28–15 overall, suggesting that he was better at bringing players on campus than he was at developing them once they arrived. Combined with the turmoil and the public relations gaffes, it was the end of the line. After the team plane arrived back in Los Angeles around three a.m., Kiffin became the first USC coach fired in the middle of a season and the first fired in the middle of the night.

GARRY PASKWIETZ: By the time of the ASU game, the program was at a real low with all the clouds surrounding Kiffin. The offense actually performed okay that night in Tempe, but the defense gave up huge numbers. At one point in the second half there was a meeting on the sideline that included Haden and his advisers. The decision was made that the players just weren't playing for Kiffin anymore and it was time to remove him from the job.

When the plane landed at LAX, Kiffin was summoned for a meeting with Haden where Kiffin passionately argued to keep his job and talked about how good the offense had looked in the game. Haden, always trying to find a way for things to work out, was starting to be swayed until one of his advisers pulled him aside and reminded him that the decision had been made and he had to fire Kiffin.

ZACH BANNER: Our plane landed, I think, around three a.m. The bus was going to take us back to school. We didn't really know what was going on yet.

When I found out, I was relieved. We needed a new direction. That was the general feeling among the players.

TIM TESSALONE: The higher-ups felt it was the right time. You could argue that it's a bit unusual to do it midseason. But the way the team performed in that Arizona State game and in some of the previous games, they felt this was the time to do it.

I've been through a lot of coaching changes. When Lane got fired, that was an amazing evening. Lane lived very close to me. I live in Redondo, and he lived in Manhattan, so our paths home that night were the same. I remember kind of following him that night down PCH [the Pacific Coast Highway]. I got home and got on my computer and wrote up our statement. I think it was 4:27 a.m. that Sunday morning. I remember pushing the Send button and how surreal that felt.

And then I recall getting on Twitter, and within thirty minutes you would have thought the baddest guy in al-Qaeda was killed and people were celebrating. That was how happy people were that Lane Kiffin was fired. And not only SC people but *everybody* in the Twitterverse. If you know Lane, he's not a bad guy. He's a good guy. But it was amazing how vilified the guy was.

PETROS PAPADAKIS: It's really hard to get fired in September as a head football coach, and it's happened to Lane twice, at the Raiders and then USC. But Haden totally botched it. In August Haden had done that YouTube video the night before Pac-12 media day, where Haden emphatically said Kiffin was not on the hot seat. Then he fires him on the tarmac in September. It was a wild 180.

I asked Papadakis, "Why the 180?"

PETROS PAPADAKIS: I have a theory. Wayne Hughes is the guy who owns Public Storage, and he's one of USC's biggest donors. He's a *real* big donor. Like, if he says to do something, you do it. I think Wayne Hughes had had enough. That's the only thing that makes sense, because until then it looked like Haden was going to go down with Kiffin. Haden was standing behind him when nobody else was. Then he fires him unceremoniously at LAX.

On Sunday Haden announced that Ed Orgeron would serve as interim head coach. USC's defensive line coach had started as an assistant under Hackett and Carroll before becoming head coach at Mississippi, where he went 10–25 in the tough Southeastern Conference. He returned to the Trojans when Garrett named Kiffin head coach in 2010.

Orgeron hadn't transformed into Mother Teresa, but he wasn't the same wild guy he was in decades gone by. He was older, of course, and also sober after publicly conceding that alcohol had caused him too many problems. But Orgeron was still a fiery motivator, whereas Kiffin was a taciturn technician.

GARRY PASKWIETZ: One of the first things Ed did was return cookies and desserts to the training table, something that really struck a chord with the media and the players. A few days after that I was talking with Ed about how quickly the mood seemed to have turned after how low things had been at the end under Lane. Ed said, "I know; I gave them a cookie, and it made national news."

ZACH BANNER: Everyone knows not to mess with Coach O because he's a very strict guy and hard-core old school. But Coach O used to take care of us. He brought us in good food, and even though it may have been bad for you, it still tasted better.

Honestly, he just brought life into the program. He wanted us to laugh and have fun. He did everything he could to be a players' coach. He made the practices shorter. Coach Kiffin believed in two-and-a-half- to three-hour practices. We used to have a lot of injuries with the longer practices. We were down to two hours under Coach O, and the tempo was faster. They just had very different styles of coaching.

After dropping to 3–2 with the embarrassing 62–41 loss at ASU, the rejuvenated Trojans won four of their next five games to improve to 7–3. Then, on November 16, they upset fifth-ranked Stanford, the eventual Pac-12 champion, 20–17. Thousands of happy fans stormed the Coliseum field after the cathartic victory. They stayed there for 20 minutes, mingling with the players and staging an impromptu Orgeron lovefest. Haden had already said Orgeron would be considered for the permanent job. On the surface at least, the Stanford game appeared to give him momentum.

The high-spirited Trojans won again the next week, 47–29, at Colorado. They were 6–1 under Orgeron, with UCLA up next in the regular-season finale. The crosstown rivals seemed evenly matched. USC came in at 9–3 overall, 6–2 in the Pac-12, and ranked No. 22. Jim Mora's Bruins were 8–3 and 5–3 and ranked 23rd. Thus, when the Trojans lost, 35–14, on their own field, almost no one saw it coming and many viewed it as the end of Orgeron's chances. But several sources say the UCLA outcome was moot.

PETROS PAPADAKIS: Ed found out the week of the UCLA game that they weren't bringing him back regardless of what happened. Ed told the players what was happening, and he allowed the players to go and speak on his behalf to an unrelenting Pat Haden. I don't think that helped Ed win the UCLA game. I don't think players play hard for a guy they feel bad for.

GARRY PASKWIETZ: The next day Haden left for a trip to the Northwest to finalize things with Steve Sarkisian. I recall the reaction from the players when they found out Orgeron didn't get the job. I've never seen so many college football players with tears in such an emotional setting.

EMON SAEE: It's pretty sad what they did to him, not giving him the head-coaching gig. I was already gone, but it upset me because of all he's done for that program over the years. I think they were looking at his Ole Miss record. Yeah, he didn't do well as the head coach at Ole Miss, but that guy knows how to coach. He knows how to take care of his players. He knows how to prepare his players, and if he ever gets a head-coaching gig, I don't doubt that he'll win a national title.

ZACH BANNER: I would say there were mixed feelings. A lot of guys wanted him to be head coach, but a lot of guys understood when he didn't get it. Me, personally, I didn't shed any tears. It didn't hurt me the way it hurt a lot of guys. I'm just going to be honest. The reason it didn't hurt me is because I learned in high school that football is a business.

Everyone else, I think, was pulling for him because we were winning football games. We were 9–4. Plus, everyone knew Coach O could recruit. He was *my* recruiting coach. People say to me, "How were you not pissed that they didn't keep him?" That's just the business. I wish I had the same coach at USC for the past four years. But I haven't.

SHELLEY SMITH: Ed was popular, but I don't think he was ever in the running. They felt he didn't have the savvy to deal with the boosters and alumni.

CHRIS HUSTON: There was a lot of sentiment for Orgeron, but it was mostly coming from people who don't follow college football real closely. I don't think he was ever really considered, and appropriately. I don't think his personality and demeanor were that of a head coach. And he had a checkered past. I think in Haden's mind, hiring Orgeron was too much of a risk. But I also don't think Sarkisian should have been the guy they hired instead. You might as well hire Orgeron if you're going to hire Sarkisian.

ARTIE GIGANTINO: At the time I thought Sarkisian was a good choice. I didn't think he would reach the heights that Pete Carroll reached, but Sark is a good coach. But I still would have preferred Jack Del Rio.

I knew Ed Orgeron never had a chance to get that job. They could have gone undefeated with Ed and he was not gonna get that job. He's a non-polished guy. That USC job, you might as well be the mayor of Los Angeles. I mean, picture Ed Orgeron in a pin-striped suit and a red tie having dinner on a Friday night at Steven Spielberg's house. That ain't going to happen. You know what I'm saying? Ed was kind of a crude good guy. A *good* guy, but Pat Haden was never going to hire that guy. Not in a million years. The emotion? Coach O had that. And he was so different from the other guy, Kiffin. But at the end of the day, they were never, ever giving that job to Ed Orgeron.

Sarkisian returned to USC directly from Washington, where he went 35–29 in five seasons while leading the Huskies to four bowl games. When he was hired on December 3, 2013, many saw it as USC's second attempt to re-create the Carroll era, pointing to Kiffin's hiring as the initial attempt. Orgeron had played a role in the Carroll years, too, but he was not a Carroll protégé. Kiffin and Sarkisian were.

Back in late September, when USC gave Orgeron the interim job, it was intended to be for the rest of the season. Orgeron abruptly resigned, though, after the UCLA game and after getting passed over. So in the three weeks before the Trojans played in the Las Vegas Bowl, their *new* interim coach was offensive coordinator Clay Helton.

ZACH BANNER: Coach O left us. It was a weird situation. He left right after our last regular-season game. Sark moved in, but Sark wasn't our official coach. Sark came in and said, "I don't know you guys. I'm not gonna take you over for one bowl game."

SHELLEY SMITH: Ed Orgeron was and is a good guy. But he should have taken the high road and coached them in the bowl. Instead he was seen as a pouter.

Over the last three decades, the USC football team often had underachieved in lower-tier bowl games. This time the unranked Trojans came into the December 21 Las Vegas Bowl with a 9–4 record. Fresno State was 11–1 and ranked No. 21. Its quarterback Derek Carr had led the nation in touchdown passes and passing yards. It was Cody Kessler, though, who won MVP when he passed for a career-high 344 yards and four touchdowns. The Trojans routed the Bulldogs, 45–20, and the game was over by halftime with USC ahead, 35–6.

What a long strange trip it was for the resilient Trojans of 2014. Their first head coach, Kiffin, was fired. Their second head coach, Orgeron, resigned. Their fourth head coach, Sarkisian, had not yet taken over and watched the bowl game with Haden in a suite. Their third head coach, Helton, said afterward, "I can't say how proud I am of this team."

I asked Banner for his impressions of Helton in the run-up to the Las Vegas Bowl and during the game itself.

ZACH BANNER: I thought he was amazing. I thought he was a pro. I think all of us did.

21

STARTING OVER TWICE:

2014–2015

It took Lane Kiffin's dismissal and Ed Orgeron's disappointment, but Steve Sarkisian finally had his dream job.

At Washington he revived the ailing program after inheriting an 0–12 team, but he never returned the Huskies to the upper echelon in the Pac-12. Sarkisian went 5–7 his first year in Seattle. He went 8–4 in his last year. The three straight 7–6 years in the middle brought him the unwanted nickname Seven-Win Sark.

After firing Kiffin in late September, Haden said he identified 20 candidates and interviewed five. Two of the strongest contenders were Boise State head coach Chris Petersen and former USC linebacker Jack Del Rio, the defensive coordinator for the Denver Broncos. Haden said he offered the job only to Sarkisian, who had coached on Carroll's staff for seven (non-consecutive) seasons.

GARRY PASKWIETZ: Sark was thought to have a bright offensive mind, and Haden felt that was important in today's college football landscape. He was known to be a very good recruiter, particularly in the Southern California area. It was clear from the way he ran his program that he had learned under Pete Carroll. Everything was positive and designed to have energy.

SHELLEY SMITH: Sark was like Pete, they thought. They wanted the Pete magic back. And Pete was very much in favor of Sark getting the job.

According to Carroll himself, he had endorsed Sarskisian as his future replacement before leaving USC for Seattle in January 2010. Carroll made that statement in February 2014, soon after he had won the Super Bowl and the Trojans had named Sarkisian head coach. As the two men shared a stage for a speaking engagement at USC's Bovard Auditorium, Carroll told the crowd, "I tried to get the administration to guarantee he [Sarkisian] would be the next coach if I was leaving."

Carroll didn't say *when* he sought those assurances, but by the time he left USC, his relationship with Mike Garrett had deteriorated. Whether that was a factor or not, Garrett passed on Sarkisian and hired Kiffin.

This time around, say multiple sources, Carroll made his pro-Sarkisian feelings known directly to Haden and also perhaps through Mark Jackson, a Carroll confidant then working under Haden as senior associate athletic director.

PETROS PAPADAKIS: Mark Jackson is now the athletic director at Villanova. Jackson worked for Carroll on the Patriots before Jackson worked at USC. Jackson's the guy that pushed Haden to keep Kiffin after the terrible loss at the Sun Bowl. He's the guy who pushed for Sark when Kiffin left. And Jackson was the link between Pete Carroll and the USC program after Pete Carroll left.

The 2014 season began with the NCAA sanctions finally lifted after four years and the Trojans ranked No. 15. They went 8–4 overall and 6–3 in the Pac-12 in the regular season, with quality wins on the road at Stanford and Arizona. But three defeats were glaring: against unranked Boston College after blowing a 17–6 lead, and to Arizona State and Utah in each of those games' final seconds. The fourth loss came against the rival Bruins, 38–20, making Jim Mora 3–0 against USC.

ZACH BANNER: We beat Stanford in our second game. It was the first time in years we beat them at their place. We got bumped up in the rankings to No. 9. We were like, *Yes! This feels great! This is the first time we've been in the top ten for a while! Let's keep it here!*

The next week we blow it against Boston College. Then we don't finish the game against Arizona State, and we lose on a Hail Mary pass. Then we also don't finish in the game against Utah. Then we were just hoping for other teams to lose. And then we choked up against UCLA at the end of the season and wound up in the Holiday Bowl.

On December 30 at Qualcomm Stadium in San Diego, the 8–4 and 24th-ranked Trojans faced 9–3 and 25th-ranked Nebraska. USC nearly squandered an 18-point third-quarter lead before holding on, 45–42. Cody Kessler passed for 311 yards and three touchdowns, one of them to Adoree' Jackson, who also ran back a kickoff 98 yards for a score.

Some said the Holiday Bowl typified an underachieving season in which the talented Trojans struggled to close out middling opponents. Others saw the postseason win and 9–4 final record as reason for optimism in the first year after the sanctions.

ZACH BANNER: I thought the season was crushing. Isn't that crazy? At any other school, if they go to a bowl game, they win the bowl game, they get a ring. I haven't had a single ring in the past years because even though we won two bowl games, they're not the

Rose Bowl and they're not a BCS game. I don't even think we know where those Holiday Bowl or Las Vegas Bowl trophies are. They're not in a case anywhere. They're probably in someone's office or at someone's house.

Sarkisian told reporters after the Holiday Bowl, "Our future is ridiculously bright." That February he signed the No. 1 recruiting class in the nation. That summer, the media picked the Trojans to win the Pac-12 and several national polls ranked them in the top ten. Then, two weeks before the 2015 season opener, the USC football program went haywire yet again.

On August 22, Sarkisian spoke at the annual Salute to Troy pep rally. In front of boosters, alumni, players, and their parents, Sarkisian used obscene language, insulted other teams, and appeared inebriated to many in attendance on that shocking Saturday night. The media weren't allowed to cover the event, but a video clip went viral. And then came the coast-to-coast headlines.

ZACH BANNER: Yeah, I was there that night. Everyone was there. I could tell something was up. I saw him and Mr. Haden and those guys talking in the back, behind the stage. It was a big situation, and it came out. I think everyone knew it was going to come out. And everyone knew something bad was going to come from it.

Sarkisian spoke at a media conference that Tuesday. He said he had mixed an unspecified medication "with alcohol, not a lot, and I responded in a way that was not acceptable for me or for the university." When asked if he had a drinking problem, he said, "I don't believe so," but added, "I'm going to find that out." He explained that he would seek treatment, but he didn't specify what for.

By then Haden had posted this brief statement on the school's own website: "I met with Coach Sarkisian and I expressed my disappointment in the way he represented himself and the University at our Salute to Troy event. While the details of our conversation will remain between us, I am confident he heard my message loud and clear."

Some called Haden's scolding insufficient, saying Sarkisian should be suspended. Others sympathized with Sarkisian, saying he needed to take a leave of absence and get away from coaching in order to regain his equilibrium. When Haden took neither course, he became the object of intense criticism.

Two weeks later, on September 15, the ill-fated season started with Sarkisian on the sidelines and his Trojans ranked No. 8. They began 2–0 by demolishing outmanned Arkansas State and Idaho by a total score of 114–15. Then sixth-ranked USC lost, 41–31, to unranked Stanford in the Pac-12 opener. The Cardinal had a strong team, though, and would not remain unranked for long.

USC improved to 3–1 with a 42–14 win at Arizona State. The Trojans had the next Saturday off and then played a Thursday night game against Sarkisian's former Washington team, which by then was coached by Chris Petersen, who many USC fans had wanted hired before the Trojans chose Sarkisian.

USC came in ranked 17th versus the unranked Huskies, but the 17–12 loss at the Coliseum was not another garden-variety upset. The Trojans had ten days to get prepared. Then they went one for 13 on third down and scored their only touchdown in the fourth quarter despite having fifth-year senior Cody Kessler playing quarterback. Washington, in contrast, won a Pac-12 road game with true freshman quarterback Jake Browning.

The Coliseum crowd, already shell-shocked by recent events, booed throughout the second half and then as the Trojans left the field. Sarkisian took the blame for the poor offensive showing but also said, "We're going to be okay." The season didn't figure to get any easier, though. Now 3–2 overall and 1–2 in the Pac-12, USC had Notre Dame next in South Bend.

The troubled Sarkisian did not make the trip. On the Sunday morning after the Washington game, he showed up at a team meeting, he later confirmed, after drinking the night before and taking prescription medication shortly before the team gathered at eleven a.m. USC players said later, Sarkisian "didn't seem right."

That Sunday afternoon, Haden placed Sarkisian on an indefinite leave of absence. "It is very clear to me that he is not healthy," said Haden. On Monday Haden dismissed Sarkisian 18 games into his tenure at USC. Haden said in his official statement, "After careful consideration of what is in the best interest of the university and our student-athletes, I have made the decision to terminate Steve Sarkisian, effective immediately."

I asked Banner how he took the news.

ZACH BANNER: I loved playing for Sark. He was a very emotional guy. I'm not saying Mr. Haden made a bad decision. I will always 100 percent completely support Mr. Haden. He cares about us as players and also as people. So I think he wanted to change that environment around us when there were some issues going around. I just felt like it was a shitty situation for everyone.

Not everyone agreed with Banner's assessment of Haden, who would ultimately retire in June 2016 after struggling with his health. In October 2015, some said Haden should step down or be dismissed for his handling of the Kiffin and Sarkisian years.

GARRY PASKWIETZ: I don't think there's any question that he bears some responsibility. He didn't hire Kiffin, but you could have made a real case for getting rid of him after the Sun Bowl. But Pat continued it on into the next year, and it just didn't work out.

So yes, the Kiffin and Sarkisian decisions—and the decision not to retain Orgeron—are squarely placed on Haden's shoulders by most Trojan fans. In hindsight, it's hard to think of the coaches that were passed on in order to hire Sarkisian: Orgeron, Jack Del Rio, Chris Petersen.

Before the game in South Bend on October 17, the Trojans named offensive coordinator Clay Helton to serve as interim coach for the second time. The first time was two years before when USC hired Sarkisian and Orgeron abruptly resigned. Helton then coached the team to its 45–20 win over Fresno State in the Las Vegas Bowl.

Now USC gained almost 600 yards against Notre Dame but was outscored 17–0 in the fourth quarter of a 41–31 loss. Still, the resolute Trojans went 5–1 the rest of the regular season, with a cathartic win at the Coliseum over third-ranked Utah (42–24) and a satisfying win over UCLA (40–21) that snapped the three-game skid against the Bruins. Between those victories, though, the suspect USC defense allowed six touchdown passes in a 48–28 loss at Oregon.

The turbulent regular season ended with USC 8–4 overall, 6–3 in the Pac-12, and first in the Pac-12 South. On the Monday before facing Pac-12 North winner Stanford in the conference championship, USC introduced Helton as the permanent head coach. Of course, other names had been floated by the media, including the far more famous NFL coaches John Harbaugh and Chip Kelly.

Still, the Trojans had gone 5–2 after Helton became the interim. He had joined the USC staff in 2010 and was not another Pete Carroll protégée. His players clearly wanted him to keep the job, launching a social media campaign and then going nuts when they heard the news. Helton also scored with USC supporters because he talked about playing physical football. Finally, the wounded program needed healing, and the 43-year-old Helton seemed equipped for that.

SHELLEY SMITH: Helton is a no-nonsense, disciplined family man. He's not a great personality like Sark and Pete were, but he knows what he's doing and the kids love him.

ZACH BANNER: Me, personally, I love Coach Helton. I think he's a great ball coach. I'm totally a Helton guy. So I felt pure happiness. I also thought when I heard it: *USC finally made a good decision.*

"I apologize for not being glitzy," Helton said at his first news conference as the permanent coach. "But I believe that mentality, that blue-collar toughness mentality, is what wins championships." Helton also recognized that some USC fans had yearned for Chip Kelly or John Harbaugh or another already-proven commodity. "Sometimes the right choice is not always the easy choice," he said. "I understand I'm not a flashy name."

In the Pac-12 championship that Saturday, the 8–4 and 20th-ranked Trojans met 10–2 and seventh-ranked Stanford for a berth in the Rose Bowl. USC was done in by the truly great running back Christian McCaffrey, who accounted for 461 all-purpose yards. The Cardinal won, 41–22, sending the Trojans to their second straight Holiday Bowl in San Diego.

First, there was additional drama. On the Sunday after the Stanford loss, four assistant coaches lost their jobs, including the much-maligned defensive coordinator Justin Wilcox. On that Monday, Sarkisian filed a lawsuit against USC alleging that it unlawfully fired him. The complaint included his version of what had transpired at the Salute to Troy: He had been suffering from anxiety and depression after going through a painful divorce and had only appeared intoxicated after mixing two of his prescribed anxiety medications with two beers that he drank earlier that day.

Sarkisian's complaint demanded the $12.6 million in salary left on his contract, but his lawyer said he would seek close to $30 million. The lawsuit repeatedly stated that USC had "kicked him to the curb" rather than help him seek treatment. The university issued a statement saying that it would defend itself "vigorously" and that much of the complaint was "patently untrue." A number of legal experts predicted an out-of-court settlement, which is how most civil lawsuits are resolved.

For the moment all that remained in this seemingly endless season was the December 30 Holiday Bowl. Both the 8–4 Trojans and 9–3 Wisconsin came into the game unranked. Then USC trailed, 20–7, charged back to lead, 21–20, and lost, 23–21, when the Badgers kicked a short field goal with 2:27 remaining.

But the details were more telling than the final score. The Trojans allowed 394 total yards and ran for just 65 while losing the battle for the line of scrimmage. USC, in short, did not play the physical football Helton had been preaching.

Helton had entered that postseason with a 5–2 record as the interim coach. He left it 0–2 as the permanent one. If the Stanford loss didn't end the honeymoon, the loss to Wisconsin might have. But Helton wasn't coaching with his own assistants or any of his own recruits. He deserves to be judged on his first full season— and arguably longer—and not on two and a half unsettled months.

What about the iconic USC football program? Can it mend its tattered image and recapture its past glory?

No one can really say with any certainty. The team in cardinal and gold is often mercurial and mystifying. And it is *always* interesting.

ZACH BANNER: It's been crazy here the past several years. We're in Los Angeles, right near Hollywood, and we're talking so much about drama, we can't really focus on football. But we can only go up from here. And it is going to happen, whether it's 2016 or the year after or the year after. There's no program in America that's like it. There's no place like USC.

ACKNOWLEDGMENTS

I am especially grateful to the USC players, coaches, and administrators who were so generous with their time and memories. This book could not have been written without their kindness and cooperation.

Every author needs someone who will help him or her unconditionally, and I had two of those people. Shelley Smith, the remarkable ESPN reporter, provided invaluable background and referrals. Former USC player Brad Leggett introduced me to many of his ex-teammates who ended up being interviewed for the book. Shelley, Brad, I owe you.

I am forever thankful to Scott Waxman, my literary agent and sounding board. My gracious editor, Nate Roberson, provided straightforward feedback every step of the way. I am especially thankful to my colleagues and friends at ESPN. It has been an honor to work on the same team with so many dedicated and gifted journalists.

Anyone writing about the history of USC football is indebted to the many strong newspapers and talented sports reporters throughout Southern California. It's a hell of a lot more fun researching a book when the clippings you're reading are so lively.

Another important resource was *Sports Illustrated,* which has covered USC football with its signature mix of substance and style.

For their various contributions, I'd also like to say thank you to Matt Gee, Tim Tessalone, Mitch Mustain, Tom Sirotnak, Dan Avila, Gary Delsohn, Penny Delsohn, Sharon Delsohn, Denis Anthony, Jennifer Anthony, David Rubenstein, Sheldon Gottlieb, and Kenneth Saul.

This book is also dedicated to the memory of Kathleen Anthony, my recently departed mother-in-law, and to the memory of my father, Norman, whose spirit will always guide me.

My mother, Eilene, has been my single biggest fan, and I love her dearly.

My three children, Grace, Hannah, and Max, are kind, compassionate, and always on the side of the underdog. I am so very proud to be their dad.

Finally, my deepest thanks to my wife, Mary Kay Delsohn. It was pretty much love at first sight, and she is still everything to me.

INDEX

ABOUT THE AUTHOR

Steve Delsohn is the author or coauthor of several notable sports books, including the *New York Times* bestseller *Out of Bounds* with NFL great Jim Brown. He is currently a reporter for ESPN television. Delsohn grew up in Chicago and now lives in Southern California.